Clinical Approaches to the
Mentally Disordered Offender

Clinical Approaches to the Mentally Disordered Offender

Edited by

KEVIN HOWELLS
Reaside Clinic, Birmingham
and
School of Psychology,
The University of Birmingham, UK

and

CLIVE R. HOLLIN
School of Psychology,
The University of Birmingham, UK
and
The Youth Treatment Service

JOHN WILEY & SONS
Chichester · New York · Brisbane · Toronto · Singapore

Other Wiley Editorial Offices

John Wiley & Sons, Inc., 605 Third Avenue,
New York, NY 10158-0012, USA

Jacaranda Wiley Ltd, G.P.O. Box 859, Brisbane,
Queensland 4001, Australia

John Wiley & Sons (Canada) Ltd, 22 Worcester Road,
Rexdale, Ontario M9W 1L1, Canada

John Wiley & Sons (SEA) Pte Ltd, 37 Jalan Pemimpin #05-04,
Block B, Union Industrial Building, Singapore 2057

Library of Congress Cataloging-in-Publication Data

Clinical approaches to the mentally disordered offender / edited by
   Kevin Howells and Clive R. Hollin.
      p.   cm. — (Wiley series clinical approaches to criminal
   behaviour)
      Includes bibliographical references and indexes.
      ISBN 0-471-93908-0 (cased)
      1. Criminals—Mental health.   2. Criminals—Mental health
   services.   I. Howells, Kevin.   II. Hollin, Clive R.   III. Series.
      [DNLM: 1. Criminal Psychology,   2. Mental Disorders—therapy.
   3. Mental Health Services.   WM 30 C6405 1993]
   RC451.4.P68C53   1993
   362.2′08692—dc20
   DNLM/DLC
   for Library of Congress   92–48423
                                                                   CIP

British Library Cataloguing in Publication Data

A catalogue record for this book is available from the British Library

ISBN 0-471-93908-0

Typeset in 10/12pt Times by Mathematical Composition Setters Ltd, Salisbury, Wilts.
Printed and bound in Great Britain by Bookcraft (Bath) Ltd.

Personal Note and Dedication

As this book was in the hands of the copy-editor we received the news from the States that Dr Saleem Shah had died just before Christmas as a result of injuries he sustained in an automobile accident. Although familiar with Dr Shah's writings neither of us had met Dr Shah personally, yet as we prepared this book we grew to gain an appreciation of him through our correspondence by fax and by letter. At all times Dr Shah was prompt, courteous, helpful, and supportive of our efforts: above all, as his chapter in this book shows, he was a clear thinker and a more than able scholar.

To record our own sense of loss of a colleague and as a token of our appreciation of his work, it is to the memory of Dr Shah that we wish to dedicate this book.

January 1993

KEVIN HOWELLS
CLIVE R. HOLLIN

Contents

List of Contributors

ESTELLA BAKER, *Faculty of Law, University of Leicester, Leicester, UK, LE1 7RH.*

RONALD BLACKBURN, *Psychology Department, Ashworth Hospital, Liverpool, UK, L31 1HW.*

CHRIS CULLEN, *Psychological Laboratory, University of St Andrews, St Andrews, UK, KY16 9JU.*

KENNETH DAY, *Department of Psychiatry, University of Newcastle upon Tyne, Newcastle upon Tyne, UK.*

ADELLE E. FORTH, *Department of Psychology, Carleton University, Ottawa, Canada, K1S 5B6.*

M. G. GROSSMAN, *Clarke Institute of Psychiatry, Toronto, Ontario, Canada, M5T 1R8.*

ROBERT D. HARE, *Department of Psychology, University of British Columbia, Vancouver, BC, Canada, V6T 1Z4.*

CLIVE R. HOLLIN, *School of Psychology, University of Birmingham, Birmingham, UK, B15 2TT; and Glenthorne Centre, Youth Treatment Service, Birmingham.*

KEVIN HOWELLS, *Reaside Clinic, Birmingham, and School of Psychology, University of Birmingham, Birmingham, UK, B15 2TT.*

S. J. HUCKER, *Clarke Institute of Psychiatry, Toronto, Ontario, Canada, M5T 1R8.*

HERSCHEL PRINS, *Midlands Centre for Criminology and Criminal Justice, University of Loughborough, Loughborough, UK, LE11 3TU.*

CAROL SELLARS, *District Psychology Service, Basingstoke & North Hampshire Health Authority, Basingstoke District Hospital, Hampshire, UK, RG24 9LZ.*

THE LATE SALEEM A. SHAH, *Division of Applied and Services Research, National Institute of Mental Health, Rockville, MD 20857, USA.*

CATHERINE E. STRACHAN, *Department of Psychology, University of British Columbia, Vancouver, BC, Canada, V6T 1Z4.*

C. D. WEBSTER, *Clarke Institute of Psychiatry, Toronto, Ontario, Canada, M5T 1R8.*

Series Preface

This series around the theme of *Clinical Approaches to Criminal Behaviour* has its origin in a sequence of conferences we organized between 1984 and 1988. Our intention, both then and now, was to make some progress towards re-establishing an approach to changing criminal behaviour which has become unfashionable, unpopular and much maligned in recent years. It should be made absolutely clear that in the present context the term 'clinical' is not intended to imply a medical model, in which criminal behaviour is viewed as pathological, but to define an approach in which the focus is on the individual and on psychological methods of producing change. Having said that, we are not blind to the crucial importance of economic, political and social factors in crime and criminological theory. We agree that change is necessary at all levels to reduce crime, and have no wish to be seen as placing the spotlight of blame and responsibility exclusively on the offender to the exclusion of environmental factors. (As behaviourists, admittedly of differing persuasions within that broad church of theoretical opinion, how could we say otherwise?) However, we would also maintain that it is important not to lose sight of the individual, and it is here that the clinical approach comes into its own. The series is intended to serve two functions: to inform clinicians of developments in the clinical approach to criminal behaviour in its many forms, and to convince others that the clinical approach has a role to play in changing criminal behaviour. There is no reason why social reform and clinical change should be incompatible: others have written on the former approach, we now seek to re-assert the latter.

CLIVE R. HOLLIN
KEVIN HOWELLS

Preface

This is the third volume in the Wiley Series in *Clinical Approaches to Criminal Behaviour*. The first book in the series, *Clinical Approaches to Violence*, was published in 1989, with a paperback edition published in 1992. The second volume, *Clinical Approaches to Sex Offenders and their Victims*, followed in 1991, and we are hopeful on sales to date that a paperback edition will be published. As we note in the Series Preface, the books in this series were the direct result of a string of conferences we organized between 1984 and 1988. At the time of writing therefore we have been immersed in this project for the best part of a decade. From the outset we had a reasonably clear idea of what we wanted to do with the series. As we also note in the Series Preface, we wanted to provide clinicians with a source that documented the important developments, as we saw them, in the field of clinical criminology. In addition, we wished to state the case for focusing on the individual, as well as social and economic factors, when attempting to change criminal behaviour. Having reached this stage in our endeavours, we felt it would be interesting to pause to consider how well we are achieving our goals.

There are four main feedback mechanisms that we use to judge our performance: our personal opinion of the books in the series; informal feedback from contributors, colleagues and students; the views of our publishers and the sales figures; and the comments made in the published reviews.

Our personal opinion is that, overall, we are pleased with all three books. We think we have been fortunate in being able to commission some excellent writing by some extremely able and talented people. Of course, as with any project, there are minor matters that with the benefit of hindsight we might have wished to have changed or added. Nonetheless, we feel we are achieving our goals.

The informal feedback from colleagues has been pleasing. Fellow academics have said that they use the books successfully on their courses, and our own students say that they find the books helpful (although there may be an element of 'faking good' here!). Practitioners have also said how useful it is to have summaries of relevant research to inform their clinical work with offenders. While no doubt the sales have helped to sustain their interest, our publishers at Wiley have been highly supportive in their comments and actions, and encouraged us to continue with the series. (The fourth book is being planned as we write.)

Which brings us to the published reviews. Both books have been reasonably widely reviewed and, overall, have been favourably and positively received by reviewers. We are particularly heartened by the strong reviews in the social work, criminology, and law journals. However, the reviewers have raised a number of points on which we feel it is appropriate to make some comment.

It is true that in some instances chapters in the same book by different authors sometimes make reference to the same studies. This is not editorial laxity: it sometimes happens that a unifying theme, reflecting current thinking in a given field, crosses chapter boundaries. A good example is the application of the concept of post-traumatic stress disorder (PTSD) to help understand the reactions of victims, both child and adult, of sex offenders. In our view, rightly or wrongly, we think it highly appropriate to have a brief discussion of PTSD in different chapters on, say, child victims and adult victims.

In addition, the books should not be taken to be all-inclusive; it is not our intention to present bibliographies of every paper ever published. The contributors were asked to present summaries of the research, not exhaustive reviews of the literature. Finally, it was never our intention to offer 'how to do it' practice manuals, nor to cover every possible theoretical perspective: anyone who expects either of these will be disappointed.

Which brings us to volume 3. This is a collection of pieces by some of the leading figures in the field, it contains summaries of relevant literatures, and it discusses some of the practical and ethical dilemmas faced by clinicians working with mentally disordered offenders. As editors we have gained a great deal from reading the work of the contributors to this volume, giving us cause to reflect on our own teaching and practice. We are confident that the thinking clinician will gain similar benefits.

KEVIN HOWELLS
CLIVE R. HOLLIN

The Mentally Disordered Offender: A Clinical Approach

CLIVE HOLLIN and KEVIN HOWELLS
School of Psychology, The University of Birmingham, UK

The mentally disordered offender poses a set of unique conceptual, empirical, and practical problems for researchers and clinicians alike. Even before reaching the empirical issue of the nature of the relationship between mental disorder and criminal behaviour, there are problems with each element of the term 'mentally disordered offender'. Taking first the *mental* element, there are conceptual difficulties surrounding the notion of mind and mental events. Flowing from this, there are associated issues concerning the nature of the relationship between mental events, biological activity, and behaviour. As Hayes and Brownstein (1987) note, the concept of mind demands that 'there are two kinds of stuff in the world: one type exists in space and time, while the other is non-spatiotemporal' (p. 213). In other words, we must accept that mental events take place in a non-physical, even metaphysical, world. This non-physical world, by definition, cannot be studied by any means known to contemporary science. Yet further, if one follows the view that mental events cause behaviour, then one has to admit the omniscience of the ghost in the machine.

What alternatives could there be to the concept of mind? One alternative lies in physiological reductionism: that mental events—or *cognitions* as the now favoured term—are synonymous with physiological, usually brain, functioning. Advocates of a metaphysical mind would, of course, object to this view outright. Others would regard it as an explanatory sleight of hand in that recourse to the interplay between brain and cognition to explain behaviour is simply to raise another ghostly presence in the machine. Another alternative lies in behaviour analysis, in which behaviour is explained not by recourse to inner events, but by reinforcing environment contingencies acting on the individual (Skinner, 1974).

About the only concrete point to make is that this debate has been running for centuries and is not about to be resolved (Russell, 1961). The point is made, however, that the term 'mental' carries with it a host of philosophical assumptions.

Clinical Approaches to the Mentally Disordered Offender
Edited by K. Howells and C. R. Hollin © 1993 John Wiley & Sons Ltd

Turning to the *disordered* element, similar issues arise. In a thought-provoking paper, Wakefield (1992) argues forcefully that 'disorder' should not be the term of choice with psychodiagnosis. The basic problem is one of definition: what is a disorder? Wakefield notes that several approaches have been used: disorder is whatever professionals treat, disorder as statistical deviance from the norm, disorder as biological disadvantage, and disorder as unexpectable distress or disability. While the diagnosis of disorder involves gathering facts about an individual's level of functioning, it must also involve value judgements. Inevitably such value judgements will be influenced by the sociopolitical climate of the times, leading to the possibility of charges of sexual, racial, and class bias against those professionals making the diagnoses. There are many historical examples of such biases, such as *drapetomania* (the 'disorder' that impelled slaves to escape from slavery) and the pathological view of homosexuality. Indeed, one argument is that the whole concept of mental disorder is a social invention, a myth, constructed for the benefit of those with the power to confer psychodiagnostic labels (Szasz, 1974).

Wakefield suggests that the term *harmful dysfunction* is preferable to disorder: that is, an individual's behaviour is due to the failure of a mechanism, mental or physical, that is endowed through the processes of natural selection. However, to equate with disorder, such a dysfunction must, in turn, be harmful to the individual concerned as seen in the context of the prevailing social and cultural standards.

When we move to the *offender* element, there are again definitional problems: is the propensity to commit crime an individual failing, an act of free will, a product of environmental contingencies, or a socially constructed mechanism of control to preserve the power of the ruling classes? Criminology texts grapple with these issues (e.g. Siegel, 1986), and psychologists struggle to translate their theories and findings within the criminological domain (e.g. Hollin, 1989, 1992).

Put these three elements of mind, disorder, and crime together to produce the compound of the mentally disordered offender and the conceptual issues multiply exponentially. Clearly there are those individuals who display what, for want of a better term, we might call mental disorder, who also commit crimes. What is the relationship between mental disorder and criminal behaviour? Anticipating what is to follow, there are several important issues to consider. Do mentally disordered people commit offences at a different rate to non-mentally disordered people? This is an empirical question, but one that is difficult to answer in practice. While it is possible to look both at criminal behaviour among persons with mental disorder and at rates of mental disorder among offenders, there is a myriad of confounding factors that blur the findings of research. However, it is possible to detect a recent change in opinion in contemporary work.

In the early 1980s the evidence leaned towards the view that the apparent dangerousness of those with mental disorder was an artifact of methodological and social processes (Howells, 1982). For example, it could be argued that the florid mentally ill were more visible, attracted greater attention and were more easily apprehended, and more likely to be penalised in court. Thus any association between mental disorder and crime was seen as an artifact produced by social processes. Thus Monahan and Steadman (1983) observed that: 'The relation between ... crime and mental disorder can be accounted for largely by demographic and historical characteristics that the two groups share. When appropriate statistical controls are applied for factors such as age, gender, race, social class, and previous institutionalization, whatever relations between crime and mental disorder are reported tend to disappear' (p. 152). In a recent paper, Monahan (1992) has reappraised this view: referring directly to the quote above, Monahan states 'I now believe that this conclusion is at least premature and may well be wrong' (p. 514). Monahan refers to the view that controlling variables in a statistical analysis may in fact mask a real relationship between the phenomena of concern, and that fresh empirical evidence has been published over the past decade. This new wave of evidence finds a consistent, if modest, relationship between violent and illegal behavior and the presence of mental disorder. In a typical 'new wave' study, Link, Andrews, and Cullen (1992) reported that 'Mental patient groups scored higher not only on official measures of violent crime, but also on indicators of violent/illegal behavior that did not involve arrest' (p. 289). It is important to emphasise that the elevated risk of offending among mentally disordered people is modest, most mentally disordered people do not commit offences. In addition, these findings can in no way account for rising levels of violent crime in society generally. Further, Link, Andrews and Cullen suggest that within the broad range of manifestations of mental disorder, a specific set of symptoms are associated with elevated crime rates. Specifically, they conclude that 'Only patients with current psychotic symptoms have elevated rates of violent behavior' (p. 290). A conclusion in keeping, for example, with the findings of Lindqvist and Allebeck (1990) that criminal behaviour is more widespread among schizophrenic patients than among the general population. Although again it must be emphasised that the absolute figures are modest: most people with schizophrenia do not commit crimes.

The unsolved mystery lies in the nature of the relationship between mental disorder, psychotic symptoms in particular, and criminal behaviour. While it is tempting to conclude that the relationship is causal, this would be to go beyond the data. There are other possible explanations: for example, there may be an interpersonal component in that it is the reaction of others to the psychotic symptoms that precipitates crimes against the person. While, as Taylor (1985) cautions, there are grave problems in omitting to consider the social, environmental, and organic antecedents to both psychosis and crime. To arrive at a full understanding of mental disorder and criminal behaviour, social and illness factors must be considered together rather than held separate.

As Long and Midgely (1992) describe, throughout history there has been a conceptual blurring of the boundaries between mental disorder and criminal behaviour. In times past the socially deviant, outcast to the margins of society, were an amorphous population of the mentally and physically disadvantaged, the socially inept and incompetent, and those who transgressed the law of the land. As the mentally disordered and the criminal formed part of the same problem, the same solution was applied—a social policy that entailed the removal of such individuals from decent society. Thus alongside such excesses as deportation to foreign lands, there was an active move towards housing the deviant in large institutions. The legacy of this social policy is still with us today in the form of large prisons, mental hospitals, and special (or state) hospitals.

One of the challenges facing the legal systems in many countries is to formulate legislation to accommodate the special demands posed by the mentally disordered offender. Such a challenge taxes not only psychologists and mental health professionals (e.g. Meyer, 1992), but also those in the legal profession. To emphasise the importance of this interface between psychology and law and to demonstrate the issues involved, the first chapter in this book is written by a lawyer, Estella Baker. While it would have been interesting to have a full discussion of legal systems around the world, limitations of space precluded a book on cross-cultural aspects of law. The opening chapter does, therefore, use English law as a vehicle to explore legal trends and policies towards the mentally disordered offender. We hope this will not be seen as narrow parochialism but as an exemplar of the way that societies respond to the issues posed by the mentally disordered offender. While advice on the exact rules of law will be available in individual cases, the broader message to be taken from Estella Baker's chapter is that clinicians need to be aware of the place of their work within a much larger system.

The second chapter in the opening section, by Herschel Prins, looks at the crucial issue of service provision and facilities for the mentally disordered offender. Again limitations of space preclude a cross-cultural analysis, but the discussion of the British systems provides an example of both institutional and community provision. It is plain that those charged with caring for the mentally disordered offender face an exceedingly daunting task.

The second part of the book moves to clinical research and practice. The chapters in this section are intended to provide an overview of the empirical research and clinical issues with a range of specific disorders. The opening chapter by Carol Sellars and ourselves considers the evidence for any special relationship between mental illness, neurological and organic disorder, and criminal behaviour. With regard to neurological and organic disorder, this chapter includes both a discussion of a range of clinical techniques used with this group of offenders and an illustrative case study. Treatment programmes for mentally ill offenders are discussed in the next chapter by Chris Webster and his colleagues. This chapter highlights the range of mental health services in both prisons and hospitals. It also includes an illustrative case study.

The long-standing view that intelligence and criminal behaviour are causally linked is one that continues to occupy contemporary researchers (e.g. Lipsitt, Buka, and Lipsitt, 1990). Within this broad concern, a body of research has looked at whether there is any special relationship between very low intelligence and criminal behaviour. Kenneth Day provides a thorough and considered overview of both the research and its implications for practice. The treatment of offenders, including the recent advances in the use of cognitive techniques such as anger control training, is described by Chris Cullen in Chapter 6.

The review of psychopathy and crime by Robert Hare, Katy Strachan, and Adelle Forth covers a great deal of essential material in this most problematic of areas. This chapter addresses the meaning of the term psychopathy, its assessment and the defining characteristics of the psychopathic person, and the relationship between psychopathy and criminal behaviour. The next chapter, by Ronald Blackburn, focuses on clinical programmes with psychopaths. Following a discussion of the 'treatability' of psychopaths, Blackburn looks at the assessment of psychopathy and personality disorders and offers an overview of the success of the various clinical techniques used with this group. A case history illustrates the treatment of a psychopathic patient in a secure institution.

The third and final section seeks to draw together the major issues pertaining to clinical approaches to the mentally disordered offender. In a masterful chapter, Saleem Shah offers a comprehensive overview of the legal, practical, and ethical issues in offering clinical treatment to mentally disordered offenders. Our endpiece gives the main points, as we see them, to emerge from the book. Few of those who work in the field would disagree with our conclusion that much remains to be achieved in furthering clinical services for mentally disordered offenders.

REFERENCES

Hayes, S., and Brownstein, A. (1987). Mentalism, private events, and scientific explanation: A defense of B. F. Skinner's view. In S. Modgil and C. Modgil (eds), *B. F. Skinner: Consensus and Controversy*. New York: Falmer Press.

Hollin, C. R. (1989). *Psychology and Crime: An Introduction to Criminological Psychology*. London: Routledge.

Hollin, C. R. (1992). *Criminal Behaviour: A Psychological Approach to Explanation and Prevention*. London: Falmer Press.

Howells, K. (1982). Mental disorder and violent behaviour. In P. Feldman (ed.), *Developments in the Study of Criminal Behaviour*, vol. 2: *Violence*. Chichester: Wiley.

Lindqvist, P., and Allebeck, P. (1990). Schizophrenia and crime: A longitudinal follow-up of 644 schizophrenics in Stockholm. *British Journal of Psychiatry*, 157, 345–50.

Link, B. G., Andrews, H., and Cullen, F. T. (1992) . The violent and illegal behaviour of mental patients reconsidered. *American Sociological Review*, 57, 275–92.

Lipsitt, P. D., Buka, S. L., and Lipsitt, L. P. (1990). Early intelligence scores and subsequent delinquency: A prospective study. *American Journal of Family Therapy*, 18, 197–208.

Long, C. G., and Midgely, M. (1992). On the closeness of the concepts of the criminal and the mentally ill in the nineteenth century: Yesterday's professional and public opinions reflected today. *Journal of Forensic Psychiatry*, 3, 63–79.

Meyer, R. G. (1992). *Abnormal Behavior and the Criminal Justice System*. New York: Lexington Books.

Monahan, J. (1992). Mental disorder and violent behaviour: Perceptions and evidence. *American Psychologist*, 47, 511–21.

Monahan, J., and Steadman, H. (1983). Crime and mental disorder: An epidemiological approach. In M. Tonry and N. Morris (eds), *Crime and Justice: An Annual Review of Research*, vol. 4. Chicago: University of Chicago Press.

Russell, B. (1961). *History of Western Philosophy and its Connection with Political and Social Circumstances from the Earliest Times to the Present Day*. London: Allen & Unwin.

Siegel, L. J. (1986). *Criminology* (2nd edn). St Paul, MN: West Publishing.

Skinner, B. F. (1974). *About Behaviorism*. New York: Knopf.

Szasz, T. S. (1974). *The Myth of Mental Illness: Foundations of a Theory of Personal Conduct* (rev. edn). New York: Harper & Row.

Taylor, P. J. (1985). Motives for offending among violent and psychotic men. *British Journal of Psychiatry*, **147**, 491–8.

Wakefield, J. C. (1992). The concept of mental disorder: On the boundary between biological facts and social values. *American Psychologist*, **47**, 373–88.

Part 1
Laws and Service Provision

1

The Social and Legal Framework

ESTELLA BAKER
Faculty of Law, University of Leicester, UK

INTRODUCTION

This chapter is divided into three sections. The first sets current English provision for mentally disordered offenders into its social context through the examination of some ideas which, historically, have shaped policy towards mentally disordered offenders together with the underlying doctrines of criminal law and the criminal justice system. The second surveys contemporary measures for dealing with mentally disordered offenders. The final section highlights some inconsistencies and tensions inherent in modern law. The chapter will conclude by identifying some causes of the conflicts involved.

I UNDERLYING PHILOSOPHIES

TRADITIONAL IDEAS ABOUT MENTAL DISORDER

The practice of treating mentally disordered offenders differently from 'normal' offenders has remarkably deep cultural roots. Documentary evidence exists that a surprisingly enlightened attitude towards insane killers was taken in Saxon England. Rather than being punished personally for their offences such individuals became the responsibility of their families who were charged with preventing repetition and required to pay compensation to the victim's family (Walker, 1968, p. 16). This was a matter of civil rather than criminal law. However, as the doctrine of guilty intent, or *mens rea*, as the basis of criminal liability developed, it became clear that there was a moral rationale for what

Clinical Approaches to the Mentally Disordered Offender
Edited by K. Howells and C. R. Hollin © 1993 John Wiley & Sons Ltd

continued to be a comparatively humane response towards mentally disordered offenders. They were not to blame and so should not be punished for their actions (Walker, 1968, pp. 16–19). This stance persists today in the availability of criminal defences specifically tailored to the needs of mentally disordered offenders (see below, 'Insanity').

The second significant idea in the historical treatment of mentally disordered offenders was the belief that to suffer the illness was itself a sufficient punishment. In other words there was a kind of moral 'double jeopardy' principle at work. This latter idea has perhaps fewer modern manifestations than the first. However, the ability of sentencing courts to impose a hospital order as an alternative to imprisonment in the absence of an established causal connection between the offending behaviour and the offender's illness provides an illustration of it (Mental Health Act 1983, section 37; see below).

The final influential strand of thought was the association of mental disorder with dangerousness; that 'bad' and 'mad' were closely intertwined. Far more than either of the first two bodies of thought, the nature of this relationship has significance today. Confusion as to definition and attribution of dangerousness, and the existence, or lack of a causal connection between dangerousness and mental disorder is rife in modern law.

THE MORAL FOUNDATION OF THE CRIMINAL LAW

Responsibility

Liability under English criminal law is founded on the doctrine of *mens rea*. For most serious offences guilt is not dependent solely upon proof of the commission of a prohibited act, the *actus reus* (literally the guilty act) of the offence, but derives from the act's performance with a proscribed state of mind, the *mens rea*. Crimes which are constituted merely of an *actus reus* tend to be regulatory in nature whereas those requiring *mens rea* are frequently referred to as 'real' or 'true' crimes. This is because they involve morally unacceptable behaviour and it is the presence of *mens rea* which allows this moral judgement to be arrived at. For example, it is the offender's knowledge that the woman does not consent to sexual intercourse, or recognition that she may not do so, which transforms what would otherwise be a lawful act into the crime of rape (Sexual Offences (Amendment) Act 1976, section 1). Simultaneously, therefore, the fact that the offender acted with *mens rea* renders him or her responsible for the wrong doing. If responsible, he or she may legitimately be blamed for the act and so liable to punishment. Thus the doctrine of *mens rea* determines who is and who is not held criminally liable for their acts and is a vitally important device to protect the morally innocent from conviction.

In order for responsibility to be attributed on this basis, however, two further qualifications are necessary. First, the act concerned must truly be the offender's. Therefore, it must be voluntary in the sense, either of being consciously willed or, alternatively, as the product of (at least partial) control by the brain (*Broome* v *Perkins* (1987)). Secondly, it must be committed by a person of sound mind (*R* v *M'Naghten* (1843) at 210, per Tindal C.J.). Both conditions are presumed to have been met unless evidence is produced to suggest otherwise.

From what has been said so far it should be clear that there are a number of reasons why it may be difficult to conclude that a mentally disordered defendant is criminally responsible for his or her acts. But, even if responsibility can properly be attributed, he or she may have a defence which none the less negates liability for the 'offence' or, more rarely, reduces it (see below, pp. 25–27).

Defences

In theoretical terms criminal defences may be categorised into justifications and excuses. The distinction between them is that a justification is a negation of the wrongfulness of the conduct owing to the circumstances in which it has occurred. For example, in appropriate circumstances, killing in self defence is regarded as justified. By contrast excused conduct is viewed as wrongful. Nevertheless, the law provides a defence because it acknowledges that the defendant lacks responsibility for it. Defences which are tailored to the needs of mentally disordered offenders are excusatory in nature and reflect the beliefs about mental disorder outlined above.

THE CRIMINAL JUSTICE SYSTEM

The fact that the legal doctrines upon which the criminal justice system is founded are supremely important with regard to the maintenance of human rights can be seen from the fact that they are enshrined in the European Convention on Human Rights [ECHR]. Whilst the Convention is of persuasive authority only in English law and is not binding, its significance appears to be growing. Certainly a number of celebrated decisions in which English law has been held to be in breach of the Convention have initiated important changes to domestic law (see below).

The fundamental presumption of the criminal justice system is that the defendant is innocent until proven guilty (Article 6(2) ECHR). This dictates that the onus of proving that the defendant committed the offence alleged lies with the prosecution. The requirement is further strengthened by providing that a high burden of proof, 'beyond reasonable doubt', must be satisfied (*Woolmington* v *DPP* [1935]). Associated with this is the right of the defendant to a 'fair trial'. Although this is a complicated concept, for the purposes of this chapter, the aspect of particular relevance is the necessity for the defendant to be able to participate both in the trial process and his or her defence, at least to the extent of understanding the proceedings and their significance. These requirements are also included in Article 6(3) of the ECHR. Clearly some mentally disordered defendants do not have sufficient capacity to meet them. The law relating to unfitness to plead exists to cater for such cases (see below, 'Unfitness to Plead').

II LEGAL PROVISION

Contemporary provision for mentally disordered offenders rests on the premise that the mentally disordered require 'special' treatment when in contact with the criminal justice system and that it is better provided by a separate system of mental health provision than through adapting penal facilities to cater for them. Therefore, although the prison system has some specialised units, comprehensive provisions exist throughout the criminal justice system to divert mentally disordered offenders into mental health care. This diversionary policy has recently been underlined by a Home Office circular, designed to heighten awareness of the available measures amongst criminal justice agencies (Home Office Circular No. 66/90).

The fact that the circular was thought necessary highlights the fact that implementation of the policy is not entirely successful. Lack of awareness of the available measures is one reason why the mentally disordered remain in the penal system. However, there are a number of others. First, the criteria for admission to hospital may not be met, either because of the nature of the illness or, in some cases, because it is not thought to be treatable. Secondly, even where the admission criteria are fulfilled, other penal aims such as retribution and desert or deterrence may be given precedence over the offender's need for treatment. Finally, in cases where treatment is felt to be desirable, service provision may be inadequate to meet the offender's needs.

As far as mental health provision itself is concerned, English law is built on the principle, enunciated in section 131(1) of the Mental Health Act 1983 [MHA 1983], that treatment for mental disorders should be available in the same way that it is for physical illnesses. This basic idea permeates facilities and services for all patients, both voluntary and compulsorily detained and whether admitted under civil or criminal powers. The 1983 Act is the major statute regulating mental health services and the entitlement approach to mental health care which it adopts has important consequences for the treatment of mentally disordered offenders. As far as possible, the Act aims to treat patients identically, regardless of whether they have been admitted under its civil or criminal provisions. Consistent with this, it creates largely parallel criteria for civil admission for treatment under section 3 and the imposition by a sentencing court under section 37 of a hospital order (and its equivalents, see page 18 below, 'Admission as an Unrestricted Patient'). Once in hospital, patients detained under these provisions have an equivalent legal status and enjoy largely similar rights.

However, there is one group of criminal patients to whom this equation does not apply. If an offender is thought to pose a risk to the public the legislation provides for admission as a 'restricted patient'. The effect of this is that the normal focus of attention on the offender's right to treatment is modified by the need to protect the public from him or her. The mechanism by which this is achieved is that autonomy over management decisions affecting restricted patients is removed from the medical authorities and given to the Home Secretary instead. In other words, restricted patients have a different legal status from 'unrestricted patients' who are admitted solely for treatment.

The discussion which follows will consider the distinction between unrestricted and restricted patients in more detail both in terms of status in hospital and route of admission. It will then go on to consider the overall scheme of provision.

STATUS IN HOSPITAL

Before clarifying the important differences between the Act's treatment of unrestricted and restricted patients, the provisions of the MHA 1983 governing consent to treatment will be examined as they apply to both groups, with the limited exceptions listed below.

Consent to Treatment

Part IV of the MHA 1983 sets out a statutory framework for the compulsory treatment of nearly all detained patients. For the purposes of this chapter the relevant categories (which will be examined more fully below) to whom Part IV does not apply are: individuals detained in a 'place of safety' under section 136, those remanded to hospital for reports under section 35, individuals subject to a guardianship order under section 37 and restricted patients who have been conditionally discharged from hospital under section 73(2). All other criminal patients may be treated against their wishes, provided that the treatment is carried out in accordance with the Act.

Section 63 of the Act lays down the general rule that the patient's consent is not necessary for any medical treatment for his or her mental disorder given under the direction of the responsible medical officer [RMO] (the doctor in overall control of the patient's treatment, defined in section 34). Although confined to treatment *for the mental disorder*, the power is still very wide since 'medical treatment' is defined in section 145(1) of the Act as including 'nursing, ... care, habilitation and rehabilitation under medical supervision'.

Where particularly invasive or irreversible treatments are contemplated (ECT, surgery carried out with the purpose of destroying brain tissue or its function and surgical implantation of hormones designed to reduce male sexual drive) sections 57 and 58 lay down additional requirements to be met before the treatment may be given. These also apply to the further administration of medication in cases where patients are taking medicine and three months have elapsed since the first dose. Special provision is made for the delivery of these treatments without the need to comply with the time consuming special procedures in urgent cases (section 62).

Where treatment is necessary for reasons other than the patient's mental disorder, normal common law principles governing the treatment of all patients apply. Therefore, treatment may only be given with consent, or to preserve the patient's life or health or, occasionally, because it is in the patient's best interests. Where treatment takes the form of restraint, it is lawful if exercised in self defence or to prevent crime, such as an assault (Criminal Law Act 1967, section 3) provided the force used is reasonable in the circumstances.

Duration of Authority to Detain

A hospital order (or equivalent) authorises the detention of an unrestricted patient for an initial six month period. It is then renewable for a further six months and annually thereafter (section 40). By contrast, the length of time for which a restricted patient may be held varies according to the nature and terms of the order (see further below). The provisions governing the duration and renewal of orders with regard to unrestricted patients do not apply to restricted patients (section 41(3)(a)).

Leave of Absence and Transfer

Section 17 of the Act permits the RMO to grant leave of absence to unrestricted patients. In addition a Mental Health Review Tribunal [MHRT] may recommend that it is granted but cannot order it. With respect to restricted patients leave of absence may be granted only with the Home Secretary's consent (section 41(3)(c)(i)).

The regulations regarding the transfer of patients are relatively complicated. However, in general, a restricted patient may not be transferred in the absence of the Minister's consent (section 41(3)(c)(ii)) whereas the hospital authorities have autonomy over the transfer of unrestricted patients.

Discharge from Hospital

Unrestricted patients

An unrestricted patient may be discharged from hospital at any time by the RMO or hospital managers (section 23(2)(a) and Schedule 1, Part I, para. 8(b)). In addition, the legality of the patient's detention is periodically reviewed by an MHRT. The Tribunal is made up of a legal, a medical and a lay representative drawn from a panel appointed by the Lord Chancellor. Its deliberations are based upon a combination of written evidence, an examination of the patient by the medical member and an informal oral hearing.

Both the patient and the patient's 'nearest relative' (defined in section 26) may apply for the patient's case to be reviewed, initially in the second six months of detention and annually thereafter (section 69(1)(a)); periods which correspond to the provisions governing duration of detention. This right to regular independent scrutiny of the patient's detention is safeguarded because, if a period of three years elapses without a review, the hospital managers are under a statutory duty to refer the case for a Tribunal hearing (section 68(2)).

The legislation is reasonably generous as regards Tribunals' powers in respect of unrestricted patients. It sets out criteria which, if met, oblige the patient's discharge but also provides the Tribunal with a degree of discretion to discharge in cases where it does not have to do so (section 72(1)). Under section 72(1)(b) the

Tribunal must discharge the patient if it is satisfied either that, at the time of the hearing,

  (i) ... the patient is not ... suffering from mental illness, psychopathic disorder, severe mental impairment or mental impairment (see below, p. 19) or from any of those forms of disorder of a nature or degree which makes it appropriate for him to be detained in a hospital for medical treatment; or
  (ii) that it is not necessary for the health or safety of the patient or for the protection of others that he should receive such treatment.

These criteria are also applied in restricted cases and, in that context, the difference in nature between the 'diagnostic question' contained in section 72(1)(b)(i) and the 'social question' (*R* v *MHRT, ex parte Pickering* [1986] per Forbes J. at 101) in section 72(1)(b)(ii) has caused considerable problems (see below, p. 17).

Restricted patients

The divorcing of management from medical decisions relating to treatment dictates that decisions regarding the discharge of restricted patients may only be made with the Home Secretary's consent (section 41(3)(iii)), subject to independent review by the MHRT.

The Secretary of State may discharge a restricted patient at any time, either absolutely or subject to conditions (section 42(2)). If discharged conditionally the Minister retains the power to recall the patient to hospital (section 42(3)). It has been confirmed recently that a recall warrant may lawfully be issued even though there is no evidence that the patient is mentally disordered (*R* v *Secretary of State for the Home Department, ex parte K* [1990], below p. 17).

The powers of MHRTs with regard to restricted patients differ from those that they possess with regard to unrestricted patients in the following respects. First, only the patient has the right to request a hearing. Secondly, the duty to refer the patient's case if three years elapse without a hearing rests with the Secretary of State, not the hospital authorities (section 71(2)). These are comparatively insignificant alterations; of far more importance are the limitations placed on Tribunals' decision-making powers in restricted cases.

Section 73(1) of the MHA 1983 requires the Tribunal to apply the section 72(1)(b) criteria to restricted patients. Except in relation to one patient group, if it is satisfied as to at least one of them, the patient is entitled to be discharged from hospital. But, unlike unrestricted cases, the Tribunal must go on to consider whether it is appropriate for the patient to remain liable to recall to hospital for medical treatment (section 73(1)(b)). If the Tribunal is satisfied that it is, then the patient's discharge is conditional only. This has the same legal effect as a conditional discharge ordered by the Secretary of State.

The effect of section 73 is to deprive the Tribunal of the discretionary power of discharge that it possesses in respect of other patients. In addition, section 74 of the Act modifies the Tribunal's powers with respect to sentenced prisoners who have been transferred to hospital under a restriction direction (see below,

p. 22). Although the Tribunal must consider the patient's case in the light of the same criteria as in an 'ordinary' restricted case, it cannot order the patient's discharge. Instead, its powers are limited to recommending the appropriate course of action to the Home Secretary. The Minister then has the option of complying with the recommendation or transferring the prisoner back to gaol. Interestingly, this was the position with respect to *all* restricted patients under the Mental Health Act 1959 [MHA 1959]. The regime under the 1983 Act was introduced in response to the European Court of Human Rights' ruling in *X* v *United Kingdom* [1981] that the 1959 Act contravened Article 5 of the ECHR as it failed to provide for adequate judicial review of detention decisions.

The extent to which the new arrangements have successfully overcome the perceived defects of the earlier legislation is controversial. Despite the reforms, research conducted into the implementation of the 1983 Act suggests that, in practice, MHRTs exercise their powers with considerable caution (Genn, 1989; Peay, 1989).

It is argued that one of the most significant causes of Tribunals' conservatism is the drafting of section 72(1)(b). In accordance with the principle, (recognised *obiter* by the Court of Appeal in *Kynaston* v *Secretary of State for Home Affairs* (1981) in the context of the 1959 Act and the European Court of Human Rights in *Winterwerp* v *The Netherlands* [1979]), that an individual who is not mentally disordered should not be made subject to mental health legislation, it clearly requires the Tribunal to discharge a patient whom it is satisfied is not disordered even though it believes him or her to be dangerous. Admirable as this may be, the Tribunal is left in a very uncomfortable position. Therefore, it is suggested that MHRTs have developed a variety of decision-making strategies to enable them to justify not releasing patients whom they believe to pose a risk to public safety. In other words, in practice, they approach their task in much the same protectionist spirit as the Secretary of State (Peay, 1989).

Furthermore the courts have not adopted a constructive approach to the review of such cases. The decision of the Court of Appeal in *R* v *Merseyside MHRT, ex parte K* [1990] affords a clear demonstration of this. In 1989 Mr K, a restricted patient at Park Lane Special Hospital (now Ashworth North), sought judicial review of an MHRT's decision to order his conditional discharge. The legal basis for the Tribunal's decision was that it was satisfied that he was not suffering from any mental disorder. Section 145 of the 1983 Act defines a 'patient' as ' . . . a person suffering or appearing to be suffering from mental disorder'. In essence, therefore, Mr K's argument was very simple. The Tribunal's finding of fact meant that he was no longer a 'patient' within the meaning of the Act. Therefore, it had been unlawful to order that he remain subject to the legislation and he was entitled to an absolute discharge.

Despite the logic of the argument, it was rejected. The court took the view that the definition of 'patient' in section 145 was to be read in the light of the discharge provisions in section 73. Consequently Mr K remained a 'patient' until he was discharged absolutely. Butler-Sloss L.J. added, at 699–700, that the power to order a conditional discharge under section 73:

... [appeared] to be a provision designed both for the support of the patient in the community and the protection of the public, and [was] an important discretionary power vested in an independent tribunal, one not lightly to be set aside in the absence of clear words.

As far as Tribunal powers are concerned, tangentially, the decision in *ex parte K* raises a particular difficulty in restricted cases. The Tribunal has no statutory power to order a patient's transfer to another institution and it has been ruled unlawful for it to conditionally discharge a patient, making residence in a hospital one of the conditions. 'Discharge' means 'release from hospital' and the Tribunal cannot achieve indirectly what it has not got the express power to do (*Secretary of State for the Home Department* v *MHRT for the Mersey Regional Health Authority* [1986]). Therefore, any desire the Tribunal may have to aid a patient's progress through the system is frustrated.

The second point is that the decision in *ex parte K* runs directly counter to the principle supported in the *Kynaston* and *Winterwerp* cases. This view is reinforced by the Court of Appeal decision in the second case initiated by Mr K, *R* v *Secretary of State for the Home Department, ex parte K* [1990].

Whilst conditionally discharged from hospital, Mr K was convicted of assaulting two young women and sentenced to six years' imprisonment. As his earliest date of release approached, the Home Secretary issued a warrant under section 42(3) of the Act recalling Mr K to hospital on the grounds that he was a danger to the public, with the result that he was immediately detained in Broadmoor Special Hospital following his release from prison. Mr K sought judicial review of the Minister's decision to recall him on the grounds, *inter alia*, that there was no medical evidence that he was mentally disordered and, consequently, that the decision to issue the warrant was unlawful. The action was unsuccessful. The court contrasted the terms of section 42(3) with other provisions of the 1983 Act which specifically required medical evidence to be considered, especially section 47 (see below, page 20), and concluded, at 570, that:

> The clear intention [was] that the Secretary of State be empowered in his discretion at any time during the continuance of a restriction order in respect of a patient to recall the patient to hospital.

In the court's view this argument was further strengthened by the Home Secretary's obligation under section 75(1) to refer the case of any recalled patient to an MHRT within one month of his or her return to hospital. This, it was felt, afforded adequate protection of the rights of the patient.

The issues with which the court is grappling in these cases (and others) are presented in an acute form because the discharge criteria in section 72(1)(b) are treated as direct alternatives despite their difference in nature. To some degree this is incongruous because, as will be seen below, in relation to admission powers, the Act requires decision makers to consider the 'diagnostic question' of the offender's mental disorder first and the 'social question' of the risk that he or she may pose to the public second (see above, p. 15). It is only if the offender is believed to pose a risk to the public that a restriction order will be made in addition to a hospital order. Viewed in that light, the approach taken by Tribunals and the courts to the discharge of restricted patients is more in tune with the Act's admission powers than the statute itself.

ADMISSION POWERS

Part III of the MHA 1983, which concerns patients involved in criminal proceedings, contains the provisions designed to give effect to the diversionary policy identified above (p. 12). For the purposes of discussion the measures it contains will be divided into two broad groups; first, powers authorising comparatively short-term detention, relevant during the early stages of the criminal justice process, and secondly the longer term disposal provisions. The latter group will be focused upon initially because it is with regard to these powers that the distinction between unrestricted and restricted patient status operates. The overall scheme of the Act and the wider framework of provision will be considered afterwards.

Admission as an Unrestricted Patient

Admission as an unrestricted patient can occur at three points in the criminal justice process. They are:

(1) Disposal by way of a hospital order under section 37 of the 1983 Act following conviction.
(2) Disposal by way of a hospital order following a finding of unfitness to plead or not guilty by reason of insanity under section 3 of the Criminal Procedure (Insanity and Unfitness to Plead) Act 1991 [CP(IUP)A 1991].
(3) Transfer of a sentenced prisoner to hospital by a transfer direction under section 47 of the 1983 Act.

The criteria for imposing each of the measures contained in the MHA 1983 are broadly the same as those set out in section 37 of the Act and the effect of each of the listed measures is identical to that of a hospital order. Therefore, section 37 will be discussed first, followed by section 47. The effect of the 1991 Act will be considered last.

The power to make a hospital order under section 37 of the MHA 1983

A hospital order is a direct alternative to imprisonment. As Mustill L. J. recently observed in *R v Birch* (1990), at 84–5,

> [The] offender is dealt with in a manner which appears, and is intended to be, humane by comparison with a custodial sentence ... The sole purpose of the order is to ensure that the offender receives the medical care and attention which he needs in the hope and expectation of course that the result will be to avoid the commission by the offender of further criminal acts.

As his statement implies, the criteria for imposing an order under section 37 have a strong medical emphasis.

The first is that the court must be satisfied, on the written or oral evidence of two registered medical practitioners (at least one of whom must be certified under section 12 of the Act as having expertise in mental health [a section 12 doctor]), that the offender is suffering from one (or more) of the following four forms of mental disorder to a nature or degree which makes it appropriate that he or she be detained in hospital for medical treatment. The four listed disorders are mental illness, severe mental impairment, mental impairment and psychopathic disorder (section 37(2)(a)).

All four are defined in section 1(2) of the Act, barring 'mental illness'. The sole guidance on its meaning derives from the Court of Appeal's comments in *W* v *L* [1974], a case decided under the MHA 1959, in which Lawton L.J. composed the 'man-must-be-mad' test (Hoggett, 1990, p. 8). He said, at 719:

> The words [mental illness] are ordinary words of the English language. They have no particular medical significance. They have no particular legal significance ... ordinary words of the English language should be construed in the way that ordinary sensible people would construct them ... [What] would the ordinary sensible person have said about the patient's condition in this case if he had been informed of his behaviour ...? [Such] a person would have said: 'Well the fellow is obviously mentally ill'. If that be right, then ... the case ... falls within the classification of 'mental illness'.

Space constraints preclude a comprehensive investigation of the statutory definitions of mental disorder here. However, it is worth noting that Lawton L. J.'s 'definition' has a number of features in common with them. All four are umbrella concepts rather than specific conditions and all involve a behavioural element. The statutory definitions refer to the presence of 'abnormally aggressive or seriously irresponsible conduct'. In the context of mentally disordered offenders this raises the problem that it is possible to classify *all* offending behaviour as irresponsible.

In terms of its overall policy, the Act draws a distinction between mental illness and severe mental impairment, the 'major disorders', which are considered to merit hospital treatment *per se*, regardless of whether it is likely to have any effect and mental impairment and psychopathic disorder, the 'minor disorders'. If the offender suffers from one of these then a hospital order may only be made if the doctors also give evidence that treatment is likely to alleviate or prevent a deterioration of the offender's condition [the 'treatability criterion'] (section 37(2)(a)(i)).

Finally, section 37(2)(b) requires the court to take into account the nature of the offence, the character and antecedents of the offender and other available methods of dealing with him or her.

Both Crown courts and magistrates' courts may impose a hospital order in respect of any imprisonable offence other than one for which the penalty is fixed by law (section 37(1)). For practical purposes the restriction is confined to murder cases. For this reason, where an identical exclusion operates in relation to measures discussed later in this chapter, the offence of murder only will be mentioned. Magistrates' courts have the additional power to make an order in the absence of a conviction if they would be able to do so following conviction and they are satisfied both that the accused suffers from one of the two major disorders, and that he or she committed the act or omission charged (section 37(3)).

It is unfortunate, given the laudable intention of section 37, that the legislation fails to provide courts with the muscle to enforce their decisions. Section 37(4) of the Act dictates that a hospital order cannot be made unless the court has evidence that a bed will be available to receive the patient within 28 days. If not, the court is effectively obliged to imprison the offender. All that it can do to prevent its intentions from frustration is to call the Regional Health Authority to account for its admissions policy (section 39) and hope that this produces a bed through embarrassment.

The power to issue a transfer direction under section 47

Section 47 of the 1983 Act enables the Home Secretary to transfer a mentally disordered sentenced prisoner to hospital by means of a transfer direction. The medical criteria for doing so are identical to those in section 37, except that the evidence must satisfy the Minister rather than a court. In addition the Minister must be of the opinion that it is expedient to make the transfer, having regard to the public interest and all the circumstances (section 47(1)). A transfer direction has the same effect as a hospital order (section 47(3)).

The power to make a hospital order under the CP(IUP)A 1991

Except in murder cases, section 3 of the CP(IUP)A 1991, permits a court to dispose of a defendant found 'under a disability' (unfit to plead) or not guilty by reason of insanity (the 'special verdict'; section 1 of the Criminal Procedure (Insanity) Act 1964 [CP(I)A 1964]) by means of a hospital order, as defined by section 37 of the MHA 1983 (section 6(2) of the 1991 Act).

The 1991 Act does not require, however, that the criteria in section 37 be applied in these cases (White, 1992, p. 10). Once the jury has returned the relevant verdict, the court may make a hospital order at its discretion. Strictly speaking, therefore, the sole criterion for making the order is the jury's verdict. Although, indirectly, it could be argued that proof of the requirements for a finding of unfitness or insanity constitutes a *de facto* set of criteria for imposing the order, the identical argument would apply to each of the orders which the court is empowered to make under the 1991 Act (see further below).

Admission as a Restricted Patient

Admission as a restricted patient may occur at almost identical stages in the criminal justice process to admission as an unrestricted patient. This is because of the two-stage admission procedure contained in the MHA 1983. The first step is fulfilment of the conditions for imposing a hospital order (or equivalent); the second, consideration of the criteria for making the patient's detention subject to the restrictions outlined above. Therefore, the measures which are relevant here are:

(1) Disposal by way of a hospital order with restrictions under sections 37 and 41 of the 1983 Act.
(2) Disposal by way of a hospital order with restrictions following a finding of unfitness or insanity under section 3 of the CP(IUP)A 1991.
(3) Transfer of a sentenced prisoner to hospital by a transfer direction with restrictions under sections 47 and 49 of the 1983 Act.
(4) Transfer of a remand prisoner to hospital by a transfer direction with restrictions under sections 48 and 49 of the 1983 Act.

Just as the Act lays down a basic framework with regard to unrestricted patients in section 37, so it does in relation to restricted patients in section 41. Therefore, section 41 will be considered first followed by the remaining powers under the 1983 Act. The effect of the 1991 Act will be dealt with last.

The power to make a restriction order under section 41 of the MHA 1983

The power to impose a restriction order is confined to the Crown court. Therefore, a magistrates' court which believes that a restriction order should be made in a case before it, must either deal with the individual in an alternative way or remit the case to be dealt with by the Crown court (section 43(1)).

The appropriate procedure to be followed in making a restriction order was set out by the Court of Appeal in the recent guideline decision of *R v Birch* (1990). Once the court has decided to make a hospital order, it should then consider whether a restriction order under section 41(1) should be imposed as well (*R v Birch* (1990) at 87). The criteria to be applied are that it appears necessary to do so 'for the protection of the public from serious harm', having regard to 'the nature of the offence, the antecedents of the offender and the risk of his committing further offences if set at large'. In other words, the court may impose restrictions if it believes the offender is dangerous.

Before imposing the order, the court must hear oral evidence from at least one of the doctors testifying to the offender's mental disorder for the purposes of section 37 (section 41(2)). However, it was made clear in *R v Birch* (1990) that this statutory requirement did not mean that the court was bound by the doctor's opinion. On the contrary, Mustill L. J. was quite categorical that it was the court's task to assess the risk posed by the offender. He cited the contrasting terms of sections 37 and 41 as support for this view. He said, at 86,

Before a hospital order can be made, the court must be satisfied of the stated conditions 'on the written or oral evidence of two practitioners'. But where a restriction order is in question, section 41(2) requires no more than that the court shall hear the oral evidence of one of the medical practitioners. It need not follow the course which he recommends. Section 41(1) makes the assessment of the risk ... [a matter] for the court.

This is not merely a linguistic distinction but is a further example of the 'diagnostic question/social question' dichotomy highlighted by Forbes J. in the context of section 72 of the Act (see above, p. 15).

A restriction order may be imposed for a determinate period or indefinitely (section 41(1)). However, in R v Birch the Court of Appeal confirmed its earlier advice that cases in which a determinate order is appropriate are scarce ((1990) at 88 approving R v Gardiner (1967)).

The power to make a restriction direction under section 49

Section 49(1) of the 1983 Act enables the Secretary of State to impose a restriction direction on a sentenced prisoner in addition to a transfer direction 'if he thinks fit'. No specific criteria have to be fulfilled (section 49(1)). A restriction direction has the same effect as a restriction order (section 49(2)).

The Minister also has the power under sections 48 and 49 of the Act to transfer a remand prisoner to hospital. However, a transfer direction may only be issued if there is medical evidence that the prisoner is suffering from one of the two major disorders and is in urgent need of treatment (section 48(1)) and the Minister must also impose a restriction direction (section 49(1)).

The power to make a hospital order with restrictions under the CP(IUP)A 1991

Section 3 of the 1991 Act requires a court to make a hospital order with restrictions in respect of any defendant found unfit to plead or not guilty on a special verdict in relation to a murder charge. Over and above that, the court has the discretion to make such an order in all other cases.

THE OVERALL FRAMEWORK OF THE CRIMINAL JUSTICE SYSTEM

The way in which the powers described thus far fit into the overall scheme for diverting the mentally disordered from the criminal justice system into mental health care will now be considered. The system is summarised in Figure 1.1.

Pre-trial Measures

Pre-trial measures fall into two categories. First, exercised by or affecting the police. Secondly, powers available to the courts and Home Secretary at the remand stage.

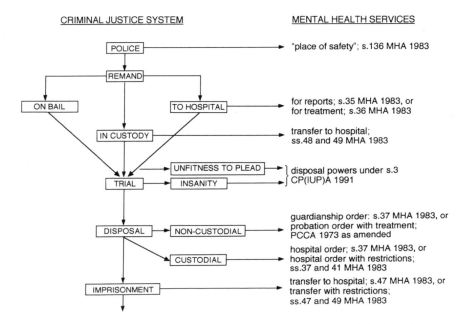

Figure 1.1   System for diverting the mentally disordered from the criminal justice system into mental health care

Powers available to the police

Section 136(1) of the MHA 1983 enables a police officer to remove a person who appears to be mentally disordered and 'in immediate need of care or control' from a public place to a 'place of safety' (defined in section 135(6)), if the officer thinks it necessary to do so in the person's own interests or for the protection of others. The power is not dependent for its exercise upon suspicion that the individual has been involved in the commission of an offence. It permits detention up to a maximum of 72 hours in order for arrangements to be made for the person's treatment or care.

The measure is controversial because the trigger for its use is the wide generic definition of 'mental disorder' under section 2(1) of the Act not the presence of one of the four specific disorders considered above (p. 19). Given its 'ordinary and natural meaning' the generic definition appears sufficiently elastic to embrace mental handicap and any recognised psychiatric condition which is sufficiently serious to be labelled abnormal (Hoggett, 1990, p. 58). Although it may be argued that section 136 authorises comparatively short periods of compulsory detention, none the less 72 hours is sufficient to constitute a serious interference with civil liberties.

The second set of measures affecting the police are the safeguards contained in the Police and Criminal Evidence Act 1984 Code of Practice for the Detention, Treatment and Questioning of Persons by Police Officers. If it is known or suspected that a person in police custody is mentally disordered, mentally handicapped or is mentally incapable of understanding questions then a 'responsible adult' should be present during the course of police interrogation. The 'responsible adult' (defined in the Code; paragraph 1.7) should never be a person employed by the police. He or she is intended actively to intervene in the questioning process in the manner that a 'normal' suspect would be expected to do in order to protect his or her rights.

Remand powers

Powers of the courts   Courts may remand a defendant to hospital for two reasons. First, under section 35, if it is suspected, on the evidence of one section 12 doctor, that an accused suffers from one of the four specific MHA disorders, he or she may be remanded to hospital for a report to be made on their mental condition (section 35(3)). Crown courts may utilise this power both in relation to defendants awaiting trial and to offenders awaiting sentence. Magistrates' courts may only use it following conviction or a finding that the accused committed the act or omission charged (section 35(2)). Secondly, section 36 permits the Crown court to remand a defendant awaiting trial or prior to sentence to hospital for treatment if it is satisfied, on the evidence of two doctors (one of whom must be a section 12 doctor), that the person is suffering from one of the major disorders to a nature and degree requiring detention in hospital for medical treatment. Both sections 35 and 36 apply only to defendants charged with an imprisonable offence, other than murder. Orders under both sections are made for 28 days, renewable up to a maximum of twelve weeks.

The Home Secretary's powers   These have already been explained above.

Measures Available to Courts during the Trial

Mental disorder may arise at trial either because the defendant is unfit to plead or through the pleading of a defence.

Unfitness to plead

The law of unfitness to plead affords protection to a defendant who is mentally disordered at the time of trial with the result that he or she lacks capacity adequately to participate in the trial process.

In order to return a verdict that the defendant is 'under a disability' the jury must be satisfied as to two conditions. The first is that the defendant committed the act or omission charged (a similar provision to section 37(3) of the 1983 Act). If the evidence fails to establish this the defendant must be acquitted (section 4A of the 1964 Act as amended by section 2 of the 1991 Act). Secondly, the jury must be satisfied that the defendant is unable:

(1) to understand the difference between the pleas of guilty and not guilty,

(2) to challenge jurors,
(3) to instruct counsel, or
(4) to understand the evidence (*R* v *Pritchard* (1836)).

The 1991 Act has also introduced a procedural requirement that the jury must have written or oral evidence from two or more registered medical practitioners (at least one of whom must be a section 12 doctor) (section 4 of the CP(I)A 1964 as amended by section 2 of the 1991 Act) before reaching a finding of unfitness. The same requirement also now applies in insanity cases (section 1 of the 1991 Act). Should the defendant recover sufficient capacity he or she may be remitted to face trial but this is not inevitable (Mackay, 1991).

Other than where the defendant is charged with murder and the court is obliged to impose a hospital order with restrictions, it may order one of the following disposals following a finding of unfitness (section 3 of the CP(IUP)A 1991):

(1) a hospital order with restrictions,
(2) a hospital order *simpliciter*,
(3) a guardianship order,
(4) a treatment and supervision order,
(5) an absolute discharge.

The custodial orders were dealt with above; the non-custodial orders will be dealt with below.

Defences

English law contains two defences which specifically cater for the mentally disordered; insanity and diminished responsibility.

Insanity   The insanity defence, which operates in relation to all crimes, is set out in the M'Naghten rules. They provide that, to rely on the defence, it must be established that,

> ... at the time of the committing of the act, the [defendant] was labouring under such a defect of reason, from disease of the mind, as not to know the nature and quality of the act he was doing; or, if he did know it, that he did not know he was doing what was wrong (*R* v *M'Naghten* (1843) at 210, per Tindal C.J.).

It will be seen that, in fact, the Rules create two alternative defences, which have in common that the defendant was suffering from 'a defect of reason from disease of the mind' at the material time. It is well established that a 'disease of the mind' is any disease, deriving from a cause internal to the body (*R* v *Quick* [1973]), which affects 'the mental faculties of reason, memory and understanding'. As Devlin J. said in *R* v *Kemp* [1957], at 407, 'the condition of the brain is irrelevant and so is the question whether the disease is curable or incurable, transitory or permanent'. The only limiting factor is that the disease must cause a 'defect of reason'. This has been held to mean that it must deprive the defendant of the ability to reason; a mere failure to use such reasoning power as is possessed is insufficient (*R* v *Clarke* [1972]).

To rely on the first limb of the Rules, the mental abnormality must cause the defendant 'not to know the nature and quality of the act he was doing'; that is, to lack *mens rea* (*R* v *Sullivan* [1984]). Alternatively, if *mens rea* was possessed, under the second limb, the abnormality must cause the defendant not to 'know he was doing what was wrong'. Under English jurisdiction 'wrong' has been held to mean legally, as opposed to morally, wrong (*R* v *Windle* [1952]).

The Rules have been the subject of wide-ranging criticism for decades, not only in England and Wales, but also in other common law jurisdictions. Suffice it to say that the response in some parts of the United States has been either to amend the Rules or to replace them entirely. Yet, despite a number of attempts at wholesale reform, no entirely satisfactory formulation has been arrived at. This is because none of the tests so far suggested has managed to strike an acceptable balance between updating the law in line with contemporary medical knowledge about brain function, addressing the potential conflict between the defendant's need for treatment and the wider interests of justice and maintaining the appropriate separation in decision-making between the judge and/or jury and the expert witness (see, for example, Morris, 1975, pp. 11–37). If insanity is successfully pleaded the court's disposal powers are identical to those following a finding of unfitness to plead.

Diminished responsibility   Section 2 of the Homicide Act 1957 creates the partial defence of diminished responsibility to the crime of murder. If successfully pleaded it reduces the defendant's liability to that for manslaughter. For the offender this carries the benefit that sentencing becomes discretionary. The court may either impose a penal or a therapeutic disposal, up to a maximum penalty of life imprisonment.

To rely on the defence it must be established that the accused

> ... was suffering from such abnormality of mind (whether arising from a condition of arrested or retarded development of mind or any inherent causes or induced by disease or injury) as substantially impaired his mental responsibility for his acts or omissions in doing or being a party to the killing (section 2(1) of the 1957 Act).

'Abnormality of mind' was defined by Lord Parker C.J. in *R* v *Byrne* [1960]. Having pointed out that it was a wider concept than 'disease of the mind' under the M'Naghten rules, he went on to state, at 403, that it was:

> ... a state of mind so different from that of ordinary human beings that the reasonable man would term it abnormal. It appears to us to be wide enough to cover the mind's activities in all its aspects, not only the perception of physical acts and matters, and the ability to form a rational judgment as to whether an act is right or wrong, but also the ability to exercise will power to control physical acts in accordance with that rational judgment.

This statement bears a striking resemblance to Lawton L. J.'s definition of 'mental illness' in *W* v *L* [1974] (above, p. 19) and produces a defence which includes a number of conditions which are excluded from insanity. The sole limiting factor is that the 'abnormality of mind' must derive from one of the listed causes.

Measures Available to Courts at the Disposal Stage

The courts have a selection of custodial and non-custodial disposals available to them for dealing with mentally disordered offenders.

Custodial measures

Hospital orders, with and without restrictions, have already been considered above (pp. 18–22). It is also appropriate to consider the role of the discretionary life sentence.

Discretionary life imprisonment   Life imprisonment is the maximum penalty for a surprising number of crimes under English law. However, in practice, its use is confined to offences which involve death or serious bodily harm, serious sexual offences and property damage aggravated by threats of harm to the person.

It is established sentencing law that cases in which it is appropriate to impose a discretionary life sentence are those where the offence is sufficiently grave to merit a long prison term and the offender is mentally unstable or disordered and poses a continuing risk to the public (*R* v *Wilkinson* (1983)). Normally the court should hear medical evidence before passing sentence, although, in exceptional cases, it may dispense with this requirement (*R* v *Virgo* (1988)). This is consistent with the approach taken to risk assessment in the context of the MHA 1983 (see above, p. 21).

Non-custodial measures

Guardianship orders   The criteria for making a guardianship order following conviction are identical to those for imposing a hospital order under section 37 of the MHA 1983 except that the treatability criterion does not apply and the offender must be 16 years of age or older and suffering from the mental disorder to a nature or degree which warrants reception into the guardianship of the local authority (section 37(2)(a)(ii)). A guardianship order may also be made following a finding of unfitness or insanity (CP(IUP)A 1991, section 3).

Probation order with a condition of treatment   A probation order may be imposed on an offender who is 16 years or over. The criteria for doing so are that the court is of the opinion that supervision by a probation officer

... is desirable in the interests of—
(a) securing the rehabilitation of the offender; or

(b) protecting the public from harm from him or preventing the commission by him of further offences ...

The order must be between six months and three years in duration (section 2(1) of the Powers of Criminal Courts Act 1973 as amended by section 8 of the Criminal Justice Act 1991). The court may impose a number of additional requirements upon the offender which include attendance for psychiatric treatment (section 9 of the Criminal Justice Act 1991).

Supervision and treatment order   Except in murder cases, a court may make a supervision and treatment order following a finding of unfitness to plead or insanity. To do so it must be satisfied on the evidence of two doctors, one of whom must be a section 12 doctor, that the defendant's mental condition requires treatment, and may be susceptible to it, but that it is not sufficiently serious to warrant the making of a guardianship order or admission to hospital (Schedule 2, Part II, para.2(1) of the CP(IUP)A 1991). The court must also be satisfied that the order is the most suitable means of dealing with the defendant. The order may be for up to two years in duration.

Transfer of Sentenced Prisoners from Prison to Hospital

The Secretary of State's powers to transfer sentenced prisoners to hospital as either unrestricted or restricted patients were considered above (pp. 20, 22).

III   THEMES, INCONSISTENCIES AND CONFLICTS

The final section of this chapter aims to highlight some of the conflicts inherent in the scheme of provision described in Part II. Although the topics selected for inclusion may seem diverse, the conclusion will attempt to knit them together through a re-examination of the status of the mentally disordered in the criminal justice system.

THE CONCEPT OF JUSTICE

Superficially, at least, many of the measures which have been developed to provide for mentally disordered offenders are founded in the ideals of 'justice' and 'humanity'. Defendants suffering an appropriate mental disability at the time they commit the *actus reus* of an offence are excused liability and a therapeutic disposal is generally ordered. Similarly, where conviction results, a mentally disordered offender may be 'excused' the punishment of imprisonment and receive the compassionate alternative of a hospital order. Individuals have the right not to be convicted of offences for which they are not legally responsible. Equally a person who is seriously mentally disordered has a right to treatment for it; or, so it is said. However, there is an alternative perspective: one which holds that the law is nothing like as philanthropic as it is claimed to be. Critics maintain, for a variety of reasons, that the price of compassion is the erosion of human rights.

First, in the sphere of criminal responsibility, it is asserted that the mentally disordered have the same right to be treated as responsible actors as the 'normal' population. However, insanity and diminished responsibility both involve at least a partial denial of rational control over, and motivation for, acts. For example, if a woman kills whilst suffering from severe pre-menstrual tension diminished responsibility may be available as a defence (*R* v *Smith* [1982]). But if the plea is successful, the offender is instantly transformed from a reasonable being into a helpless victim of her hormones. Even if she believes that her self-control was reduced, *she* may none the less view her behaviour as rational. Therefore, a tension is created between the woman's image of herself and her right to rely on the defence which may cause her to feel that her dignity and respect have been undermined. The difference in legal outcome between the mandatory life sentence for murder and the court's discretionary sentencing powers following a manslaughter conviction which hinges upon acceptance of the defence only serves to make the dilemma more acute.

The second line of argument is even more potent. An offender made subject to a hospital order is likely to be compulsorily detained for far longer than his or her counterpart sentenced to a term of imprisonment for the same offence, especially if a restriction order is also imposed. From the outset fixed terms of imprisonment, by definition, have an identified point at which further detention becomes unlawful. Hospital orders do not. The rationale is that only in an exceptional case is it possible to predict recovery. It has been passionately argued by C. S. Lewis (Lewis, 1972) that the upshot is that the offender's discharge becomes dependent upon the effecting of a 'cure' which is itself difficult to define and identify. Therefore, the patient's civil liberties are sacrificed to doctors and other professionals who operate in a realm which is divorced from the criminal justice system and thus from any concept of natural justice or desert.

Lewis' argument may be regarded as over-exaggerated in the light of the powers of MHRTs. Nevertheless the significance of Tribunals can also be over-stated in view of the increasing body of research pointing to their cautious approach (see above, p. 16). Overall there is ample evidence to suggest not only that detention for mentally disordered offenders is prolonged but that, once caught up in the system, it is extremely difficult to shake free of it.

THE ROLE OF NON-LEGAL EXPERTS

Expert witnesses, particularly psychiatrists, play a central role in the decision-making process. This makes it important to consider the inter-relationship of law with other disciplines and the demands made by the legal process of expert witnesses. The discussion which follows will focus upon the interaction between law and psychiatry.

In common with all specialisms, discourse in law and in psychiatry is conducted in its own technical vocabulary. As a consequence each discipline tends to be impervious to the other and communication between lawyer and psychiatrist can be a fraught process. Breakdown can occur in a number of ways. For example, legal and medical concepts of mental disorder bear scant relationship to each other. Therefore, the psychiatrist must bring his or her diagnosis within one of the legal labels in order to trigger a 'mental health' response from a court. But the mismatch penetrates further. Take the question 'Was the defendant responsible for his or her acts at the time of the offence?' For the lawyer 'the state of a man's mind is as much a fact as the state of his digestion' (*Edgington* v *Fitzmaurice* (1885) at 483, per Bowen L. J.). Therefore, what is expected is the answer 'yes' or 'no'. However, to the psychiatrist this complex issue demands an elaborate explanation of behaviour.

Divergence in relation to questions like this stems both from a disparity of approach to the cognitive process and a different focus of interest. The product of the incoherence may be to distort the medical evidence. The doctor is likely to be pressed to respond in black and white terms. If unwilling to do so, he or she may find that their expertise is undermined through apparent inability 'to give a simple answer to a simple question'. Alternatively, by giving in, the witness may feel that professional expertise has been sacrificed to the demands of the court room. In essence this is one of a variety of ethical dilemmas with which the expert may be confronted.

Preparation of psychiatric reports may also lead to ethical problems, caused by the fact that the task cannot be undertaken in a vacuum. It may be said that reports should be prepared without reference to the context in which they are to be used. But how is the psychiatrist to exclude extrinsic matters from his or her consideration? For example; should the patient's wishes be seen as relevant? Should the psychiatrist take into account the fact that a therapeutic disposal is likely to lead to longer detention than a penal sentence? In drafting a report to what extent should the psychiatrist be sensitive to alternative interpretations of its contents or other uses to which it may be put? The solution to these issues is heavily dependent upon identifying whose interest(s) the psychiatrist is intended to serve.

THE LOCATION AND NATURE OF DECISION-MAKING POWER

The decision-making process is given heightened complexity by the array of interests involved and the distribution of authority to take decisions amongst a variety of individuals and institutions. To some extent power has been spread deliberately, for instance, in deciding the composition of MHRTs, as a means of ensuring competent decisions as well as enhancing balance between the competing interests of the patient's right to treatment, the needs of justice and public protection. Presenting these matters in shopping list fashion, though, suggests that they are discrete items, susceptible to independent consideration and readily identifiable with the actors involved. But this is a questionable supposition.

In reality the demarcation of role between decision-makers is blurred. Moreover, even where there has been some attempt at clarification, it has not been outstandingly successful. Referring back, for example, to the 'medical question/social question' distinction (see above, pp. 15, 17, 22, 27), the demarcation between the role of the psychiatrist and that of the court is not a sharp one. In each context where the division has been identified either the court is required to hear medical evidence before adjudicating on dangerousness or, where that is not the case, it has been emphasised that only exceptionally should risk assessments be made in the absence of medical evidence. Therefore, interdependence between the disciplines involved is encouraged. In addition, in some situations, the nature of the decisions being taken means that it is difficult to divorce wider legal and social questions from proper medical comment. This is an additional problem entailed in writing a psychiatric report. It is also the issue under scrutiny when lawyers ask doctors about responsibility. Attribution of responsibility is a conclusion of law. Therefore, it should not be decided by a psychiatrist.

THE POLITICAL DIMENSION

Seen at its most basic, the political process determines policy and thus, the nature, level and extent of service provision. Recent political activity has not been confined to the Home Office circular promoting diversion but has produced a Department of Health review of health and social services for mentally disordered offenders (Department of Health/Home Office, 1992).

It is easy to lose sight of the importance of service provision but it is crucial in enabling effective implementation of other policies. For example, the problems associated with Community Care have not been confined to civil and informal patients but have affected criminal patients too. Secure facilities have found difficulty moving patients on through the system. Simultaneously the closure of asylums has resulted in vulnerable people finding their way onto the streets, heightening the likelihood that they will end up in prison. It is ironic, therefore, that the Home Office is urging the transfer of the mentally disordered away from the criminal justice system.

CONCLUSION

In seeking to draw together the various strands of argument presented in this chapter, two inter-related points have particular importance. The first is to emphasise the challenging nature of the problems posed by mentally disordered offenders, both for the professional groups with which they come into contact, and for society in general. The second is to highlight the conflict of beliefs and interests which pervades the current scheme of provision for coping with them.

As a feature it is likely to outlive any proposed reform, although enhanced inter-disciplinary understanding and communication should mitigate its effects.

Expanding on the first point; the challenge springs from the fact that decisions regarding the treatment and disposal of mentally disordered offenders involve the balancing of moral and ethical principles, considerations of civil liberties and human rights, jurisprudential and penological theory and political and social doctrine regarding service provision and delivery. Prioritising, let alone recon-ciling, these diverse and disparate requirements is a highly demanding task.

Given the fundamental nature of many of these ingredients, this in itself would amount to a powerful recipe for conflict. However, the task is made still more difficult by two further factors. First, the system requires co-operation between mental health and criminal law, despite the fact that the former is designed to facilitate treatment and containment whilst the latter is primarily concerned with securing the just conviction and punishment of the guilty. Therefore, their focuses of concern, principles and priorities are very different. Secondly, there are the tensions produced as a result of the multi-disciplinary basis of the system and the hierarchy of professional groups involved. Viewed in combination, it is not surprising that conflict results from these pressures.

The product of a challenging problem with multi-disciplinary implications ought to be the promotion of informed, interested debate aimed at enhanced understanding. However, in practice, the reverse has been the case. Mentally disordered offenders have been of marginal interest to the committed few in the relevant disciplines. It is to be hoped that one of the effects of the current renewed interest in this area, seen, for example, in the establishment of the Department of Health review, will be to promote the discussion and collabo-ration that is so badly needed in order to find more satisfactory solutions to the problems of the existing system.

REFERENCES

Department of Health/Home Office (1992). *Review of Health and Social Services for Mentally Disordered Offenders and Others Requiring Similar Services*, Cm. 2088. London: HMSO.

European Convention on Human Rights (1950), *Cmd. 8969*.

Genn, H. (1989). *The Effectiveness of Representation at Tribunals: A Report to the Lord Chancellor*, London: Lord Chancellor's Department.

Hoggett, B. (1990). *Mental Health Law*, 3rd edition. London: Sweet & Maxwell.

Home Office Circular No. 66/90, *Provision for Mentally Disordered Offenders*.

Lewis, C. S. (1972). The Humanitarian Theory of Punishment. In Gerber, R. J. and McAnany, P. D. (eds), *Contemporary Punishment*, Indiana: University of Notre-Dame Press.

Mackay, R., The Decline of Disability in Relation to the Trial [1991] Crim LR 87.

Morris, G. H. (1975). *The Insanity Defence: A Blueprint for Legislative Reform*. Lex-ington, MA: Lexington Books.

Peay, J. (1989). *Tribunals on Trial: A Study of Decision-Making under the Mental Health Act 1983*. Oxford: Clarendon Press.

Walker, N. (1968). *Crime & Insanity in England*. Edinburgh: Edinburgh University Press.

White, S. The Criminal Procedure (Insanity and Unfitness to Plead) Act 1991 [1992] Crim LR 4.

Cases

Broome v *Perkins* (1987) 85 Cr App Rep 321.
Edgington v *Fitzmaurice* (1885) 29 Ch D 459.
Kynaston v *Secretary of State for Home Affairs* (1981) 73 Cr App Rep 281.
R v *Birch* (1990) 90 Cr App Rep 78.
R v *Byrne* [1960] 2 QB 396.
R v *Clarke* [1972] 1 All ER 219.
R v *Gardiner* (1967) 51 Cr App Rep 187.
R v *Kemp* [1957] 1 QB 399.
R v *M'Naghten* (1843) 10 Cl & Fin 200.
R v *MHRT, ex parte Pickering* [1986] 1 All ER 99.
R v *Merseyside MHRT, ex parte K* [1990] 1 All ER 694.
R v *Pritchard* (1836) 7 C & P 303.
R v *Quick* [1973] QB 910.
R v *Secretary of State for the Home Department, ex parte K* [1990] 3 All ER 562.
R v *Smith* [1982] Crim LR 531.
R v *Sullivan* [1984] AC 156.
R v *Virgo* (1988) 10 Cr App Rep (S) 427.
R v *Wilkinson* (1983) 5 Cr App Rep (S) 105.
R v *Windle* [1952] 2 QB 826.
Secretary of State for the Home Department v *MHRT for the Mersey Regional Health Authority* [1986] 3 All ER 233.
W v *L* [1974] 1 QB 711.
Winterwerp v *The Netherlands* [1979] 2 EHRR 387.
Woolmington v *DPP* [1935] AC 462.
X v *United Kingdom* [1981] 4 EHRR 181.

Statutes and Statutory Instruments

Criminal Justice Act 1991.
Criminal Law Act 1967.
Criminal Procedure (Insanity) Act 1964.
Criminal Procedure (Insanity and Unfitness to Plead) Act 1991.
Homicide Act 1957.
Mental Health Act 1959.
Mental Health Act 1983.
Powers of Criminal Courts Act 1973.
Sexual Offences (Amendment) Act 1976.

Police and Criminal Evidence Act 1984 Codes of Practice No.2 (SI 1990: 2580).

2

Service Provision and Facilities for the Mentally Disordered Offender

HERSCHEL PRINS
Midlands Centre for Criminology and Criminal Justice, University of Loughborough, UK

> We remain uncertain how to treat them ... [mentally disordered offenders] ... We are unwilling to leave them alone, yet most agencies seek to avoid responsibility for their care. We confine them to prisons and to prison-like hospitals where they are sometimes treated worse than other offenders.
>
> (Halleck, 1987, p. 11)

INTRODUCTION

This chapter reviews the service provision and facilities for mentally disordered offenders with special reference to England and Wales. However, where appropriate, brief reference is made to the law and provision in Scotland, Northern Ireland and Ireland. In the space available it has not proved possible to review the provisions in the North Americas or in other European countries. Readers who wish to study these will find the *International Journal of Law and Psychiatry* a valuable resource. They will also find much helpful information on law and services in the *Principles and Practice of Forensic Psychiatry* (Bluglass and Bowden, 1990) and hopefully in the references cited in this chapter. The chapter is divided into four parts. Part I is concerned with a brief survey of the legal context of provision for mentally disordered offenders, the somewhat idiosyncratic and serendipitous nature of disposals, and concludes with some brief comment upon the relationship between mental abnormality and crime. Part II offers some indication of the extent of mental abnormality in penal and other populations and some of the problems of assessing this with any degree of

Clinical Approaches to the Mentally Disordered Offender
Edited by K. Howells and C. R. Hollin © 1993 John Wiley & Sons Ltd

accuracy. Part III outlines the main provisions for dealing with mentally abnormal offenders and Part IV deals with the community, social and psychiatric supervision of potentially dangerous offender-patients.

I   CERTAINTY OR SERENDIPITY

Those with experience in the field of forensic services would probably agree that whether an offender receives a psychiatric or a penal disposal sometimes seems to rest as much upon chance as upon any more clearly discernible factors. The more cynical might go on to observe that much will depend upon the credibility and/or public performing skills of one's psychiatrist, what the judge had for breakfast, the prejudice of the jury and the talents of one's advocate. Certainly the determination of many cases involving mental abnormality and crime appears to be idiosyncratic. This is largely because the law is a clumsy instrument for determining such issues. Two famous statements encapsulate opposing views in this matter. The famous jurist Lord Coke said 'The Law is the perfection of reason' and Dickens' Mr Bumble suggested that 'The Law is a ass—a idiot'. The following three well-known cases are put forward in an attempt to illustrate the above points.

Case One—Peter Sutcliffe

Peter Sutcliffe pleaded not guilty on the grounds of diminished responsibility to the murder of thirteen women and guilty to the attempted murder of seven others. His defence to the charges of murder was that his delusional belief that he had a Divine mission to rid the world of prostitutes constituted a sufficient abnormally of mind (namely a paranoid schizophrenic illness) as to diminish substantially his mental responsibility for his acts within the meaning of Section 2 of the English Homicide Act, 1957. Counsel for the prosecution had indicated that they were happy to accept their own experts' views to this effect and they were also in agreement with the defence's similar psychiatric evidence. Thus, there was no dispute as to his mental state. However, the judge, no doubt because he regarded the case as one of great public importance, decided, as was his right, to place the matter of Sutcliffe's mental state before a jury and thus not leave it to the 'experts'. As a result of this decision we had the unedifying spectacle of the prosecution having to discredit the evidence of their own psychiatric witnesses which up to then they had been prepared to accept unreservedly. The psychiatric witnesses for the defence received the same treatment, and the case received a great deal of publicity (see for example Prins, 1986, ch. 2). The result of this sad case (sad for the law, and sad for psychiatry) is well known. The jury reached a majority (10:2) verdict that Sutcliffe was guilty of murder and he was sentenced to life imprisonment with a minimum recommendation that he serve 30 years. It is important to note that the jury did *not* by this finding necessarily conclude that Sutcliffe was not mentally abnormal, merely that the abnormality was not of sufficient degree to diminish substantially his responsibility within the meaning of the Homicide Act. Many people—and not only mental health professionals—thought this a somewhat strange verdict in respect of a man who by any accounts seemed grossly abnormal.

In the event, the psychiatric view prevailed. Within two years the Home Secretary found it necessary to have Sutcliffe transferred from prison to Special Hospital under the terms of Section 47/49 of the Mental Health Act, 1983, but not before he had been violently assaulted by a fellow prisoner and not before his psychiatric condition had continued to deteriorate steadily. It might not be unreasonable to question whether the case would have had a happier outcome for all concerned if the judge had acquiesced in the agreed course of action put forward by both prosecution and defence in the first instance.

Case Two—Dennis Nilsen

Nilsen admitted to killing fifteen young men and dissecting, boiling and burning their bodies. No doubt he would be described by observers in the United States as a 'serial killer' (see Holmes and De Burger, 1988; Norris, 1990). He was sentenced to life imprisonment, the judge adding a recommendation that he serve a minimum of 25 years. The jury had convicted him, as in Sutcliffe's case, of murder by a majority (10 : 2) verdict. In arguing for a manslaughter verdict on the grounds of diminished responsibility Nilsen's counsel had tried to convince the jury (not unreasonably one might think) that 'anyone guilty of such horrific acts must be out of his mind' (*The Times*, 5 November 1983). For not only did he kill them, but he lived with the decomposing products of his activities for many months. It was claimed for Nilsen that he was suffering from a severe enough form of personality disorder to constitute an abnormality of the mind within the meaning of the Homicide Act. Nilsen's activities were, if anything, even more grotesque and abnormal than Sutcliffe's and his case illustrates, once again, the problem of trying to fit the inevitably imprecise concepts used in psychiatry into the confining strait-jacket of the current legislation.

Case Three—Michael Telling

In June 1984, Michael Telling was gaoled for life for the manslaughter (on the grounds of diminished responsibility) of his second wife. Following a nine-day trial, the jury took only *two and a half hours* to reach a unanimous verdict. By all accounts, Telling had received a difficult upbringing, had been highly disturbed as a child and shown poor control of his impulses. The facts in Telling's case are only minimally less bizarre than those in Sutcliffe's and Nilsen's. Admittedly, he had committed only one murder, but the circumstances of that single killing seem singularly grotesque. According to press accounts (*Guardian*, 30 June 1984) Telling shot his wife after she had allegedly taunted him beyond endurance with details concerning her sexual encounters with both sexes. After killing her, he moved her body round the house for a week or so, calling in occasionally to kiss and talk to the corpse as it lay on a camp-bed. He then placed the body in a half-burnt sauna in the house. *Five months* later it is alleged he tried unsuccessfully to bury the body but, before doing so, he decapitated it, taking the head with him in the boot of his car. In Telling's case, two psychiatrists testified that his responsibility was diminished and one testified against that view. It is difficult to tell whether the jury was more influenced by the opinions of the two psychiatrists, who considered him to be suffering from an abnormality of mind that would diminish his responsibility, or by his bizarre activities following the killing, when they, no doubt, took the view that anybody who behaved in such a fashion 'must have been mad'. It is to be noted that even after a finding of an abnormality of mind (in this case a severe disorder of personality) Telling did not receive a hospital disposal, no doubt on the grounds that such a disorder of personality was not a treatable condition within the strict criteria for the compulsory detention of persons suffering from psychopathic disorder under the Mental Health Act. However, in over a decade of experience as a member of the Mental Health Review Tribunal and having had to review a large number of fairly similar cases, the present writer has come across cases which *did* attract a hospital disposal. In these the examining doctors no doubt took the view that hospital detention would at least (as the Act requires) alleviate the condition or prevent its deterioration. These three cases illustrate the vagaries of the current law. Before proceeding further it will be helpful if the law is put briefly into context.

Brief Legal Context

A short statement of the current provisions for the disposal of mentally disordered offenders through the courts, the penal and health care systems in England and Wales may be found at Appendix I. Briefer reference to the legal position in Scotland, Northern Ireland and Ireland may also be found there. (The complex provisions in the North American States may be found by perusal of the *International Journal of Law and Psychiatry*).

The law has always made some allowance for mental abnormality in determining capacity and culpability for crime. However, at the risk of considerable over-simplification, it appears from the three examples given above that such allowance has often appeared to be capricious and, in some instances, idiosyncratic. Briefly put, the following are the main forms of psychiatric exculpation from responsibility for crime:

(1) Severe insanity of the McNaghten variety may result in the 'special verdict' of not guilty by reason of insanity. That this is pleaded very rarely today is largely due to the severity of the test of insanity that is applied, to the extent that its use in murder cases has become virtually redundant since the passing of the Homicide Act, 1957, and because capital punishment has been abolished.

(2) Inability to follow the proceedings, to challenge jurors and instruct counsel may permit a plea of 'unfitness to plead' (or being 'under disability' as it is now called). One of the main problems with both these defences is that detention in hospital, sometimes under conditions of maximum security,

was, until 1991, the automatic outcome. In addition, in the case of unfitness to plead, the facts of the case might never be heard unless the patient recovered sufficiently to be remitted for trial (see Appendix I).

(3) Since 1957 (but only in murder cases) as already indicated, the accused may plead diminished responsibility on the grounds of an 'abnormality of mind'. If successful, such a plea will result in a verdict, or finding, of manslaughter, leaving the court unrestricted in its choice of disposal. If such a plea fails, the sentence is, of course, a mandatory one of life imprisonment, with or without a recommendation from the trial judge as to its length. As we have seen, the implementation of the Homicide Act has proved to be highly contentious and an area in which psychiatry and law have often proved to be incompatible. Various useful proposals for reform have been put forward, but have not as yet been acted upon (for summaries see Home Office and DHSS, 1975; Prins, 1986).

(4) In other cases, psychiatric evidence may be called in order to mitigate penalty. Generally speaking, courts do not request psychiatric reports very often. When they do, it is in cases where there would appear to be an important element of suspected mental abnormality. Examples are: homicide; serious repeated assault, sexual and non-sexual; cases in which the offence seems 'out of the blue'; repetitive crimes committed over a short period of time without obvious reason; or where the accused has a past or current history of mental disorder. (See Campbell, 1981 and Prins, 1980 for reviews of some of the research.) Where courts do find, on the evidence, that mental disorder has played a significant part in the offending, or the offender is obviously ill at the time of the hearing, they may make orders under the relevant mental health legislation. They may also make probation orders with requirements for in- or out-patient treatment if the offender appears to require it, and is susceptible to informal, as distinct from compulsory, treatment (see Appendix I). They may, of course, also deal with the case in such a manner that permits the offender to continue with treatment without any sanction for it being imposed. This is often the case when a defendant has been under medical care prior to the offence and/or the hearing. It is worth noting that even if mental disorder is present courts are not obliged to follow psychiatric advice, although they usually do (Prins, 1980). It is also worth observing that cases do not always come to court; the police will sometimes exercise their discretion in the case of a mentally abnormal offender, perhaps by implementing the relevant section of the Mental Health Act, 1983 (s 136); or they may merely caution the person concerned in order to allow informal psychiatric care.

II HOW MANY MENTALLY ABNORMAL OFFENDERS?

It is very difficult to answer this question. There are disagreements not only about the aetiology of many mental disorders, but also about whether they actually exist (see e.g. Szasz, 1987, and for a less rhetorical view, Roth and Kroll, 1986). There is little doubt that the prevalence and presentation of mental disorders appear to change over time. For example, disorders that presented in the middle ages and earlier are now rare because of changes in diet and life-style. Some workers also suggest that the schizophrenias, as we know them today, probably did not exist in pre-industrial English society (see e.g. Hare, 1983; Scull, 1984). Crime is not a static phenomenon either. Changes in public attitudes are reflected in changes in the criminal law; crime may be said to 'come and go'. It is therefore not hard to see that since much criminal behaviour is 'somewhat arbitrarily defined and there are arguments over the existence and definition of mental abnormality, it is hardly surprising that we find difficulties in trying to establish connections between these two somewhat ill-defined and complex forms of behaviour' (Prins, 1990a, p. 248). In a recent article, Verdun-Jones (1989) suggests four quite helpful categories of mentally disordered offenders: (i) the predominantly mad who are *not* considered to be dangerous; (ii) the predominantly mad who *are* considered to be dangerous; (iii) the predominantly bad who are not considered dangerous; and (iv) mentally disordered offenders who have committed a serious offence and who are considered to be dangerous. Groups (ii) and (iv) are of particular concern in this presentation. Despite many methodological difficulties considerable efforts have been made over the years to study the prevalence of mental disorder in penal and criminal populations.

It is, of course, comparatively easy to produce the numbers of formally diagnosed and classified mentally disordered offenders in prisons and hospitals and to provide figures for those made subject to psychiatric supervision on probation. However, there are large numbers of mentally disordered offenders not classified in this way who are living in the community, some known to general practitioners and social workers, some not. For reasons referred to below, accurate statistics would be very hard to obtain. The population is neither clearly identifiable nor static enough for head-counting purposes.

Studies of Penal and Criminal Populations

These studies have been conducted on inmates of penal and correctional establishments and attenders at specialists court clinics. The populations are therefore highly selected. This fact has important implications. For example, it is quite likely that the act of incarceration may well exacerbate certain underlying psychiatric conditions; or the effects of such incarceration may be so severe as to precipitate mental abnormality in vulnerable individuals (see e.g. Coid, 1984, 1988a, b; Gunn, Robertson, Dell and Way, 1978; Schorer, 1965. Feldman (1977) has also suggested that those who are, in fact, mentally abnormal may be less skilful in crime and thus caught more easily. He further suggests that the police may tend to charge some of these offenders more readily. In addition, pleas of guilty may be more frequent; a point confirmed in a recent paper by Robertson (1988). Scott (1969) once suggested that even if we allowed for the high degree of selectivity in penal and remand populations, the proportion of clearly identifiable psychiatric diagnoses was only somewhere in the order of 15%. Gunn *et al.* (1978) have estimated that about one-third of a sample of 629 prisoners they studied could have been regarded as requiring psychiatric attention at the time of interview. More recent figures appear to indicate that the number of English prisoners assessed as formally mentally disordered within the meaning of the mental health legislation has shown a decline in recent years: from about 800 in 1977 to about 350 in 1986 (NACRO, 1987) and 235 in 1988 (House of Commons, written reply, 22.12.88). Estimates indicate that these numbers have been rising again—350 in 1988–9 (*Independent*, 10 July 1990). In a recent study by Gunn, Maden and Swinton (1991), of *sentenced* prisoners it was considered that about 1100 would warrant transfer to hospital for psychiatric treatment. Recently a slight upward trend has again been noted with a disquieting increase in prison suicides (Griffiths, 1990). However, in addition to prisoners formally classified as mentally disordered, there are, of course, an unknown number of mentally abnormal prisoners who are not classified under the mental health legislation. These will range from a very small number of people who have committed notorious crimes, to a not inconsiderable number of socially inadequate people, many of whom are continually in and out of prisons and other institutions. The latter constitute the 'stage army' described so graphically by Rollin (1969). During the year ending 31 March 1986, 14 228 prisoners were referred to prison psychiatrists; the Principal Medical Officer for the Prison Department has estimated that on any one day there could be about 1500 male prisoners who were formally mentally disordered. Of these some 250 would be mentally ill (NACRO, 1987). Although the remit of the Mental Health Act Commission does not extend to persons detained in penal institutions, the Commission has been able to make some assessment of the problems of mentally disordered persons in prison and has passed on its concern to the Home Office. It has also published the results of a survey of how the provisions of the Mental Health Act, 1983, which relate directly to mentally disordered offenders, have been working (MHAC, 1987). It concluded that the provisions were not being implemented as well as they might be, and that some modification of the legislation might be needed to bring about improvement.

About ten years ago the present writer examined some twenty studies that had been undertaken on penal and court clinic populations during a 50-year period. The results are described in detail elsewhere (Prins, 1980). In 1982, Howells, as part of a study of the relationship between mental disorder and violent behaviour, summarised the findings in roughly the following fashion. The studies showed substantial disparities. The percentage of offenders found to be suffering from psychoses (affective disorders and the schizophrenias) ranged from 0. 5% to 26%; from mental subnormality from 2.4% to 28%; from psychopathy from 5.6% to 70% and from alcoholism/excessive drinking from 11% to 80%. As Howells says, 'such variation is likely to be in part a function of the different populations surveyed' (1982, p. 165), ranging as they did from homicides to approved-school boys. However 'in spite of these disparities, these studies do suggest a high level of mental disturbance in criminal groups' (Howells, 1982, p. 165). The point has also been made by Taylor (1986) in a study of life-sentenced prisoners in custody and in the community. It is also relevant to note here that some observers have suggested that suicide in prisons is roughly three times more frequent than in the general population (Topp, 1979). After having made allowances for methodological weaknesses, the overall impression from most of these studies is that severe psychiatric illness (psychosis), organic disorders and serious mental handicap are comparatively uncommon in criminal populations. However, personality disorders (which may of course be accompanied by various forms of formal mental illness or mental impairment), alcohol and other drug-related and sexual problems figure quite prominently. Such findings should come as no great surprise.

Criminality in Psychiatric Hospital and Similar Populations

To provide reasonable evidence of a clear association between mental disorder and criminality, it would be desirable to demonstrate the prevalence of criminality in psychiatric hospital patients and similar groups. To date, little work of substance has been carried out in this area, largely, as Gunn (1977) suggests, because of the considerable ethical problems involved in investigating the possible criminal backgrounds of hospitalised psychiatric patients. However, a few workers have attempted to explore certain aspects of this field. Walker (1968) estimated, on the basis of various epidemiological studies, that about twelve persons in every thousand would suffer from some kind of identifiable psychiatric disorder. Gunn (1977), on the basis of calculations made by McClintock and Avison (1968), suggests that approximately one in three of the male population and one in twelve of the female population would be convicted in their lifetime of a 'standard list' (fairly serious) offence. Thus, as Gunn suggests, in the light of these figures, it would be surprising if psychiatric hospitals and clinics did not contain an appreciable number of persons with criminal records. In the USA, a number of workers have examined mental hospital populations and the records of persons attending psychiatric clinics. Guze (1976), who surveyed a population of some 500 such patients, found that 4% had committed a serious offence. All the studies tend to show that the relationship between mental disorder and crime is not straightforward; however, one thing is clear, namely, support for Rollin's 'stage army' of persons drifting between hospital and penal containment (Rollin, 1969). A more recent, and somewhat unusual, study was carried out by Cook (1983). This was a retrospective survey in Bristol of 78 men without previous convictions, who had at least one psychiatric hospital admission of not less than three months before the age of 30. The subsequent conviction rate of these men was determined and found to be comparable with that of men of the same age in the general population. However, as Cook suggests, some caution is necessary on drawing too many general conclusions from these results as his sample was a small one and may not be typical of the country as a whole.

   In conclusion, it is worth emphasising that most of the studies referred to have been carried out on heterogeneous populations of *remand* prisoners and inmates. Coid (1984) rightly points out, on the basis of a review of the more reliable studies, that when *sentenced* prisoners are compared with the general population they appear to be comparatively normal psychiatrically. Psychosis predominates as a diagnosis but such disorder often appears to be secondary to the imprisonment itself. However, he does suggest, as have others, that the mentally handicapped and epileptic show a higher than expected prevalence in prison populations. Smith (1988) has recently examined the forensic problems presented by the mentally impaired and the borderline mentally impaired. At a more general level, Weller and Weller (1988a, b) have drawn attention to the likelihood that, given the present inadequacies of 'community care', more mentally disturbed persons will be drawn into the penal system. This fact has important implications for the community social work and probation services and is the subject of later comment.

III DEVELOPMENT AND DEPLOYMENT OF SERVICES

Brief Historical Background

The history of provision for mentally disordered offenders is inextricably linked with the history of the provision for the treatment of the mentally ill in general. As such, both reflect the fluid concepts of criminality and mental disorder already noted in this chapter. There have also been cyclical patterns of care that have sometimes had a 'flavour of the month' quality, often demonstrated by passion rather than any objective appraisal of need. However, in writing about English practice, Parker (1980) has suggested that: 'From early times the mentally disordered in England seem to have been afforded some protection, in principle at least, from the customary consequences of wrongdoing' (p. 461). She goes on to illustrate the various ways in which this has occurred from very early times to the twentieth century. As she says in her more recent and detailed historical review:

> The practice of confining some of the insane stretches back more than 600 years in England. The type of detained patient has varied, always including those considered to be dangerous ... The forms of security employed have changed little over the period; perimeter security, internal locks and bars, and individual restraint by both physical and chemical means have been in continuous use to a greater or lesser degree in various guises up to the present day. (Parker, 1985, p. 15)

A similar somewhat haphazard and fear-ridden approach can be seen in the development of community-care services, bedevilled as they have been by underfunding and lack of co-ordination. At the time of writing it seems unlikely that some of the more sensible proposals in the Griffiths report (1988) and in the Government White Paper—*Caring for People* (1989) will be uniformly implemented. There is little doubt that the history of this topic reveals that to be both 'mad and bad' places those so designated at the bottom of the social priority heap; and those who work with them may sometimes feel 'contaminated', 'alienated' and as vulnerable to adverse public opinion as their patients or clients.

Space does not permit a detailed account of the legislative background, but a few general comments may be helpful in order to provide context. Legislation from as early as the beginning of the eighteenth century provided for the detention of those who might be dangerous, but it was not until the nineteenth century that special provision was introduced for the *public* as opposed to the *private* care and treatment of the mentally disordered. However, such provisions were almost entirely of a custodial nature and services for criminal lunatics, as they were then called, developed separately and in piecemeal fashion. That they arose at all was largely as a result of notorious cases such as Hadfield and McNaghten. In the early twentieth century the trend to provide specific legislation for mentally disordered offenders continued, as for example in the Mental Deficiency Act of 1913 which enabled courts to deal more effectively with mentally defective (handicapped) people who committed crimes by removing them from the penal system and placing them in hospital care. Refinements to the 1913 legislation were made in the 1920s and the 1948 Criminal Justice Act enabled courts to make psychiatric treatment a formal condition of a probation order. The 1959 Mental Health Act and the 1983 Act made further provision for the compulsory detention of mentally disordered offenders (see Appendix I). We have already seen how the provisions of the Homicide Act, 1957 widened the scope for eroding criminal liability for those accused of murder, thus reducing the number of pleas of not guilty by reason of insanity under the more restricted 'McNaghten Rules'. In the last 30 years, several trends may be discerned which have been influential in the treatment, and in some cases the non-treatment, of the mentally disordered in general and the mentally disordered offender in particular. Briefly these may be summarised as follows:

(1) A growing demand for the run-down of the older mental hospitals. With hindsight, such demands have proved to be somewhat premature, based as they were on rather unreliable predictions about the future size of psychiatric populations and psychiatric needs, and an over-optimistic estimate of the power of some forms of chemotherapy (see Prins, 1992).

(2) A lack of adequate community care provision, both in terms of finance and professional and public attitudes towards this gravely disadvantaged group of people.

(3) Challenge to long-held assumptions about the nature of mental disorder; such challenges were often led by psychiatrists, particularly in the early 1960s.

(4) Increasing concern and activity about mental patients' rights and a concentration on civil liberties issues. This concern and activity was much in evidence in the background of events leading up to the 1983 Mental Health Act. Much of this concern and activity has been laudable, but in some respects it has led to the practice of defensive psychiatry and may have led to some patients and their relatives being denied access to treatment. Such a phenomenon is very familiar on a larger scale to those working on the North American continent.

(5) A justified and growing concern about the degree to which black and other ethnic minority groups appear to be over-represented in penal and psychiatric populations.

(6) A reduction in the primacy of medicine in the treatment of the mentally disordered. This is evidenced by the psychiatric profession's own acknowledgement that a team approach may well be preferable in the treatment of mental disorder and the parallel jostling for improved positions on the part of nurses, psychologists, and social workers in the mental health field, particularly in the field of forensic psychiatry (see Prins, 1984).

With this brief background in mind we can now examine some of the current facilities and services for the care and management of mentally disordered offenders, paying special attention to those adjudged to be dangerous.

HOSPITAL, PENAL AND OTHER SERVICES

Mentally disordered offenders should of course be able to avail themselves or be helped to avail themselves of the general provisions that are there for all people suffering from mental disorder (Department of Health and Home Office, 1992). Such services may be provided by the National Health Service, local social service authorities, the probation service, voluntary bodies or, increasingly, by the private sector. Apart from hospital care, a variety of types of residential facilities are also available to help in management and rehabilitation, but sadly never enough in terms of either buildings or staff. The overall aim, of course, is for all patients, whether criminal or not, to be enabled to live reasonably self-sufficient and trouble-free lives in the community. Although, as already indicated, very many mentally disordered offenders will be managed by the ordinary hospital and allied services, a number present problems of disordered and deviant behaviour of such a degree as to warrant special provisions; it is to these that we now turn.

Hospital Provisions

As already noted, a number of offender-patients will be detained in an ordinary hospital; however, those who have committed very grave crimes and who are thought to be an immediate danger to the public will, most likely, be detained in one or other of the Special Hospitals—see below. In the latter stages of their rehabilitation they may well be transferred to a local psychiatric hospital or special unit as part of a phased return to the community. In recent years, local psychiatric hospitals have been highly reluctant to accept difficult, potentially dangerous and/or restricted offender-patients. Their reasons include a concern that such patients cannot be easily contained on open wards, may prove too disruptive for staff to manage and be upsetting to other patients. Such reluctance has resulted not only in an accumulation of such patients in the Special Hospitals, but also in consequent delays in implementing their return to the community. For many years there was a serious concern about the overcrowding in the Special

Hospitals and delays in discharge. This was so serious that the Butler Committee produced an *Interim Report* recommending that urgent priority be given to the establishment of secure and medium-secure units (Home Office and DHSS, 1974). Although the government of the day gave rapid acceptance to these proposals to the extent of earmarking special funds for their development, many years went by before any form of national system of secure units was implemented. Today there are about 500 places available in England and Wales, a figure far short of the original estimate of some 1000 places (Department of Health and Home Office, 1992). There have been a number of problems in developing the units and establishing a uniform ethos of patient selection and management. First, they were seen as panaceas for the management of all difficult patients in psychiatric hospitals. Second, they were seen to some extent as 'mini' Special Hospitals. Third, most units saw themselves as offering a maximum stay for patients of about two years; some patients clearly need longer than this. Fourth, it has proved very difficult to get local hospitals to take certain patients on transfer who clearly were not yet ready to go from a secure unit to the community. This merely re-created the problem formerly faced by the Special Hospitals. Fifth, it has allegedly proved difficult to recruit adequate numbers of trained nursing staff at some units. Sixth, the very mixed population at many secure units and the floridly unstable condition of some of their patients are likely to have an unfortunate impact on those transferred to them from a Special Hospital where they have, over the years, reached a degree of stability and freedom from psychotic symptoms. To be placed in an establishment where such psychotic behaviour is inevitable can be decidedly unsettling and has frequently produced a breakdown in the Special Hospital patient's rehabilitation. It may be that too much has been expected of such units. As Snowden (1990) has suggested, Regional Secure Units and Interim Secure Units are not the only answer: There 'needs to be development in the prison service and some flexibility in the Special Hospitals to improve the system of dealing with the mentally abnormal offender further' (p. 1386). See also Berry (1985), Bluglass (1985), Faulk (1985), Faulk and Taylor (1986), Gostin (1986, ch. 5), Gudjonsson and MacKeith (1983) and Treasaden (1985) for more detailed accounts of developments and problems.

Special Hospitals

Under Section 4 of the National Health Service Act of 1977 for England and Wales, the Secretary of State for Social Services is required to provide and maintain such institutions as are necessary for persons subject to detention under the mental health legislation who, in his or her opinion, require treatment in conditions of special security because of their dangerous, violent or criminal propensities. However, it should be noted that about one-third of all Special Hospital patients are *not* offenders, but have been admitted because of their difficult or disruptive behaviour in ordinary psychiatric or mental handicap hospitals. There are three (formerly four) Special Hospitals in England, Broadmoor, Rampton and Ashworth (formerly Moss Side and Park Lane), and none in Wales or Northern Ireland. The State Hospital at Carstairs in Scotland is the equivalent of a Special Hospital in England and the Central Hospital at Dundrum in Dublin performs some of the functions of an English Special Hospital. Formerly the English Special Hospitals were administered directly by the Department of Health. Following various enquiries and reports, it was decided to bring them into line with other National Health Service Hospitals and there is now a special health authority for all of them (The Special Hospitals Service Authority). Because Northern Ireland has no Special Hospital it sends a few of its more dangerous offender-patients to Carstairs or, more rarely, to Ashworth. We shall consider each of these hospitals briefly. For fuller accounts of the English Special Hospital system see Gostin (1986, ch. 3), Hamilton (1985, 1990); for Carstairs see Hamilton (1990); and for the Central Hospital, Dundrum, Dublin, see Smith (1990a).

Broadmoor (Berkshire)

This is the oldest of the Special Hospitals, being established in 1863. It currently has a population of about 400 patients. Once beset by severe overcrowding, some relief has been afforded by the building of Park Lane (now Ashworth) Hospital. It takes mostly mentally ill and psychopathic patients. Its management has been the subject of extensive recent reviews, most notably by the National Health Advisory Service, whose 1988 report was highly critical of some practices within the hospital. The report stated that 'An unfortunate air of uniformity and consistency reinforces the atmosphere of an institution, albeit tempered by changes in furnishing' (p. 3).

Rampton (North Nottinghamshire)

This hospital (established in 1914), like Broadmoor, has also suffered from overcrowding and isolation in the past. Unfortunately it has also suffered from allegations of ill-treatment of patients; in 1980 it was the subject of a highly critical review (DHSS, 1980) in which it was described as 'a backwater ... the main currents of thought about the care of mental patients have passed it by' (p. iii). Rampton is now much less overcrowded, containing some 450 patients, mainly, but not exclusively, mentally impaired and psychopathic. In recent years it has been revitalised as a result of an energetic review board and the appointment of younger and more forward looking staff in all disciplines and at all levels. Certainly it is no longer the 'backwater' of a decade ago although sadly some problems remain.

Ashworth complex (Maghull, Liverpool)

This complex consists of the former Moss Side (established 1933) and Park Lane (established 1974) Hospitals. Moss Side at one time took mainly mentally impaired patients but now that it is integrated with Park Lane it takes all three categories, although there is some degree of specialisation. Park Lane is the newest of the Special Hospitals, taking mainly the mentally ill and the psychopathic. The population of both hospitals numbers some 600 patients.

Although the English Special Hospitals have at various times come in for a good deal of justified criticism, even their severest critics have acknowledged that these institutions have to undertake a tremendously difficult task in attempting to combine containment, clinical treatment, and rehabilitation in a climate of opinion that, as has already been suggested, does not give high priority to the care of the 'mad and the bad'. A good deal of research has been carried out into the characteristics and needs of Special Hospital patients, not only by the former Special Hospitals Research Unit, but by a variety of psychiatric professionals working on an individual basis. Although the climate has to be one of containment and the security of the public given paramount importance, much valuable therapy is being carried out by nursing, psychiatric, psychology, social work and occupational staffs. The Hospitals now have stronger links with various academic departments and are recognised as training centres for all psychiatric professionals working in forensic settings. Hopefully, the new administrative arrangements that have been set in train to establish closer links with National Health Service care will maintain the impetus for change and development that has been established recently (but see postscript, p. 64 below).

Other parts of the United Kingdom

Scotland   The State Hospital at Carstairs (established in 1944), in Lanarkshire, has its functions defined by Section 90 of the Mental Health (Scotland) Act of 1984: 'The Secretary of State shall provide such hospitals as appear to him to be necessary for persons subject to detention ... who require treatment under conditions of special security' (Hamilton, 1990, p. 1371). Currently it houses over 200 patients, the majority suffering from psychotic illness. As already indicated, it occasionally receives patients from Northern Ireland.

Ireland   The Central Hospital, Dundrum, Dublin, has a predominantly male population of some 100 offender-patients, about half of whom are said to be suffering from psychosis (mainly schizophrenic illness). A large number of admissions appear to come from prison transfers. Smith (1990a), writing rather pessimistically (but perhaps also realistically) says: 'There are treatment triumphs, but there are many failures, suggesting that remission of illness is not encouraged by security hospitalisation' (p. 1353).

Prison Psychiatric Services

Acts of 1774 and 1779 required prisons to appoint a physician and an organised full-time medical service began with the establishment of the Prison Commission in 1877 (Bluglass, 1990; Gunn, 1985). Such appointments were the forerunners of a range of other professional appointments which were to swell the ranks of prison staffs (chaplains, psychologists, specialist nursing officers, probation officers, education personnel and works and occupations staff).

The history of the prison medical service reveals that there have been a number of attempts to describe and classify mentally disordered offenders received into prison. Perhaps the most significant of all of these was a report which appeared from East and Hubert (1939) which paved the way for the foundation of Grendon Psychiatric Prison in 1962 (see below). In 1985, the Directorate of the Prison Medical Service consisted of Director, Deputy and three Principal Medical Officers. In the prisons, there were 4 principal medical officers, 26 senior and 68 full-time medical officers. There were in addition 117 part-time medical staff (Bluglass, 1990). In 1982, about half had post-graduate psychiatric qualifications. (It should be remembered that the prison medical service has general oversight of the total care both of prisoners and of staff and also a concern with environmental health matters.) Psychiatric assessment and management is only one aspect of the work. There have been a number of suggestions for the integration of the prison medical service with the National Health Service and on balance the present writer tends to view this as a desirable thing, as did the Royal College of Psychiatrists in evidence to the May Committee on the Prison Service (Home Office et al., 1979; see also Smith, 1984). However, in the most recent and comprehensive study of prison medical services, the House of Commons Select Committee, reporting in 1986, concluded that this was too simple a solution and that some specialist service would always be required (see also Prins, 1992).

As we have already noted, there is still a small number of mentally disordered offenders who should be in hospital and an even greater number who, while not fulfilling the strict criteria for transfer under the mental health legislation, require psychiatric management. Prisons are obviously not the best places for managing mental disorder, the more so since notions of treatment have been abandoned from the late 1970s for 'positive custody' (Home Office et al., 1979). Be this as it may, the prison service has designated certain prisons and units as places where prisoners may be offered the advantage of psychiatric help. The most notable of these is Grendon Psychiatric Prison in Buckinghamshire. Established under medical governorship in 1962, it aimed to be a therapeutically orientated institution for those offenders who showed mental disorder or whose offences suggested a degree of psychiatric morbidity (Faulk, 1990). Inmates are not sent there directly by the courts; indeed the High Court has made it clear that courts are not empowered to make such directions or requests. Prisoners are selected by the prison medical service in conjunction with Grendon staff. Since Grendon opened much has been written about its success or otherwise. If one takes mere reconviction rates as a yardstick, then Grendon probably does no better than any other penal establishment. However, if one takes social adjustment, or rather lack of personal maladjustment, then Grendon does seem to do rather better than other prisons. It can offer useful pointers to the management of prisoners in a more effective and humane way, much as Barlinnie has done for the Scottish prison service (Whatmore, 1990a). Currently, a non-medical governor is in charge of Grendon and the main therapeutic thrust is upon offering psychiatric help to other penal institutions and to working with more rigorously selected inmates, notably suitable psychopaths and sex offenders (Faulk, 1990). More recently, a wing for the treatment of acutely psychiatrically ill inmates has been established. The latter are sent to Grendon because of their acute mental disturbance and in the knowledge that formal transfers under the Mental Health Act, 1983, take a considerable time to put into effect in some cases (see Selby, 1991). Other therapeutic work is being carried out at Parkhurst Prison Hospital and the prison's C Wing. The prison hospital, housed in a separate building, accommodates some 90 inmates, the majority of whom are there for psychiatric assessment and treatment. There is a good inmate/nurse ratio, including female staff. The hospital provides a specialist psychiatric service to the three other large prisons on the Isle of Wight and Kingston Prison, Portsmouth—a small specialist prison for mainly domestic life-sentence prisoners. It also offers an assessment and treatment facility for inmates referred from other parts of the prison system and guidance on the long-term management of chronically mentally disordered prisoners who do not fall within the categories of the Mental Health Act, 1983, or for whom it has proved impossible to find an NHS bed. C Wing aims to manage some 25 inmates with long sentences who have proved difficult and disruptive in other prisons and whose behaviour indicates long-standing psychological difficulties. It seems to bear some comparison with the special unit at Barlinnie (Cooper, 1990; see also Evershed, 1991). There are special units in other prisons: for example, at Wormwood Scrubs, Wakefield and the Youth Custody establishment (Young Offender Institution) at Feltham. As already indicated, if an inmate fulfils the strict criteria of the Mental Health Act for compulsory admission to hospital, the Home Secretary, on medical evidence, may authorise a transfer to hospital either before or after sentence (Sections 47, 48). The relationships between various parts of the health care and penal systems are complex. In Figure 2.1 an attempt is made to outline these in simple fashion as they relate to England and Wales. The arrangements for the rest of the United Kingdom and Ireland are similar in intentions but organisationally different.

Community Services

Many mentally disordered offenders will be able, or encouraged, to make use of the range of community psychiatric provisions that are available for the mentally disordered generally. In addition, there are a number of specialist provisions available. These include hostels, other residential establishments and day centres run by the social services departments of the local authorities, the probation service and by voluntary organisations. In England and Wales the social services are organised and funded locally, the probation service is also organised on a local basis, but has considerable central government subvention. In Scotland the social and probation services are combined into single departments (Departments of Social Work); in Northern Ireland both services are more centrally controlled than in England and Wales. As already indicated, in the discussion of hospital provision, the availability and deployment of services for the mentally disordered and the delinquent are very much dependant upon public and political attitudes. There is little doubt that what is now provided falls woefully short of what is required and offender-patients seem to be tossed backwards and

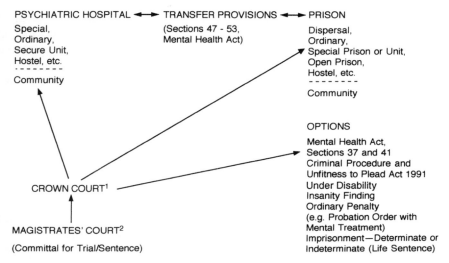

PSYCHIATRIC HOSPITAL ◄──► TRANSFER PROVISIONS ◄──► PRISON

Special,   (Sections 47 - 53,   Dispersal,
Ordinary,   Mental Health Act)   Ordinary,
Secure Unit,   Special Prison or Unit,
Hostel, etc.   Open Prison,
- - - - - - - -   Hostel, etc.
Community   - - - - - - - -
                                                              Community

                                                              OPTIONS

                                                              Mental Health Act,
                                                              Sections 37 and 41
                                                              Criminal Procedure and
                                                              Unfitness to Plead Act 1991
                                                              Under Disability
             CROWN COURT[1]   Insanity Finding
                                                              Ordinary Penalty
                                                              (e.g. Probation Order with
                                                              Mental Treatment)
MAGISTRATES' COURT[2]   Imprisonment—Determinate or
                                                              Indeterminate (Life Sentence)
(Committal for Trial/Sentence)

Figure 2.1   Disposal of mentally disordered offenders through the health care and penal systems—E and W
[1] The powers available to the Crown Court are also exercisable on appeal by the Court of Appeal
[2] All grave offences will be sent for trial from the Magistrates' Court to the Crown Court. A Magistrates' Court may also commit to the Crown Court with a view to a hospital order being made *with restrictions*. Commital for trial may be in custody, on bail, or by *remand* to hospital

forwards like frail barks on the seas of hospital and so-called community care (Prins, 1990a).

IV   THE SOCIAL AND PSYCHIATRIC SUPERVISION OF POTENTIALLY DANGEROUS OFFENDER-PATIENTS

There is a small group of offenders and offender-patients whose past psychiatric, social histories and records of offending pose particular problems of management; it is assumed that these will be of special interest to readers of this volume. It is for this reason that Part IV of this chapter is devoted to detailed commentary on their management.

The Population

The population under review consists mainly of those who have committed very serious offences of violence against persons or property *and* who it is thought have the potential to do so again. Such offences will include homicide and attempted homicide, grievous bodily harm with intent, serious sexual assault, both homosexual and heterosexual, and certain crimes against property such as aggravated burglary and arson. The number of such persons being supervised under statutory supervision in the community each year is comparatively small in relation to total psychiatric and penal populations. For example, in England and Wales, there are some 600–700 offender-patients under social and psychiatric supervision under the terms of a conditional discharge from hospital (Sections 42(2) and 73(2)(4b) Mental Health Act, 1983). In addition, there are about the same number of offenders under supervision on life-licence; some of these will have conditions for psychiatric treatment in their licences (Criminal Justice Act, 1967, Sec. 61; Prins, 1990b). There will also be a number of persons in the community who at some stage have been under supervision but who have been discharged from it, either by order of the Parole Board, the Home Secretary or by a Mental Health Review Tribunal. (For an incisive and detailed recent review of the functions of Mental Health Review tribunals see Peay, 1989.) There will be others, whose potential for dangerous behaviour has not, as yet, brought them to official attention. There will be an even larger number who have been discharged from prison or hospital without any statutory sanctions for supervision, or whose period of supervision has expired. A sense of proportion in dealing with this comparatively small number of identified potentially dangerous offender-patients is enhanced if it is remembered that the majority of offender-patients discharged into the community following the commission of grave offences, such as homicide, do comparatively well; that is, further homicide is very rare (Tennent and Way, 1984; Tidmarsh, 1982). More recently Murray (1989) has reviewed a large number of UK and North American studies into re-offending by mentally disordered offenders. Allowing for methodological weaknesses (such as differences in populations and follow-up periods), it appears that re-offending rates are not significantly higher than for other types of offenders and that further very serious offending continues to be a comparatively rare event. The author concludes that methods of prediction based upon a *combination* of actuarial and clinical approaches are probably to be preferred. As with offenders in general, past offence behaviour seems to be the best predictor of form and frequency of future offending. Offender-patients certainly go on to commit further offences, but many of these will not be grave. However, when a further *grave* offence is committed, it understandably attracts a good deal of public and media attention and questions are asked about the management of the case; that of the late Graham Young, the so-called St Albans Poisoner, is a good example, since it led not only to a formal enquiry into his particular case (Home Office and DHSS, 1973) and the establishment of a committee to advise the Home Secretary on particularly difficult cases (now called the Advisory Board; see Baxter, 1991; Egglestone, 1990), but also paved the way for the more wide-ranging enquiry by the Butler Committee (Home Office and DHSS, 1975). Over the years, there have had to be a small number of further 'social inquests', one of the more recent being the internal enquiry conducted by Wiltshire County Council (subsequently made public) into the supervision of Daniel Mudd, who was charged with murder while on conditional discharge from a Special Hospital (Wiltshire County Council, 1988). The remainder of this chapter is devoted to a consideration of some case management techniques that might limit the repetition of mayhem still further. We begin with a brief consideration of the concept of dangerousness and its prediction.

Dangerousness as a Concept

Dangerousness means different things to different people. Indeed, If asked to rank a group of people in order of dangerousness we would probably find ourselves in great difficulty, thus emphasising what a dangerous concept it is. Of the following who, for example, is the more dangerous? The bank robber, the bigoted patriot or blinkered politician, the over-zealous chief officer of police, the persistent paedophile, the person who peddles heroin to children for profit, the person who drives, knowing himself or herself to be unfit through drink or other drugs, the swimmer who uses the public baths knowingly suffering from a highly contagious and dangerous disease, or the consortium who dispose of toxic waste without proper safeguards? All of the foregoing present potential hazards of some kind; it is this capacity to create a potential hazard to the safety of others that is of central concern. This safety of others implies a relationship. Dangerousness does not exist in isolation; the relationship between proximate persons and events is best demonstrated in Scott's deceptively simple equation:

Offender + victim + circumstances = offence. (Scott, 1977, p. 130)

For present purposes we can best define dangerousness (briefly paraphrasing Scott, 1977) as a tendency to inflict serious physical injury or psychological harm on others.

Can Dangerousness be Predicted?

If we mean by prediction the capacity to be right every time, the short answer is *no*. If we have more modest goals and ask, are there measures, based upon past experience, that we can take to reduce the possibility of dangerous conduct, then the answer is *yes*. Some of these measures will be described shortly. Pollock and Webster (1990) put the issue clearly: 'From a scientific perspective ... [the] ... question is impossible to answer since it is based on an unscientific assumption about dangerousness, namely that it is a stable and consistent quality existing within the individual'. Translating the question into more appropriate terms would require the following question ... 'what are the psychological, social and biological factors bearing on the defendant's violent behaviour and what are the implications for future violence and the potential for change?' (p. 493).

Psychiatrists appear to be no worse at predicting dangerousness than other professions, and in relation to potentially dangerous *mentally ill* offenders are better at it than others (Greenland, 1980, 1985). All professionals might perform better if attempts at prediction were less global and were confined to specific types of offender-patients. (See for example the discussion in Hamilton and Freeman, 1982, and a review of recent research findings in Prins, 1990c.) It is probably wisest to assert that our endeavours in this field are currently more at the 'art' than the 'science' stage. Because of this, great caution should be observed before labelling anyone as dangerous. For this reason a greater degree of toleration of ambiguity and uncertainty has to be shown in this area of psychiatric practice than in many others. The work is made additionally difficult because some of it has to be carried out under legal and administrative constraints (Prins, 1990a).

Management

Workers of all disciplines will bring to the task of managing dangerous offender-patients in the community a degree of what the present writer has described elsewhere as 'ambivalent investment' (Prins, 1988). Three aspects may be discerned. First, the difficulty in having to come to terms with the feelings of revulsion and horror that some of these offender-patients engender because of the crimes they have committed (see for example the three cases cited at the beginning of this chapter). Second, the need to deal with the very considerable burden of responsibility presented by the conflicting needs of the offender on the one hand and the public on the other. Third, a high therapeutic investment of the worker in seeing that things are going well because of their personal and professional motivation to nurture and assist people in a variety of difficulties—medical, social and psychological. Having had to work very hard to overcome these hurdles there is likely to be an overall investment in seeing that things are going well. For this reason, workers may not only be ambivalently receptive to the disclosure of 'bad news', but may ignore half-spoken and hinted-at messages that this is so from both offender-patient and/or family. This may result in missed opportunities for the release and catharsis of frightening thoughts and phantasies and for the confrontation of undesirable or seriously anti-social behaviour. Thus there is a need for personal preparation by workers to enable them to remain 'tuned in' to what is happening and to exercise continuing professional vigilance. The work will be much enhanced if workers obtain as accurate and detailed a picture as possible. As Scott suggested in his seminal contribution on this topic.

> It is patience, thoroughness and persistence in this process [data collection], rather than any diagnostic or interviewing brilliance that produces results. In this sense the telephone, the written request for past records and the checking of information against other informants, are the important diagnostic devices. Having collected the facts under the headings (1) the offence; (2) past behaviour; (3) personal data; (4) social circumstances, it is useful to scan them from a number of different directions with a view to answering certain key questions relating to dangerousness. (Scott, 1977, p. 129)

As Scott suggests, there are some very simple (but easily overlooked) techniques which facilitate the assessment of potential dangerousness. Full details of the index (original) offence(s) and what a variety of professional observers thought at the time of sentencing about the individual's motivation and attitudes are essential. Equally important are details of *previous* convictions, if any. For example, most indecent exposers do not go on to commit more serious sex offences (though they frequently continue to expose themselves). Those that accompany their exposure by threats, gestures and masturbation *may* go on to commit more serious sexual offences (Bluglass, 1980). In similar fashion, rape, which is always a very grave offence and an assault on a woman's rights, may offer valuable prognostic distinctions when it occurs under so-called 'normal' conditions or when it occurs against a background of highly sadistic and deviant sexual activity shown by some sexual psychopaths. Persistent and coercive paedophiles often try to present themselves in the best possible light, blaming their child victims for their crimes. Only close and persistent questioning and confrontation will reveal a different picture—usually one of slow, determined seduction on the part of the offender (Wiest, 1981). In working with potentially dangerous offender-patients it is useful to adopt a position of scepticism or disbelief—taking nothing at face value. The male burglar who steals only the shoes belonging to the female occupant of the house or slashes the bedclothes with a knife clearly needs to be distinguished from the burglar who behaves in a more conventional fashion (Morneau and Rockwell, 1980). Sometimes understanding is further enhanced by obtaining the photographs and scene-of-crime reports from the police and/or the forensic science service. Such data serve to remind workers of the gravity of the crime and may be useful in helping them to confront evasion and denial on the part of offender-patients. A degree of scepticism is also useful in relation to so-called institutional success. Intellectual achievement (such as that obtained on an Open University course) is very laudable and a matter for congratulation on the part of all concerned. However, it should not blind the worker to the need for a degree of equal achievement in relation to the development of personal awareness and social maturation. In somewhat similar fashion, the man with a life-long history of achieving his goals by violent means may win praise for his involvement in body-building classes in prison. A more realistic appraisal might be to assume that he was preparing himself for further mayhem on discharge. The supervision of potentially dangerous offender-patients often requires intrusiveness in respect of their domestic environment. Had those responsible for the supervision of the late Graham Young gained access to his living accommodation they would have found revealing pictorial evidence of his continuing preoccupation with poisons and death (Holden, 1974; Prins, 1986). The case of Simcox affords another illustration of the need for a high degree of sensitivity to changing social circumstances. Simcox's first marriage ended in divorce, but not before he had assaulted his wife and mother-in-law. His second marriage ended even more violently. He was convicted of murdering his wife with a knife wound to the throat. He was sentenced to death and reprieved. Ten years later, he was released from prison on licence. In 1961 he married for the third time and was soon in court again for carrying an offensive weapon. The judge made a probation order with a condition that he never saw his wife again. In less than two weeks he had breached that order, killed his sister-in-law and wounded another of his wife's relatives. At his second trial for murder, evidence was given that he had a paranoid personality. As Blom-Cooper, in his description of this and similar cases, suggests, a paranoid personality is not developed overnight, nor is it a temporary condition. It is suggested that Simcox telegraphed his future homicidal plans by the fact that he told people he intended to kill himself and his wife, and by actually prowling around his wife's house with a dangerous weapon, ten days before the killing

(Blom-Cooper, 1965). Detailed knowledge of the social history is essential. Blair (1971) provides a sensitive portrayal of the sad history of Richard Holmes who, at the age of 22, was sentenced to life imprisonment for attempted murder. Shortly after sentence Holmes killed himself. Apparently no one had interviewed his parents and obtained information about his past disturbed history. Tragedy *might* have been averted had they done so. This is a sad reminder of the need for careful history-taking at a time when there is justified concern about suicides in prison. The case of Daniel Mudd has already been referred to. Had those responsible for supervising Mudd adopted a more questioning stance about his interests, behaviour and activities, it is possible that a murder *might* have been averted. Such a lack of questioning sometimes comes about because the worker over-identifies with the offender-patient—for some of the reasons given earlier. Johnston (1967) suggests that mental health professionals 'identify too closely with the patient and become too sympathetic with his problem and, as a result, come up with a judgement which is not based on the stark reality of the situation' (p. 31). Such views may prevent the worker from taking essential action to set in motion procedures to have an offender-patient recalled to hospital. The guilt attendant upon such action is not the sole prerogative of non-medical staff. MacGrath (1969) suggests that it 'is shared by doctors who do not take delight in incarcerating the legally defenceless' (p. 126). In Young's case there was evidence that he appeared to be engaging in a rich phantasy life which *was also accompanied by murderous activity*. Such phantasies, which sometimes may be more readily accessible to workers than is realised, may be evidence of a wishful rehearsal for actual behaviour. This material, provided it is viewed alongside other evidence, may be of considerable diagnostic and prognostic value (see MacCulloch, Snowden, Wood *et al.* 1983).

Those with a capacity for evasion, self-deception and the projection of blame need to be firmly confronted with their tendencies from the outset. The implications of supervision, the obligations of the supervisor and of the offender-patient must be made abundantly clear; these will probably have to be repeated on more than one occasion. The special nature of such a relationship cannot be 'fudged'. If such fudging occurs, it is likely to make the need for confrontation of reality that much more difficult when it does arise (as for example when procedures for recall on the grounds of adverse behaviour have to be invoked). Management is likely to be greatly enhanced if such nettles are grasped firmly from the outset (see Walker, 1991). The need for careful preparation and adequate links between institutions and those who are to supervise the offender-patient in the community has recently been more formally recognised by central government. In 1987, the Home Office and the Department of Health and Social Security issued three very valuable sets of guidelines for social supervisors, psychiatrists and staffs in discharging hospitals; the guidelines stress the need for very careful pre-discharge liaison and planning (Home Office and DHSS, 1987a, b, c). It is also likely to be enhanced if the worker has certain areas of questioning in mind. Such questions are often very difficult for the worker to confront, but failure to do so might result in further harm to both offender-patient and community. In trying to reduce the risk of the repetition of mayhem one is inevitably trying to make the offender-patient less vulnerable (Prins, 1988, 1991). The following is a list of possible areas of questioning to be borne in mind, but they are not listed in any order of priority.

(1) How much 'unfinished business' (Cox, 1979, p. 310) does this person have to complete? For example, it would be wrong to assume that those convicted of, and sentenced for, matricide or patricide will not seek surrogate victims, or that the delusionally jealous offender-patient will not seek to take further revenge once released, even though many years have elapsed since the original incident. Close and continuing scrutiny of the social environment and the psychological state of the offender-patient is essential.

(2) Have we observed with sufficient care that current employments may be all too similar to past employments, thus increasing the offender-patient's vulnerability? Graham Young was allowed to obtain employment with a firm of optical equipment manufacturers that could have given him easy access to the means to do further serious harm. As Shakespeare's King John aptly says, 'How oft the sight of means to do ill deeds makes deeds ill done' (Act IV, sc.ii). Employments may also afford useful prognostic hints. Brittain (1970), in his classic paper on sadistic sexual murderers, notes how such killers frequently have worked in abattoirs or the butchery trade. It is interesting to note that the serial killer Nilsen probably acquired the skills needed to dissect his victim's bodies whilst employed as an Army cook.

(3) To what extent have past precipitants and stresses been removed? Has the history been scanned sufficiently, in Scott's terms (above), to determine whether forseeable vulnerability has been avoided or at least recognised as far as possible?

(4) What is this person's current capacity for coping with provocation? It is as well to remember Scott's (1977) advice that aggression may be displaced 'from a highly provoking source to one that may be scarcely provoking at all, as for example in the case of the legendary Medea who, wishing to get back at her husband, killed her baby saying "that will stab thy heart"' (p. 130). Careful scanning of the immediate environment may enable us to sense (and perhaps seek to avoid) potentially inflammatory situations. To what extent has the over-flirtatious wife of a jealous husband courted a potentially disastrous situation by sarcasm, making denigrating remarks about sexual competence (as in the case of Telling quoted earlier), been otherwise contemptuous, or worn provocative dresses? In similar fashion, to what extent has a male homosexual lover courted disaster by behaving provocatively in the presence of others, or by wearing provocative clothing such as overtight jeans? In trying to understand and manage such instances, detailed accounts of previous provoking incidents are essential.

(5) How does this offender-patient continue to view himself or herself? The need for a 'macho' self-image in the highly deviant male sex offender,

based upon unresolved conflicts around relationships with women, may make him likely to continue to take his revenge by way of serious sexual assaults accompanied by extreme violence and degradation of his victims.

(6) To what extent can we assess changes for the better in this offender-patient's capacity to empathise with others? Does this person still treat others as objects rather than as persons upon whom to indulge their deviant desires (see for example, Masters, 1985, 1993)? The true psychopath tends to see all those around him as malevolently disposed. For this reason their behaviour may be less likely to be indulged in as a reaction to the 'last straw' in a series of stressful events than is the case in the psychotic or near-psychotic offender-patient.

(7) To what extent does the behaviour seem person-specific, or a means of getting back at society in general, as in the case of some arsonists who, like the Monster in Mary Shelley's *Frankenstein* was 'malicious' because he was 'miserable' (Prins, 1987)? The person who says with continuing hatred in their voice 'I know deep down that some day I'm going to kill somebody' (MacDonald, 1967, p. 60), has to be taken seriously. To what extent are thoughts of killing or injury still present? Is there a pleasurable feel to their talk about violent acts, or is there continuing interest in such items as violent pornography, horror films, the occult, atrocities, torture, etc.?

(8) If the offender-patient's condition is responsive to medication, what are the chances of their continuing to take it on discharge? Even if the answer is a positive one, is there a likelihood that their compliance will be spasmodic or associated with the ingestion of alcohol or other non-prescribed drugs? What are the resources for ensuring continuing care and compliance? And, perhaps even more important, what are the attitudes of non-medical supervisors to the place of drugs in treatment for mental disorder? Ill-founded ideologies have no place in this highly sensitive area of work.

(9) How much regard has been paid to what the offender-patient actually did at the time of the crime? Was it so horrendous that they blotted it out of consciousness? It is necessary to stress again that we need to be in possession of the full facts. For example, did they wander off in a semi-amnesic state or, upon realising what they had done, summon help immediately? Or did they, having mutilated the body, go off happily to a meal and a good night's sleep? Have we assessed adequately the role played by alcohol or other drugs? Hospitals, and to a much greater extent, prisons are not the ideal places for testing such proclivities in offender-patients. Escorted periods of leave with close supervision may enable alcohol intake to be assessed, as they may likewise enable the assessment of a paedophile's continuing interest in small children as they play on the beach.

(10) How far has this offender-patient come to terms with what he or she did? It has been suggested that offenders and offender-patients may go through five stages during incarceration in their attempts to work through guilt and remorse, (i) confession; (ii) acceptance of punishment; (iii)

denial; (iv) grieving; (v) remorse (Wiest, 1981). Distortion and denial can occur at any of these stages and each needs sensitive appraisal. It is important to regard protestations of guilt with a degree of caution. 'A person who expresses guilt is to be regarded with vigilance. His next move ...' may be ... 'to engineer a situation where he can repeat the activities (about which he expresses guilt), but this time with rationalisation and hence without guilt. He will therefore try to manipulate his victim into giving him a pretext' (Russel and Russel, 1961, p. 60). Some offender-patients are highly reluctant to acknowledge their guilt because of the distress it would cause family and/or close friends. In other cases, the crime may have been committed so long ago that a degree of distortion or clouding of memory may have occurred. The possibility should also be considered that the offender-patient may not, in fact, be guilty, a point to be borne in mind in cases where detention had been ordered after a finding of 'disability' (unfitness to plead) and where this had never been subsequently reviewed by the courts. (For a fuller discussion see Prins, 1986, 1988.)

The community supervision of potentially dangerous offender-patients by mental health and other professionals necessitates a higher degree of surveillance than is usual in other types of work, an acknowledgement of the importance of accountability to the public and to central government (notably the Home Office) and of good liaison practices with close professional colleagues. There is no place for 'prima donna' activities in this field of activity. It is essential to overcome a reluctance to ask 'unaskable' questions and to be aware of one's own blind spots. Finally, it is worth noting some observations in the Report of the Aarvold Committee which enquired into the arrangements made for the supervision of Graham Young.

> The making of recommendations and decisions about the discharge and continuing care of ... [dangerous] ... mentally disordered offenders entails, fundamentally, the assessment and prediction, by one group of human beings, of the probable future behaviour of another. Prescribed procedures can offer real safeguards against the chance of human error going undetected, but we do not believe that in this situation there can be an absolute guarantee of infallibility. Indeed, there might be a risk that the adoption of over-elaborate proceedings could reduce the quality of judgements made, by weakening the sense of personal responsibility which those who care for these unfortunate individuals bring to their tasks ... (Home Office and DHSS, 1973, p. 20)

It behoves all those working in the field to try to aspire to the standards of professional competence envisaged by Sir Carl Aarvold and his colleagues.

SUMMARY

In this chapter, an attempt was made to review the major provisions and facilities for the management of mentally disordered offenders against a background of legal complexities and constraints. The main focus has been on England and Wales with only brief reference to Scotland, Northern Ireland and Ireland. Some attempt was made to assess the numbers of mentally abnormal offenders in penal and other populations and the limitations of such assessments acknowledged. The chapter concluded with an extended examination of case management techniques of those mentally disordered offenders adjudged to be dangerous or potentially dangerous. It is suggested that these latter observations can also be applied to offender-patients who are not subject to statutory supervision. The special nature of the supervisory task with dangerous offender-patients was emphasised.

NOTE

Any correspondence should be addressed to 1 Home Close Road, Houghton-on-the-Hill, Leicester, UK, LE7 9GT.

REFERENCES

Baxter, R. (1991). The Mentally disordered in hospital: The role of the Home Office. In K. Herbst and J. Gunn (eds), *The Mentally Disordered Offender*. London: Butterworth-Heinemann.

Berry, M. J. (1985). *Special Hospitals Research Report No. 18. Secure Units: A Bibliography*, Birmingham: Birmingham University.

Blair, D. (1971). Life-sentence then suicide. The sad case of Richard Holmes. *Medicine, Science and The Law*, **11**, 162–79.

Blom-Cooper, L. (1965). Preventable homicide. *Howard Journal of Penology*, **XI**, 297–308.

Bluglass, R. (1980). Indecent exposure in the West Midlands. In D. J. West (ed.), *Sex Offenders in the Criminal Justice System*. Cambridge: Cambridge University Institute of Criminology.

Bluglass, R. (1985). The development of Secure Units. In L. Gostin (ed.), *Secure Provision: A Review of Special Services for the Mentally Ill and Mentally Handicapped in England and Wales*. London: Tavistock.

Bluglass, R. (1990). Prison medical services. In R. Bluglass and P, Bowden (eds), *Principles and Practice of Forensic Psychiatry*. London: Churchill Livingstone.

Bluglass, R., and Bowden, P. (eds), (1990). *Principles and Practice of Forensic Psychiatry*. London: Churchill Livingstone.

Brittain, R. P. (1970). The sadistic murderer, *Medicine, Science and the Law*, **10**, 198–208.

Campbell, I. G. (1981). The influence of psychiatric pre-sentence reports. *International Journal of Law and Psychiatry*, **4**, 89–106.

Caring for People, (1989). Cmnd. 849. London: HMSO.

Coid, J. W. (1984). How many psychiatric patients in prison? *British Journal of Psychiatry*, **145**, 78–96.

Coid, J. W. (1988a). Mentally abnormal prisoners on remand. (I) Accepted or rejected by the NHS. *British Medical Journal*, **296**, 1779–882.

Coid, J. W. (1988b). Mentally abnormal prisoners on remand: (II) Comparison of services provided by Oxford and Wessex regions. *British Medical Journal*, **296**, 783–4.

Cook, D. A. G. (1983). A study of criminal behaviour in discharged male psychiatric patients. *Medicine. Science and the Law*. **23**, 279–82.

Cooper, D. (1990). Parkhurst Prison: C Wing. In R. Bluglass and P. Bowden (eds), *Principles and Practice of Forensic Psychiatry*, London: Churchill Livingstone.

Cox, M. (1979). Dynamic psychotherapy with sex offenders. In I. Rosen (ed.), *Sexual Deviation*. Oxford: Oxford University Press.

Department of Health and Home Office (1992). *Review of Health and Social Services for Mentally Disordered Offenders and Others Requiring Similar Services. Final Summary Report*. (Chairman Dr John Reed). CM 2088. London: HMSO.

DHSS (1980). *Report on the Review of Rampton Hospital* (Boynton Report), Cmnd. 8073. London: HMSO.

East, W. N., and Hubert, W. H. de B. (1939). *The Psychological Treatment of Crime*. London: HMSO.

Egglestone, F. (1990). The Advisory Board on Restricted Patients. In R. Bluglass and P. Bowden (eds), *Principles and Practice of Forensic Psychiatry*. London: Churchill Livingstone.

Evershed, S. (1991). Special Unit, C Wing, H.M. Prison, Parkhurst. In K. Herbst and J. Gunn (eds), *The Mentally Disordered Offender*. London: Butterworth-Heinemann.

Faulk, M. (1985). Secure facilities in local pychiatric hospitals. In L.Gostin (ed.), *Secure Provision: A Review of Special Services for the Mentally Ill and Mentally Handicapped in England and Wales*. London: Tavistock.

Faulk, M. (1990). Her Majesty's Prison Grendon. In R. Bluglass and P. Bowden (eds), *Principles and Practice of Forensic Psychiatry*. London: Churchill Livingstone.

Faulk, M. C., and Taylor, J. C. (1986). Psychiatric interim-secure unit: Seven years experience. *Medicine, Science and the Law*, **26**, 17–22.

Feldman, P. (1977). *Criminal Behaviour: A Psychological Analysis*, London: Wiley.

Gostin, L. (1986). *Institutions Observed: Toward a New Concept of Secure Provision in Mental Health*. London: King Edward's Fund for London.

Greenland, C. (1980). Psychiatry and the prediction of dangerousness. *Journal of Psychiatric Treatment and Evaluation*, **2**, 97–103.

Greenland, C. (1985). Dangerousness, mental disorder and politics. In C. D. Webster, M. H. Ben Aron and S. J. Hucker (eds), *Dangerousness: Probability and Prediction, Psychiatry and Public Policy*. Cambridge: Cambridge University Press.

Griffiths, A. W. (1990). Correlates of suicidal history in male prisoners. *Medicine, Science and the Law*, **3**, 217–18.

Griffiths, R. (1988). *Community Care: Agenda for Action*. London: HMSO.

Gudjonsson, G. H., and MacKeith, J. A. C. (1983). A Regional Secure Unit at the Bethlem Royal Hospital—the first fourteen months. *Medicine, Science and the Law*, **23**, 209–19.

Gunn, J. (1977). Criminal behaviour and mental disorder. *British Journal of Psychiatry*, **130**, 317–29.

Gunn, J. (1985). Psychiatry and the Prison Medical Service. In L. Gostin (ed.), *Secure Provision: A Review of Special Services for the Mentally Ill and Mentally Handicapped in England and Wales*. London: Tavistock.

Gunn, J., Maden, A., and Swinton, M. (1991). *Mentally Disordered Prisoners*. London: Home Office.

Gunn, J., Robertson, G., Dell, S., and Way, C. (1978). *Psychiatric Aspects of Imprisonment*, London: Academic Press.

Guze, S. B. (1976). *Criminality and Psychiatric Disorder*. Oxford: Oxford University Press.

Halleck, S. (1987). *The Mentally Disordered Offender*. Washington: American Psychiatric Press.

Hamilton, J. R. (1985). The Special Hospitals. In L. Gostin (ed.), *Secure Provision: A Review of Special Services for the Mentally Ill and Mentally Handicapped in England and Wales*. London: Tavistock.

Hamilton, J. (1990). Special Hospitals and the State Hospital. In R. Bluglass and P. Bowden (eds), *Principles and Practice of Forensic Psychiatry*. London: Churchill Livingstone.

Hamilton, J. R., and Freeman, H. (eds), (1982). *Dangerousness: Psychiatric Assessment and Management*. London: Gaskell Books.

Hare, E. (1983). Was insanity on the increase? *British Journal of Psychiatry*. **142**, 439–55.

Holden, A. (1974). *The St Albans Poisoner: The life and crimes of Graham Young*. London: Hodder & Stoughton.

Holmes, R. M., and De Burger, J. (1988). *Serial Murder*. London: Sage.

Home Office and DHSS (1973). *Report on the Review of Procedures for the Discharge and Supervision of Psychiatric Patients Subject to Special Restrictions*. (Aarvold Committee). Cmnd. 5191. London: HMSO.

Home Office and DHSS (1974). *Interim Report of the Committee on Mentally Abnormal Offenders* (Butler Committee). Cmnd. 5698. London: HMSO.

Home Office and DHSS (1975). *Report of the Committee on Mentally Abnormal Offenders* (Butler Committee). Cmnd. 6244. London: HMSO.

Home Office et al. (1979). *Report of the Committee of Enquiry into the UK Prison Services* (May Committee). Cmnd. 7673. London: HMSO.

Home Office and DHSS (1987a). *Mental Health Act 1983, Supervision and After-Care of Conditionally Discharged Restricted Patients: Notes for the Guidance of Social Supervisors*. London: Home Office and DHSS.

Home Office and DHSS (1987b). *Mental Health Act, 1983, Supervision and After-Care of Conditionally Discharged Restricted Patients: Notes for the Guidance of Supervising Psychiatrists*. London: Home Office and DHSS.

Home Office and DHSS (1987c). *Mental Health Act, 1983, Supervision and After-Care of Conditionally Discharged Restricted Patients: Notes for the Guidance of Hospitals Preparing for the Conditional Discharge of Restricted Patients*, London: Home Office and DHSS.

House of Commons (1986). *Third Report from the Social Services Committee, Session, 1985–1986*. London: HMSO.

Howells, K. (1982). Mental disorder and violence. In P. Feldman (ed.), *Developments in the Study of Criminal Behaviour*, vol. 2, *Violence*. Chichester: Wiley.

Johnston, W. C. (1967). Releasing the dangerous offender. In J. R. Rappeport, (ed.), *The Clinical Evaluation of the Dangerousness of the Mentally Ill*. Springfield, Ill.: Charles C. Thomas.

MacCulloch, M. J., Snowden, P. R., Wood, P. J. W., et al. (1983). Sadistic phantasy, sadistic behaviour, and offending. *British Journal of Psychiatry*, **143**, 20–9.

MacCullum, G. (1990). Northern Ireland. In R. Bluglass and P. Bowden (eds), *Principles and Practice of Forensic Psychiatry*. London: Churchill Livingstone.

MacDonald, J. R. (1967). Discussant in J. R. Rappeport (ed.), *The Clinical Evaluation of the Dangerousness of the Mentally Ill*. Springfield, Ill.: Charles C. Thomas.

McClintock, F. H., and Avison, N. H. (1968). *Crime in England and Wales*. London: Heinemann.

McGrath, P. G. (1969). Custody and release of dangerous offenders. In A. V. S. de Rueck and R. Porter (eds), *The Mentally Abnormal Offender*. London: J. and A. Churchill (for CIBA).

Masters, B. (1985). *Killing for Company: The Case of Dennis Nilsen*. London: Cape.

Masters, B. (1993). *The Shrine of Jeffrey Dahmer*. London: Hodder & Stoughton.

Mental Health Act Commission (1987). *Second Biennial Report; 1985–1987*. London: HMSO.

Morneau, R. H., and Rockwell, B. S. (1980). *Sex, Motivation and the Criminal Offender*. Springfield, Ill.: Charles C. Thomas.

Murray, D. J. (1989). *Review of Research on Re-Offending by Mentally Disordered Offenders, Research and Planning Unit Paper, 55*. London: Home Office.

National Association for the Care and Resettlement of Offenders (1987). *NACRO Briefing: Mentally Disordered Offenders*. Clapham, London.

National Health Advisory Service and DHSS Social Services Inspectorate (1988). *Report on Services Provided by Broadmoor Hospital*, HAS/SSI/88/8H/1. London: Department of Health.

Norris, J. (1990). *Serial Killers: The Growing Menace*. London: Arrow Books.

Parker, E. (1980). Mentally disordered offenders and their protection from punitive sanctions. *International Journal of Law and Psychiatry*, **3**, 461–9.

Parker, E. (1985). The development of secure provision. In L. Gostin (ed.), *Secure Provision: A Review of Special Services for the Mentally Ill and Mentally Handicapped in England and Wales*. London: Tavistock.

Peay, J. (1989). *Tribunals on Trial:. A Study of Decision-Making under the Mental Health Act, 1983*. Oxford: Clarendon Press.

Pollock, N., and Webster, C. (1990). The clinical assessment of dangerousness. In R. Bluglass and P. Bowden (eds), *Principles and Practice of Forensic Psychiatry*. London: Churchill Livingstone.

Prins, H. (1980). *Offenders, Deviants or Patients: An Introduction to the Study of Socio-Forensic Problems*. London: Tavistock.

Prins, H. (1984). Attitudes toward the mentally disordered. *Medicine, Science and the Law*, **24**, 181–91.

Prins, H. (1986). *Dangerous Behaviour, The Law and Mental Disorder*. London: Tavistock.

Prins, H. (1987). Up In smoke: The psychology of arson. *Medico-Legal Journal*, **55**, 69–84.

Prins, H. (1988). Dangerous clients: Further observations on the limitation of mayhem. *British Journal of Social Work*, **18**, 593–609.

Prins, H. (1990a). Mental abnormality and criminality: An uncertain relationship. *Medicine, Science and the Law*, **30**, 247–58.

Prins, H. (1990b). Annotation: Some observations on the supervision of dangerous offender-patients. *British Journal of Psychiatry*, **156**, 157–62.

Prins, H. (1990c). Dangerousness—A review. In R. Bluglass and P. Bowden (eds), *Principles and Practice of Forensic Psychiatry*. London: Churchill Livingstone.

Prins, H. (1991). Dangerous people or dangerous situations?—Some further thoughts. *Medicine, Science and the Law*, **31**, 25–37.

Prins, H. (1992). The diversion of the mentally disordered: Some problems for criminal justice, penology and health care. *Journal of Forensic Psychiatry*, **13**, 431–443.

Report of the Committee of Inquiry into Complaints About Ashworth Hospital, Vols I and II (1992). (Chairman Sir Louis Blom-Cooper, QC) CM 2028 (I) and CM 2028 (II). London: HMSO.

Robertson, G. (1988). Arrest patterns among mentally disordered offenders. *British Journal of Psychiatry*, **153**, 313–16.

Rollin, H. (1969). *The Mentally Abnormal Offender and the Law*. Oxford: Pergamon.

Roth, M., and Kroll, J. (1986). *The Reality of Mental Illness*. Cambridge: Cambridge University, Press.

Russel, C., and Russel, W. M. S. (1961). *Human Behaviour*. Boston: Little Brown.

Schorer, C. E. (1965). The Ganser syndrome. *British Journal of Criminology*, **5**, 120–31.

Scott, P. D. (1969). Crime and delinquency. *British Medical Journal*. **I**, 424–6.

Scott, P. D. (1977). Assessing dangerousness in criminals. *British Journal of Psychiatry*, **131**, 127–42.

Scull, A. (1984). Was insanity on the increase? A response to Hare. *British Journal of Psychiatry*, **144**, 432–6.

Selby, M. (1991). H. M. P. Grendon: The care of acute psychiatric patients. A pragmatic solution. In Herbst, K. and Gunn, J. (eds), *The Mentally Disordered Offender*. London: Butterworth-Heinemann.

Smith, C. (1990a). The Central Mental Hospital, Dundrum, Dublin. In R. Bluglass and
P. Bowden (eds), *Principles and Practice of Forensic Psychiatry*. London: Churchill
Livingstone.

Smith, C. (1990b). Mental health legislation in Eire. In R. Bluglass and P. Bowden (eds),
Principles and Practice of Forensic Psychiatry. London: Churchill Livingstone.

Smith, J. (1988). An open forensic unit for the borderline mentally impaired offender.
Bulletin of the Royal College of Psychiatrists, **12**, 13–15.

Smith, R. (1984). *Prison Health Care*. London: British Medical Association.

Snowden, P. (1990). Regional Secure Units and forensic services in England and Wales.
In R. Bluglass and P. Bowden (eds), *Principles and Practice of Forensic Psychiatry*.
London: Churchill Livingstone.

Szasz, T. (1987). *Insanity: The Idea and its Consequences*. New York: Wiley.

Taylor, P. J. (1986). Psychiatric disorder in London's life-sentenced offenders. *British
Journal of Criminology*, **26**, 63–78.

Tennent, G., and Way, C. (1984). The English special hospital—a 12–17 year follow-up
study: a comparison of violent and non-violent offenders and re-offenders. *Medicine,
Science and the Law*, **24**, 81–91.

Tidmarsh, D. (1982). Implications from research studies. In J. R. Hamilton and H.
Freeman (eds), *Dangerousness: Psychiatric Assessment and Management*. London:
Gaskell Books.

Topp, D. O. (1979). Suicide in Prison. *British Journal of Psychiatry*, **134**, 24–7.

Treasaden, I. H. (1985). Current practice in secure units. In L. Gostin (ed.), *Secure
Provision: A Review of Special Services for the Mentally Ill and Mentally Handicapped
in England and Wales*. London: Tavistock.

Verdun-Jones, S. N. (1989). Sentencing the partly mad and the partly bad: The case of
the Hospital Order in England and Wales. *International Journal of Law and
Psychiatry*, **12**, 1–27.

Walker, N. (1968). *Crime and Insanity in England*, vol. I. Edinburgh: Edinburgh
University Press.

Walker, N. (1991). Dangerous mistakes. *British Journal of Psychiatry*, **158**, 752–7.

Weller, M. P. I., and Weller, B. G. A. (1988a). Crime and mental illness. *Medicine,
Science and the Law*, **28**, 38–46.

Weller, M. P. I., and Weller, B. G. A. (1988b). Mental illness and social policy. *Medicine,
Science and the Law*, **28**, 47–53.

Whatmore, P. (1990a). The Special Unit at Barlinnie Prison, Glasgow. In R. Bluglass and
P. Bowden (eds), *Principles and Practice of Forensic Psychiatry*. London: Churchill
Livingstone.

Whatmore, P. (1990b). The Mental Health (Scotland) Act, 1984. In R. Bluglass and P.
Bowden (eds), *Principles and Practice of Forensic Psychiatry*. London: Churchill
Livingstone.

Wiest, J. (1981). Treatment of violent offenders. *Clinical Social Work Journal*, **9**, 271–81.

Wiltshire County Council, (1988). *Report of a Departmental Enquiry into the Discharge
of Responsibilities by Wiltshire Social Services in Relation to Daniel Mudd from his
Release from Broadmoor in May, 1983 until his Arrest In December, 1986 for the
Murder of Ruth Perrett*. Trowbridge: County Hall.

POSTSCRIPT

Since this chapter was written the report of the inquiry into complaints at Ashworth
Hospital has been published (*Report of Committee of Inquiry...*, 1992). It reveals serious
cause for concern about the care and management of patients at the Ashworth complex.
As a result, the future of maximum security provision for all offender patients is currently
being reviewed by a Department of Health and Home Office Committee.

APPENDIX I   SUMMARY OF THE TREATMENT OF MENTALLY DISORDERED OFFENDERS THROUGH THE COURTS, THE PENAL AND HEALTH CARE SYSTEMS— ENGLAND AND WALES

The provisions of the Mental Health Act 1983, the Criminal Procedure (Insanity and Unfitness to Plead) Act, 1991 and the Powers of Criminal Courts Act 1973 (as amended by the Criminal Justice Act, 1991), enable Courts in *England and Wales* to investigate and deal with a wide range of behaviour from the more mildly disturbed to the seriously mentally abnormal. The provisions may be summarised very briefly as follows:

Hospital Guardianship and Other Orders

(1) Section 37(1) of the Mental Health Act 1983 enables courts to make hospital orders or guardianship orders, in the event of:

   (a) Conviction for an offence (but in certain cases, in the magistrates' courts, without proceeding to conviction).
   (b) Two doctors (at least one of whom is approved by a local health authority for the purpose under Section 12 of the Act), stating that the offender is suffering from mental illness, psychopathic disorder, mental impairment, severe mental impairment of a nature or degree which makes it appropriate for him/her to be detained in hospital for medical treatment *and*, in the case of psychopathic disorder or mental impairment, that such treatment is likely to alleviate or prevent a deterioration of his/her condition.
   (c) *A hospital is willing to accept the person or, in the case of guardianship, the local authority is willing to receive him or her provided they are over sixteen.*
   (d) The circumstances being such that a hospital order *is the most suitable method of dealing with the case.*

(2) Courts may also make orders for *remand for treatment* and may make *interim* hospital orders.

   (a) Section 36 enables the Crown Court to remand an accused to hospital *for treatment* if he or she is suffering from mental illness or severe mental impairment. Such a person may be detained up to 28 days—renewable for periods of 28 days up to a maximum of 12 weeks.
   (b) Section 38 enables a court to make an *interim* hospital order in the case of a person *convicted* of an offence punishable by imprisonment (other than murder). The court must be satisfied that the person is suffering from mental disorder as defined in the Act. Period of detention—up to a maximum of 6 months in all.

(3) *Medical Reports*
   In order for the medical evidence to be obtained the following provisions may be used:

   (a) The person may be remanded *in custody* for three weeks (renewable) for the appropriate reports to be prepared.
   (b) Remand *on bail*—for periods of *four weeks* at a time. Reports may be prepared in this way on an in-patient or an out-patient basis.
   (c) Remand *to hospital* under Section 35 of the Mental Health Act 1983. (The court must be of the belief that the person concerned is suffering from mental disorder

as defined in the Act.) This provision gives courts a stronger option than a remand or bail with a requirement for medical examination.

The period of detention under this section is up to 28 days, renewable for 28 days at a time to a maximum of 12 weeks in order for this examination and assessment to be made.

(4) *Power to Transfer*
A person already in custody (either undergoing sentence or awaiting trial), whose mental state becomes such as to require compulsory detention in a hospital, may be transferred under Sections 47–49 of the Mental Health Act 1983.

(5) *Restriction Orders* (Section 41 of the 1983 Mental Health Act)
These may be made by Crown Courts in order to protect the public from serious harm. The Court must also have regard to the nature of the offence, the antecedents of the offender, and the risk of them committing a further offence if set at liberty prematurely. Such an order may be made with or without limit of time. The Secretary of State may order discharge from a Restriction Order, as may a Mental Health Review Tribunal. Conditions may be attached to release, such as supervision and conditions as to residence.

Probation and Mental Treatment

Section 3 of the Powers of the Criminal Courts Act, 1973 (as amended by the Criminal Justice Act, 1991), allows this form of treatment provided:

(1) The offender-patient consents.
(2) A hospital (or other establishment) will receive them, and is willing to provide treatment.
(3) The oral or written evidence of one doctor (approved under Section 12 of the Mental Health Act) indicates that the offender's condition requires, and may be susceptible to treatment, but is not such to warrant their detention in pursuance of a hospital order.

Other Disposals

(1) *A defence of insanity* may be raised before a Crown Court and if accepted by the jury (in the form of a special verdict of 'not guilty by reason of insanity'), may lead to detention in a hospital but not necessarily a special hospital, or to an absolute discharge or a supervision and treatment order. (On a successful plea in a murder case, the Court must impose a restriction order (Section 37/41).)
(2) *A finding of unfitness to plead* (now known as being 'under disability'). This has the same effect as a finding of insanity, see (1) above.
(3) *A defence of diminished responsibility* under the Homicide Act 1957 may be raised in *murder* cases only; if accepted it leads to a conviction for manslaughter, leaving the court free to make any order it wishes, including those outlined above.
(4) No action in respect of the mental disorder. (By this is meant that the court makes a non-psychiatric disposal.)

Other Parts of the United Kingdom

The following is a very brief statement of the mental health legislation relevant to mentally disordered offenders in other parts of the UK and in Ireland.

Scotland

The relevant legislation is the Mental Health (Scotland) Act, 1984. In many respects it is similar to the England and Wales Mental Health Act, but does not use the category psychopathic disorder. But if an offender-patient can be shown to be suffering from a persistent mental disorder which is manifested by abnormally aggressive or seriously irresponsible conduct compulsory powers can be used if it can be shown that the patient is likely to benefit from treatment (for further details see Whatmore, 1990b).

Northern Ireland

The relevant legislation in Northern Ireland is contained in the Mental Health (Northern Ireland) Order, 1986. The Northern Ireland legislation combines many of the features of the England and Wales and Scottish legislation, but psychopathy is not referred to as a category of mental disorder (see MacCullum, 1990).

Ireland

Mental health legislation is contained currently in the Mental Treatment Act, 1945, as amended by the Mental Treatment Act 1961. It is very different from England and Wales, Northern Ireland and Scotland; new legislation, said to be long overdue, is expected shortly (see Smith, 1990b).

Part 2
Clinical Research and Practice

3

Mental Illness, Neurological and Organic Disorder, and Criminal Behaviour

CAROL SELLARS
*District Psychology Service, Basingstoke, Hampshire, UK**
CLIVE R. HOLLIN and KEVIN HOWELLS
School of Psychology, The University of Birmingham, UK

Our aim in this chapter is to cover two areas of concern: firstly the relationship between mental illness and criminal behaviour; followed by neurological and organic disorder and criminal behaviour. Treatment aspects for the former are discussed in the next chapter, while treatment for the latter is also included here.

MENTAL ILLNESS AND CRIMINAL BEHAVIOUR

The relationship between mental illness and criminal behaviour has been an issue that has concerned criminologists, lawyers, and psychiatrists for many years (Whitehead, 1983). When considering the association between mental illness and criminal behaviour three positions can be defined: (i) there are people who experience mental illness and do not commit offences; (ii) there are people who commit crimes and are not mentally ill; (iii) there are people who display both mental illness and criminal behaviour. It is this third group, falling into the population sometimes referred to as mentally abnormal offenders (e.g. Craft & Craft, 1984), that is of concern in the first part of this chapter.

In their discussion of crime and mental illness in the nineteenth century, Long and Midgley (1992) describe the way in which the conceptual boundaries were blurred between these two phenomena. At that time the notion of insanity was

---

*Formerly Psychology Department, Broadmoor Hospital, Crowthorne, Berkshire, UK.

Clinical Approaches to the Mentally Disordered Offender
Edited by K. Howells and C. R. Hollin © 1993 John Wiley & Sons Ltd

extended to include all those on the margins of mainstream society, including the physically malformed, the socially inept, and those who transgressed against the law of the land. The same penalty of exclusion from society was delivered to these social outcasts, criminals included. As the mentally ill and the criminal were thrown together, literally and metaphorically, so explanations and theories for mental illness and crime began to merge. As Long and Midgely note, this was not to the advantage of either group: both became tarred with the same brush of unpredictability, dangerousness, and violence.

It is no surprise that studies of prison populations in the nineteenth century showed high levels of mental disturbance among prisoners. The interpretation of the findings of these studies was not in social terms, reflecting the practice of imprisoning the mentally ill, but in terms of psychopathology: that is, in terms of a close association between mental disorder and criminal behaviour. Thus the actions of the criminal were accounted for in medical terms with crude biological explanations of criminal behaviour, and the criminal was seen as mentally and morally pathological and diseased. Thus criminal behaviour was understood as the product of a sickness or disease of the mind that afflicts the criminal: as Long and Midgely argue, this belief in the psychopathology of offenders is still very much evident today.

Contemporary thought has moved away from the view that criminal behaviour is somehow equated with psychopathology, and two alternative options have received particular attention: (i) mental illness can be a *cause* of criminal behaviour (which, of course, is not the same as saying that criminal behaviour is evidence of psychopathology); (ii) that the relationship between mental disorder and crime is *correlational*. There are two areas of the empirical literature that can be used to attempt to shed light on the relationship between mental illness and criminal behaviour. The first group of studies is concerned with mental illness in offender populations; the second with criminal behaviour in psychiatric populations.

Psychopathology in Offender Populations

In a typical study Gunn, Robertson, Dell, and Way (1978) assessed the psychiatric status, using both questionnaires and interviews, of a sample of 600 prisoners. Gunn *et al.* found that over 20% of the prisoners had a marked or severe psychiatric condition: a figure much higher than would be expected in the general population. In most cases the prisoners were depressed, with anxiety states next most commonly found. In addition, drug and alcohol addiction were also common, but schizophrenia was rare. McManus, Alessi, Grapentine, and Brickman (1984) found a similar pattern, a predominance of alcohol addiction and mood disturbances, with incarcerated delinquent adolescents. Similarly, a study reported by Taylor (1986) of male and female prisoners serving life sentences found that approximately two-thirds of these prisoners showed evidence of psychiatric disorder. In Taylor's study depression and personality disorder were most common, with an estimated 10% of the life-sentenced prisoners being schizophrenic. Overall, it is safe to conclude that the general pattern from the empirical studies is that psychiatric problems, including mental illness, are common in prison populations (Abram and Teplin, 1991; Hodgins and Côté, in press; Prins, 1986).

However, a higher than expected prevalence of psychopathology in offender populations is not evidence for a causal link between mental illness and criminal behaviour. Alternative explanations include the possibility that mentally ill people may carry out their offences more clumsily, thereby leading to easier detection; or that with the mentally ill the authorities may be more willing to arrest, charge, and accept guilty pleas, perhaps in an attempt to access a treatment facility. Further, because an offender exhibits a mental illness in prison, it does not follow that the illness was extant at the time of the offence. It is possible that the adverse aspects of a prison environment could precipitate the onset of a disorder in vulnerable prisoners. Thus, while prison populations are characterized by higher than average levels of psychopathology, as Gunn (1977) suggests, 'This may be more closely related to their function as institutions than to any special relationship between crime and mental disorder' (p. 327). In addition, as discussed further below, there are well documented research difficulties including sample selection, sample size, the accuracy of diagnosis of the mental disorder, and measurement of criminal behaviour.

Criminal Behaviour in Psychiatric Populations

The broad consensus from the literature is that criminal behaviour is higher in psychiatric populations, including the mentally ill, than in the general population (Howells, 1982; Prins, 1980, 1986). While there are various points that qualify this broad position, considerable attention has been paid to type of offence. For some offences, mainly non-violent offences, the rates are similar both in psychiatric populations and in the general population. For more serious offences, such as robbery and possibly rape, the incidence is probably higher in psychiatric populations than in the general population (Monahan, 1992). Similarly, some studies suggest that there are high rates of crime among discharged psychiatric patients (e.g. Shore, Filson, and Rae, 1990), although a recent study specifically with a schizophrenic population did not reach this conclusion (Rice and Harris, 1992).

However, even if violent behaviour is more common among patients in psychiatric hospitals this does not mean that causal relationships are involved. Hospitalized populations are not a random sample of people with mental illness and may well include people with higher levels of criminal and antisocial behaviour than other parts of the mentally ill population. In addition, there are methodological problems in that studies may only cover a short follow-up period, hospital records may be used rather than diagnostic interviews, and there are the usual difficulties in gathering data about criminal behaviour.

It can be stated with some degree of confidence, on the basis of the evidence discussed thus far, that there is some overlap between criminal behaviour and mental disorder including mental illness. Whether this overlap is causal or correlational is impossible to say. Another way to approach this issue is to look more closely at the relationship between specific mental disorders and criminal behaviour.

While mental illness is a much used term, it lacks a legal definition, so that in practice much depends on medical opinion (Ashworth and Gostin, 1985). With particular reference to serious offenders, by far the greatest number of mentally ill offenders are diagnosed as schizophrenic, with depression the next most frequent diagnosis (Hamilton, 1985). The question then becomes: Does any special relationship exist between these two forms of mental illness and criminal behaviour?

Schizophrenia

Acknowledging the debate about even the concept of schizophrenia (Boyle, 1990), it is prudent to see schizophrenia as a group of disorders rather than a single disorder. Spry (1984) reviews the evidence on the incidence of schizophrenia in offender populations and notes that with studies of normal offender groups (usually prisoners) an incidence of schizophrenia around the 1% mark that is typical of the general population as a whole. However, for offenders selected on the basis of referral for psychiatric treatment, typically after committing serious, violent offences, the incidence is much higher. Taylor's (1986) figures for the incidence of schizophrenia among a sample of life-sentenced offenders, the majority of whom had committed murder, were substantially higher than the 1% baseline. Hodgins and Côté (in press) report rates of schizophrenia and schizophreniform disorder in excess of 6% among Canadian penitentiary inmates: these data indicated an over-representation of convictions for homicide among the inmates with schizophrenia. It is, of course, hazardous to extrapolate the findings from such select samples to the whole of the schizophrenic population: whether or not schizophrenia is closely associated with violent criminal behaviour remains a matter for debate (Chuang, Williams, and Dalby, 1987; Cirincione, Steadman, Robbins, and Monahan, 1992; Monahan, 1992; Taylor and Gunn, 1984).

As well as problems with sampling, many studies have difficulties in generating large representative samples. For example, Lindqvist and Allebeck (1990) examined the offence history of 644 schizophrenic patients discharged from Swedish hospitals in 1971. Using a retrospective longitudinal design, Lindqvist and Allebeck were able from police records to see what offences had been committed by this population during the period 1972–1986. The first level of analysis was concerned with the incidence of criminal offences. They found that of the 644 discharged patients, only 45 out of 330 men and just 9 out of 314 women had committed offences. As Lindqvist and Allebeck caution, it is unwise to extrapolate unduly from this small sample who do commit offences. Nonetheless, with regard to the type of offence committed by the schizophrenic population: 'Violent crimes were four times more frequent among schizophrenics than "normals"' (Lindqvist and Allebeck, 1990, p. 348). However, to put this in context, the schizophrenic group committed far more non-violent than violent crimes, mainly theft and petty theft; and the violent offences were almost exclusively minor in nature, mostly assault with no cases of manslaughter or murder.

Overall, while schizophrenia may have some association with violent behaviour, most people with schizophrenia are not violent, and such violence as occurs is mostly trivial. For those people with schizophrenia who do commit violent offences, the nature and function of delusional and paranoid beliefs appear to be of crucial importance. As Taylor (1982) observes: 'It is not unusual to find that the violent act of a schizophrenic cannot be directly explained by the current psychopathology. This does not, however, negate the relevance of the illness ... social and illness variables must be considered together' (p. 280).

Taylor's observation is important in its implication that when considering the association between schizophrenia and violence, it is necessary to consider not only the person but also the environment. Rather than seeing schizophrenia as a direct cause of violent behaviour, the schizophrenia and violence can be seen as the interactive consequences of common adverse environmental conditions. Indeed, from a survey of psychotic offenders, Taylor (1985) was able to conclude that in about one-fifth of cases the psychotic symptoms played an active part in the offence. However, when environmental factors such as homelessness were considered so that 'the direct and indirect consequences of psychosis are considered together, then over 80% of the offences of the psychotic were probably attributable to their illness' (Taylor, 1985, p. 497). To understand the relationship between schizophrenia and criminal behaviour it is not sufficient simply to focus on the illness and on the offence. An accurate picture of schizophrenia and crime must include interactive effects of the relevant organic, psychological, social, environmental, and legal variables.

Depression

While most research has concentrated upon schizophrenia, depression is also common among some offender groups. In a typical study, Hodgins and Côté (in press), looked at rates of major mental disorder among male Canadian penitentiary inmates. They reported rates of bipolar disorder in excess of 4% of the population, and rates of major depression of the order of 11% of the population. As with schizophrenia, there are difficulties in establishing the nature of the association between depression and criminal behaviour. There are several possibilities: the offence may have been committed because the offender was depressed; the offender's guilt after the offence may have precipitated the depression; or the offender may have been depressed when committing the crime, but the depression was not a direct cause of their criminal behaviour.

One of the more familiar and tragic associations between depression and criminal behaviour occurs in cases of murder followed by suicide, Typically, the depressed person kills their children and other members of their family before committing suicide. West (1965) discussed 78 cases of murder followed by suicide, estimating that in 28 of these cases the offender was depressed at the time of the killing. It is tempting to conclude that in this type of tragedy the depression caused the offence but, as with schizophrenia, the broader picture must be considered. Studies of the general pattern of murder by people who have become depressed suggest that adverse social factors, such as a breakdown in a long-term relationship, may play an important role (Lawson, 1984).

As well as murder, depression has been linked with other crimes including shoplifting and violence (particularly towards relatives); with the additional suggestion of a particular link between a manic state and arson. Given that depressed in-patients are not generally thought of as a violent population, it seems likely that the relationship between depression and criminal behaviour is mediated by social factors, especially those concerned with close personal relationships (Prins, 1986).

Conclusion

While psychopathology and criminal behaviour do, at times, co-exist, the nature of this relationship is altogether less clear. In some cases, perhaps with paranoid schizophrenia, the relationship appears, in part at least, to be causal: however, as Taylor has stressed, both disorder and crime must be placed in a broad social context. If paranoid delusions are one cause of violent conduct, what causes the delusions and determines their content? It is unlikely that hard and fast theoretical formulations will be made regarding the relationship between mental functioning and criminal behaviour. It is more likely that cases will have to be considered on their individual merits to determine, in that particular instance, the nature of the relationship for that person at the time the offence occurred. Of course, this is a point of practical significance both for the courts and, as discussed in detail in the following chapter, for clinicians working with this type of offender.

NEUROLOGICAL AND ORGANIC DISORDER AND CRIMINAL BEHAVIOUR

The relationship between biological factors and criminal behaviour is a topic that has generated a great deal of heat but little light. A range of possible biological factors have been associated with criminal behaviour including genetic and chromosomal factors, central nervous system functioning, autonomic nervous system functioning, laterality, and hormonal activity (for a review see Hollin, 1992). However, with an eye to the potential for bringing about individual change through clinical intervention, the focus here is on neurological and organic disorder.

It is long recognized that tumours, head injuries, or strokes can result in changes in behaviour, and several studies have been concerned with the nature of the relationship between organic functioning and criminal behaviour. Some studies suggest that offenders, particularly violent offenders, tend to show rather high rates of organic and neuropsychological disorder. Hodgins and Côté (in press) found a prevalence rate of 0.4% of organic brain syndrome among male penitentiary inmates. Studies by Spellacy (1978) and Bryant, Scott, Golden, and Tori (1984) report distinct differences in neuropsychological functioning between violent and non-violent men. Yeudall, Fromm-Auch, and Davies (1982) also reported a greater incidence of neuropsychological disorders in serious young offenders. On a note of caution, however, Hsu, Wisner, Richey, and Goldstein (1985) conclude their investigation with the statement that there is no compelling reason to believe that abnormal EEGs are a major cause of juvenile delinquency. In addition, several studies have also pointed to the possibility of frontal lobe dysfunction in psychopathic and violent offenders (Devonshire, Howard, and Sellars, 1984; Gorenstein, 1982; Hare, 1984).

Studies such as those cited above are having an increasing impact as theoretical accounts of criminal behaviour struggle to incorporate physiological, psychological, and social environmental factors (e.g. Ellis and Hoffman, 1990). At a practical level, however, the effects of an organic disorder are compounded by the difficulties that disorder creates in personal and social development. One of the functions of assessment should be, therefore, to establish as exactly as possible the nature and effect of any neurological or organic disorder.

Assessment of Neurological/Organic Disorder in Offenders

The first step in assessment of neurological and organic disorder in offenders is simply to be alert to the possibility of its existence. Often only the most gross and obvious disorder will be noticed, for example when the offender also suffers from epilepsy, or has had a severe head injury. However, once one becomes sensitive to the possibility that organic factors may be relevant to the offender's behaviour, the evidence to support this view often becomes more apparent.

A first and most important step, is to examine any existing information that is available about the offender and his/her history. Although liable to distortion and error, reports from childhood, adolescence, and from the offender's family can be invaluable sources of information. It is, however, wise to beware of the kind of family folklore which may sometimes be produced, for example: 'Well, he's never been the same since he fell off that swing when he was five.' While this may actually be true, one needs to be sensitive to the need that the family may have to blame some exterior force for the problems of their deviant family member, rather than to face the fact that they may have contributed in some way, albeit unwittingly, to the difficulties. There is a need therefore, for corroborating medical or other evidence to support any statement of this kind.

What kinds of information are important and relevant, therefore? Begin at the beginning, and endeavour to discover what were the circumstances of the birth. Prolonged labour, forceps deliveries, caesarean births (especially if associated with foetal distress), premature birth and multiple births are all known to be associated with a higher incidence of organic damage. Convulsions, anoxia or breathing difficulties in the early days or weeks of life can be relevant also. All of these events may lead to loss of brain tissue, with the possibility of resulting impairment.

Similar information should be sought about childhood problems. Frequent febrile convulsions, falls, concussions, toxic episodes, illnesses such as measles, encephalitis, etc. and any episodes of unconsciousness, should all be noted. Admissions to hospital for injuries sustained either accidentally or non-accidentally may also be important. This is especially true if there is an association with reports of a violent parent, step-parent or sibling, and perhaps alcohol abuse by such a person. In these circumstances, there is always the possibility that the child was physically abused, with a consequent head injury, or that the child suffered from foetal alcohol syndrome.

The social and academic performance of the growing child is also important. School reports, and reports from child guidance clinics, social workers and family may all help here. Was the child a 'loner', or did he or she mix well? Were there reports of learning difficulties, attentional problems or conduct disorder? Reports of oddities of appearance or behaviour may give clues. A child who is described as disruptive, distractible or hyperactive, may, for example, fulfil the criteria for minimal brain damage (MBD). However, this is where the picture may become confused. Such children may have been impaired by birth trauma, or the problem may be congenital. Children with MBD syndrome can present severe management problems to parents and teachers, and may as a result be more prone to abuse, which might add to their difficulties.

In adolescence and young adult life, note the use of drugs, or alcohol to excess. Look for any episodes of overdosing, coma or periods of amnesia. As with children, any reports of unconsciousness, concussion or convulsions may be significant. Road accidents are a common cause of brain injury in younger people, and even quite minor accidents can result in damage to brain tissue.

All the information that can be gathered helps to create a picture of the individual and his or her background. This picture is a context in which to put the information gathered from the clinical and psychometric assessments, and may suggest hypotheses to be tested, and appropriate test materials to use.

Clinical Observation

The next part of the assessment is the careful observation of the subject, both before, during, and after the formal testing. Notice the patterns of movement. Is the gait unusual? Are there jerky, uncoordinated movements? Is there any hand tremor? Are there signs of unilateral weakness? Is there evidence of facial distortion, or an unusual head shape? While none of these may be of any significance alone, in the context of other information, they may become so.

All aspects of the subject's non-verbal behaviour should be noted, including posture, handedness, indications of problems with vision or hearing, articulation difficulties, and use of space. These observations can be usefully cross-referenced with the background information already collected, and may support or eliminate the hypotheses which the clinician has begun to develop.

Formal Assessment

The nature of the assessments carried out on offenders who may also suffer from neuropsychological abnormalities is in some ways more difficult than the assessment of such abnormalities in other settings. Where such assessments are carried out on patients who have suffered head injury, or stroke, for example, there is often clear evidence as to the probable location of the injury, and this can guide the clinician in the choice of suitable assessments. In addition, if it is known that some kind of neurological damage has occurred, then the clinician's role is to define its extent, and the nature of the handicaps it causes.

When assessing offenders, the picture is often far less clear. There may be uncertainty as to whether there is any neurological damage at all, and the diagnosis may be further confused by the presence of additional psychiatric or behavioural disorders, which may be wholly functional in origin. The clinician is therefore faced with the difficult task of attempting to differentiate between problems of organic origin, and those which appear to be largely functional. Often, as described above, the two may confound each other.

The problems of discriminating between psychiatric disturbance, especially schizophrenia, and organic disorder are well known. Heaton, Baade, and Johnson (1978) have reviewed a number of studies, using a variety of psychometric tests, and conclude that this is almost impossible to do reliably. Moses and Golden (1980), have attempted to do the same, using the recently devised Luria–Nebraska Neuropsychological Battery, and claim that it is possible to discriminate reliably between the two populations.

In the case of offenders with behavioural problems who have not been diagnosed as psychiatrically disturbed, the assessment process might be expected to be simpler. However, these individuals are often difficult and uncooperative, and their motivation to complete the assessments may be very low. Furthermore, it is likely that the deficits are subtle, and may be easily overlooked by inexperienced clinicians, or not detected by insufficiently sensitive assessment methods.

Because of these difficulties, it is important to devise an assessment battery which is both comprehensive, and sensitive to subtle deficits. It is also important to make clinicians aware of the need for careful observation, and systematic analysis of their clinical information. As far as actual test materials are concerned, the Luria–Nebraska Neuropsychological Battery has proved useful in this context. Malloy and Webster (1981) have demonstrated its usefulness in identifying mild brain impairment, and it has the advantage of providing a comprehensive assessment of neuropsychological functioning. Its disadvantage is that it is rather long, and may be unnecessarily comprehensive in some situations. A compromise may be to use the initial short-screening battery, which can be used to identify those who might benefit from further and more detailed investigation, although of course, there is then the risk that subtle deficits may be missed.

The selection of test materials should also be governed by the hypotheses generated by the information already collected about the offender. Hyperactivity, distractibility, or disinhibition, for example, should suggest the need for investigation of frontal lobe function. Speech, language or memory problems should suggest the need for investigation of temporal lobe function, and so on. Lezak (1983) is an invaluable source of information and ideas for assessment, containing a review of a variety of suitable short tests of neuropsychological functioning. Tests of frontal lobe function appear to be particularly relevant to the offender population, but the possibility of other deficits should not be overlooked.

It is perhaps worth emphasizing the point that our assessment techniques are still crude, and our understanding of brain function is equally so. We may be able to demonstrate functional abnormalities without being able to localize them in particular pieces of brain tissue. However, it would seem logical that if these abnormalities are a persistent characteristic of a given individual, it is likely that they will affect his or her social and intellectual adaptation, and may therefore be of relevance in the development of offending behaviour.

It seems sensible therefore to conceptualize our idea of 'organic disorder' in terms of persisting vulnerability which certain individuals have that makes their adjustment to adult life and its problems more difficult. It would appear that a useful model is that prevalent amongst those who work with individuals who are defined as mentally impaired. What is important here, is to define clearly both the strengths and weaknesses of the individual. The aim of therapy should be to use the strengths to compensate for the weaknesses, as far as is possible. However, what is equally important is clearly to define the nature of the support systems that this individual will need in order to adapt and survive. In the case of the offender this will include the avoidance of re-offending.

Treatment of the Offender with Neurological/Organic Disorder

Labelling an offender as organically impaired commonly seems to result in one of two responses, neither of which is particularly helpful. The first is a defeatist attitude towards treatment. The assumption is made that the problem is biologically determined and therefore unchangeable. Since one of the defining characteristics of biological organisms is their ability to change and grow, this response is a curiously negative one.

The second kind of response is to pay lip service to the individual's impairment, but to continue in care and management of the person concerned as though the impairment did not exist. Hence, for example, one finds clients with frontal lobe disorders in social skills groups, where they are expected to be able to analyse and respond appropriately to very subtle cues from others; clients with memory and communication difficulties are placed in group psychotherapy sessions, where they have to understand and interpret complex emotional messages from a variety of others. In both cases, failure to succeed is often interpreted as wilful; the client is 'uncooperative' or 'unmotivated'.

The problem of attribution is a crucial one for professional staff who have to work with organically impaired clients, whether offenders or not. It is very easy, when faced with clients who have to be told the same things over and over again, or who in spite of strict instructions to the contrary will go out and drink too much, or disappear home for the weekend, to believe the worst of the person concerned.

Interventions With and Through Care Staff

It is often very difficult to get care staff to accept and understand that the client's behaviour is not necessarily deliberately rebellious but simply uncontrolled. The individual may be actually incapable of remembering the instructions given, if no one is there to remind him or her. Similarly, those who appear to contradict rules without regard for the consequences, and in spite of repeated warnings about the outcome, may simply be unable to inhibit their responses without help from others.

In consequence, a very important aspect of the care and management of organically impaired clients is the education of care staff who have to work with them, so that key workers, of whatever discipline is involved, have clear understanding of the client's problems and limitations, and how these may affect his or her day-to-day functioning. This is not a one-off task; the psychologist responsible for the assessment will have to keep prompting and reminding care staff of the client's difficulties, and modelling appropriate responses.

The next area of intervention may be in the development of behaviour modification programmes. Careful evaluation of the client should enable the therapist to define the sorts of environment in which the client will respond more appropriately. Certain reinforcers can be identified, either by the client themselves, or by those who know him or her well. The aim is to build up patterns of behaviour for the client which are socially acceptable, reinforcing to both client and carers, and ideally which compete with or prevent the undesirable behaviours. The behavioural techniques are the same as those that would be used in any applied setting (e.g. Kazdin, 1989). In addition, as well as organizational difficulties there can be practical constraints, such as shortages of care staff or frequent staff changes, that make consistency of approach difficult to achieve.

Treatment of the Individual

Working with and through care staff constitutes treatment of the individual, but there is also scope for specialist individual work. Individual programmes offer the opportunity to explain the client the nature of the deficits identified, and how these will affect his or her behaviour. Often clients are aware at some level that they have always had difficulties with some aspects of life which others appear to handle with ease. They may, in the past, have been made painfully aware of their limitations, and feel victimized and bitter as a result. Taking time to explain the problems to the clients in language that they will understand, together with sympathetic acceptance of their limitations, is important if any treatment intervention is to be effective.

It is important to try and devise a treatment programme which will be effective and meaningful to the client. To do this, a problem-solving approach can be invaluable. It is important to establish goals with the client which are acceptable and easily understood. These goals should be written down, and agreed. The next stage is to break down each goal into a series of manageable steps, so that the client can see how the goal might be achieved. Clients with problems in language or sequencing may have difficulty here and it may be necessary in these cases to introduce each goal separately. The client may be unable to conceptualize the overall programme, but each stage should be agreed with him or her.

It is also important that the client should learn to appreciate the feedback that he or she receives about their behaviour. This can be particularly difficult for patients with frontal lobe impairments who often perceive feedback but are unable to utilize it to modify their own actions. Thus patients with frontal lobe impairments often appear to act without thinking of the consequences of their actions. After the event, having suffered the consequences of their actions, which may include arrest and imprisonment, they are mortified and repentant.

Overall, it can be seen that the strategies that can be used with organically impaired offenders are not new or unique to this population. Techniques can be taken from behaviour therapy and cognitive psychotherapy, and lessons learnt from work with other client groups such as the mentally impaired, adolescents, and adults with and without organic impairment. In addition, the same principles of good practice apply so that the clinical work is conducted in the context of a trusting relationship between clinician and client.

CASE ILLUSTRATION

The problems posed by the organically impaired offender are illustrated in the following case discussion prepared by the first author of this chapter. The case in question concerns a man, called here Brian, charged with attempted murder: specifically, he had attempted to stab a stranger in the back as they entered a railway station.

Brian was said to have had a normal birth, but to be a sickly child, who suffered both from diphtheria and from a severe attack of whooping cough as a child. He had poor eyesight, and was described as a 'gormless kid with glasses, who was bullied a lot'. Academically, his performance was poor, and he had few friends.

His father was a violent man, who is known to have attacked both Brian and his mother on occasions. There is a report of Brian having been hospitalized as a result of at least one of these attacks.

On leaving school, Brian obtained a job in an office, but was sacked because he was unable to do the job. He was frequently unemployed, and worked as a packer and a lavatory attendant. He married his first and only girlfriend, but soon there were problems and he was violent towards her.

He suffered from chronic headaches, for which there were doubtful physical origins, and he began to complain of tension, irritability, and lack of concentration. He slept poorly, and complained of feeling depressed, and eventually made several suicide attempts. He also began to express ideas about harming his wife. However, it is also noted that he stated that he felt much better when he was in hospital, and that his symptoms largely disappeared once he was admitted. It seems possible that the threats towards his wife were at least partly to secure readmission.

Brian presented as a miserable, complaining, and abrupt individual, who was constantly seeking attention and reassurance from those around him. He felt constantly dissatisfied with the level of care he received, and criticized his carers relentlessly. Yet he resisted attempts to help him, saying that he was happy the way he was, in spite of very obvious cues that he was anything but happy. He had few friends, because not many others would tolerate his negativity. He seemed unable to delay gratification, and complained bitterly if he had to wait for anything. He failed to understand that his own behaviour could influence the situations in which he found himself, and was anxious and aggressive when faced with new situations which he found threatening. Physically, he appeared stiff and uncoordinated, with an unexpressive face, and rapid speech.

On assessment, he was found to have a fairly low IQ, with the pattern of scatter in the subtest scores suggestive of pathology. The report that he was sacked for being unable to do his job on leaving school, together with reports from earlier hospital admissions of his inability to make use of therapy, suggested the need for further investigation. Furthermore there was the report of the attack by his father, which required hospitalization, suggesting that the injuries could have been serious.

A more thorough assessment, using the Luria–Nebraska Neuropsychological Battery, indicated that there were abnormalities of motor control, rhythm perception, and memory, located mainly in the left hemisphere. More detailed examination of his responses indicated particular difficulties with language, especially complex language, some tendency to perseverate, and abnormalities in both sensory and motor functioning. The latter may account for his preoccupation with his physical condition. The aetiology of these abnormalities is unclear, but could either be the result of unspecified or undetected complications of childhood illnesses, or more likely, the result of the serious assault by his father.

It seems that Brian may have been experiencing bodily sensations in an abnormal way, and his stiff and awkward movements have already been noted. His headaches are likely to have been related both to his motor awkwardness and to his impaired sensory functioning. His demanding and querulous presentation probably resulted from his difficulty in understanding or remembering the explanations that he was given. He felt that his distress was being ignored or minimized, and his escalating attempt to gain attention and readmission to hospital appear to have been in response to the frustration generated as a result. His attacks on his wife also appear to have arisen from his frustration at what he perceived as her lack of care of him. It seems from Brian's account that his index offence was intended to secure further attention and care in some way and to call attention to his own distress.

Brian's treatment has taken a considerable time, amounting to some eight years so far. During that time, he has received both individual and group treatments. Initially, he resisted all attempts to engage him in treatment, but gradually he came to understand that he had to take responsibility for what happened to him, and that if he was to improve his life, then he must make efforts to change.

It quickly became evident during individual sessions, that Brian has always felt overlooked and misunderstood, and that he often had difficulty following what other people said to him. This was worse when he was emotionally distressed, and made him feel powerless and frustrated in arguments with his wife. He also tends to appear very anxious and tense, but at the same time finds this emotional state difficult to recognize or express.

Therapy sessions have been characterized by the need to present information repeatedly and very simply, until by repetition and rehearsal, he was able both to remember and understand the ideas and suggestions which were made to him. Brian now recognizes that he has a memory problem, and finds that it helps him to write things down. He carries a large diary everywhere with him for this purpose. He has been taught relaxation exercises and has a tape which he uses every day. The regularity of use of the tape is important to help him develop the habit of relaxation, and it also avoids the necessity of him being able to recognize specific cues of tension in himself.

Considerable time was spent trying to explain to Brian the possible reasons for his headache and his concern with bodily symptoms generally. This idea has been much more difficult for him to grasp. He tends to become defensive, feeling that he is being told that he is imagining his symptoms. At present the best strategy seems to be to ensure that there is someone available to listen sympathetically to his complaints at least once a day. Even though little is done in terms of actual treatment (apart from occasional painkillers if requested) the attention and sympathy appear to be sufficient. It is hoped that in time, this behaviour might be reduced, using behavioural strategies to substitute more appropriate behaviours. So far this has not been possible. Brian's history as a sickly child seems to have established a strong pattern of using sickness and bodily symptoms to gain attention and a sense of acceptance by others, and this is confounded by his impaired functioning in this area.

A major benefit seemed to result from a decision to involve him in a very simple communication group, aimed at encouraging and promoting conversation and personal confidence. Simple role plays were used, and although Brian often had difficulty in following the discussions, he was able to gain useful experiences and reinforcement of appropriate behaviours by his participation in the role plays. Brian's pleased and positive responses to the feedback he received were in turn rewarding to the other group members, who consequently became more positive towards him. The effects of such changes then become self-reinforcing, because the changes in behaviour result in changes in the responses of other people, which are in themselves a reinforcement of the new behaviours. Brian is also developing the confidence to ask people to explain further if he cannot understand, rather than pretending he has done so, and thereby often making himself look silly by having misunderstood or responded in an inappropriate way.

Overall, Brian has presented a long-term challenge to those charged with his care. Through careful assessment and intervention some real changes in his behaviour have taken place. This process will continue with the goal of his successful return to the community.

CONCLUSION

It is clear that there are two major areas of work for the future in working with offenders with neurological and organic disorder. The first is the assimilation of basic empirical research into theories of offending: this draws on mainstream research and research specifically with offender groups. The second area of work is to continue to develop clinical assessment techniques and intervention programmes for this group of offenders. In clinical psychology enormous strides are being made in rehabilitation for brain-damaged people and much is to be gained by drawing on this expertise. Indeed, if these trends are followed by clinical criminologists then work with the offender with neurological and organic impairment may well make significant progress in the years ahead.

REFERENCES

Abram, K. M., and Teplin, L. A. (1991). Co-occurring disorders among mentally ill jail detainees. *American Psychologist*, **46**, 1036–45.

Ashworth, A., and Gostin, L. (1985). Mentally disordered offenders and the sentencing process. In L. Gostin (ed.), *Secure Provision*. London: Tavistock Press.

Boyle, M. (1990). *Schizophrenia: A Scientific Delusion?* London: Routledge.

Bryant, E. T., Scott, M. L., Golden, C. J., and Tori, C. D. (1984). Neuropsychological deficits, learning disability and violent behavior. *Journal of Consulting and Clinical Psychology*, **52**, 323–4.

Chuang, H. T., Williams, R. W., and Dalby, J. T. (1987). Criminal behavior among schizophrenics. *Canadian Journal of Psychiatry*, **32**, 255–8.

Cirncione, C., Steadman, H. J., Robbins, P. C., and Monahan, J. (1992). Schizophrenia as a contingent risk factor for criminal violence. *International Journal of Law and Psychiatry*, **15**, 347–58.

Craft, M., and Craft, A. (eds) (1984). *Mentally Abnormal Offenders*. London: Baillière Tindall.

Devonshire, P. A., Howard, R. C., and Sellars, C. (1984, December). *Frontal lobe functions and antisocial personality in mentally abnormal offenders*. Paper presented at the British Psychological Society London Conference, University of London, London.

Ellis, L., and Hoffman, H. (eds) (1990). *Crime in Biological, Social and Moral Contexts*. New York: Praeger.

Gorenstein, E. (1982). Frontal lobe functions in psychopaths. *Journal of Abnormal Psychology*, **91**, 368–79.

Gunn, J. (1977). Criminal behaviour and mental disorder. *British Journal of Psychiatry*, **130**, 317–29.

Gunn, J., Robertson, G., Dell, S., and Way, C. (1978). *Psychiatric Aspects of Imprisonment*. London: Academic Press.

Hamilton, J. R. (1985). The special hosptials. In L. Gostin (ed.), *Secure Provision*. London: Tavistock Press.

Hare, R. D. (1984). Performance of psychopaths on cognitive tasks related to frontal lobe function. *Journal of Abnormal Psychology*, **93**, 133–40.

Heaton, R. K., Baade, L. E., and Johnson, K. L. (1978). Neuropsychological test results associated with psychiatric disorders in adults. *Psychological Bulletin*, **85**, 141–62.

Hodgins, S., and Côté, G. (in press). Major mental disorder among Canadian penitentiary inmates. In C. D. Webster, L. Stermac, and L. Stewart (eds), *Clinical Criminology*.

Hollin, C. R. (1992). *Criminal Behaviour: A Psychological Approach to Explanation and Prevention*. London: Falmer Press.

Howells, K. (1982). Mental disorder and violent behaviour. In P. Feldman (ed.), *Developments in the Study of Criminal Behaviour*, Vol. 2: *Violence*. Chichester: Wiley.

Hsu, L. K. G., Wisner, K., Richey, E. T., and Goldstein, C. (1985). Is juvenile delinquency related to abnormal EEG? A study of EEG abnormalities in juvenile delinquents and adolescent psychiatric inpatients. *Journal of the American Academy of Child Psychiatry*, **24**, 310–15.

Kazdin, A. E. (1989). *Behaviour Modification in Applied Settings* (4th edn). Pacific Grove, CA: Brooks/Cole.

Lawson, W. K. (1984). Depression and crime: A discursive approach. In M. Craft and A. Craft (eds), *Mentally Abnormal Offenders*. London: Baillière Tindall.

Lezak, M. (1983). *Neuropsychological Assessment*. Oxford: Oxford University Press.

Lindqvist, P., and Allebeck, P. (1990). Schizophrenia and crime: A longitudinal follow-up of 644 schizophrenics in Stockholm. *British Journal of Psychiatry*, **157**, 345–50.

Long, C. G., and Midgley, M. (1992). On the closeness of the concepts of the criminal and the mentally ill in the nineteenth century: Yesterday's professional and public opinions reflected today. *Journal of Forensic Psychiatry*, **3**, 63–79.

McManus, M., Alessi, N. E., Grapentine, M. D., and Brickman, A. (1984). Psychiatric disturbance in serious delinquents. *Journal of the American Academy of Child Psychiatry*, **23**, 602–15.

Malloy, P. F., and Webster, J. S. (1981). Detecting brain impairment using the Luria-Nebraska Neuropsychological Battery. *Journal of Consulting and Clinical Psychology*, **49**, 768–70.

Monahan, J. (1992). Mental disorder and violent behaviour: Perceptions and evidence. *American Psychologist*, **47**, 511–21.

Moses, J. A., and Golden, C. J. (1980). Discrimination between schizophrenic and brain-damaged patients with the Luria–Nebraska Neuropsychological Battery. *International Journal of Neurosciences*, **10**, 121–8.

Prins, H. (1980). *Offenders, Deviants, or Patients? An Introduction to the Study of Socio-Forensic Problems*. London: Tavistock Press.

Prins, H. (1986). *Dangerous Behaviour, the Law and Mental Disorder*. London: Tavistock Press.

Rice, M. E., and Harris, G. T. (1992). A comparison of criminal recidivism among schizophrenic and nonschizophrenic offenders. *International Journal of Law and Psychiatry*, **15**, 397–408.

Shore, D., Filson, C. R., and Rae, D. S. (1990). Violent arrest rates of White House case subjects and matched control subjects. *American Journal of Psychiatry*, **147**, 746–50.

Spellacy, F. (1978). Neuropsychological discrimination between violent and non-violent men. *Journal of Clinical Psychology*, **34**, 49–52.

Spry, W. B. (1984). Schizophrenia and crime. In M. Craft and A. Craft (eds), *Mentally Abnormal Offenders*. London: Baillière Tindall.

Taylor, P. J. (1982). Schizophrenia and violence. In J. Gunn and D. P. Farrington (eds), *Abnormal Offenders, Delinquency and the Criminal Justice System*. Chichester: Wiley.

Taylor, P. J. (1985). Motives for offending among violent and psychotic men. *British Journal of Psychiatry*, **147**, 491–8.

Taylor, P. J. (1986). Psychiatric disorder in London's life-sentenced offenders. *British Journal of Criminology*, **26**, 63–78.

Taylor, P. J., and Gunn, J. (1984). Violence and psychosis II—Effect of psychiatric diagnosis on conviction and sentencing of offenders. *British Medical Journal*, **289**, 9–12.

West, D. J. (1965). *Murder Followed by Suicide*. London: Heinemann.

Whitehead, T. (1983). *Mental Illness and the Law* (2nd edn). Oxford: Blackwell.

Yeudall, L. T., Fromm-Auch, D., and Davies, P. (1982). Neuropsychological impairment in persistent delinquency. *Journal of Nervous Disease and Mental Disorders*, **170**, 257–65.

4

Clinical Programmes for Mentally Ill Offenders

C. D. WEBSTER
S. J. HUCKER
and
M. G. GROSSMAN
*Clarke Institute of Psychiatry, Toronto, Canada
and University of Toronto, Canada*

> Much more has been written about the legal issues in providing psychiatric treatment in jails and prisons than has been written about the treatment itself. Little is available in the literature to guide decisions about designing treatment programs. Mentally ill offenders present difficult operational issues, legal dilemmas, and philosophical paradoxes. They are viewed as different from the 'typical inmate' in a prison, the 'typical patient' at a state hospital, or the 'typical client' at a community mental health center. They are stigmatized by their mental illness and by their criminal behaviour.
>
> (Jemelka, Trupin, and Chiles, 1989, p. 485)

This chapter centres on the clinical treatment of seriously mentally ill prisoners and parolees and on forensic psychiatric patients in secure hospitals and community facilities. Although there are doubtless differences between the characteristics of these populations, they also share many similarities (The authors are familiar with the expression 'being sent to cottage country', meaning that the patient is threatened with being sent to a particular large remote secure hospital. This seems similar to the practice in corrections of facing prisoners with the prospect of additional security and privations.) Whether a seriously disordered person ends up in the hospital wing of a penitentiary or in a locked ward of a secure hospital depends on many 'front end' considerations which may have little to do with the characteristics of the offender, the offence or the illness (Quinsey,

Clinical Approaches to the Mentally Disordered Offender
Edited by K. Howells and C. R. Hollin © 1993 John Wiley & Sons Ltd

1981). Either way, the individual's only hope for transfer to reduced security and supervision is through parole boards on the one hand or tribunals or review boards on the other. In practical terms the onus is on the patient or prisoner, legally assisted or not, to demonstrate that the illness has abated and that he or she is no longer a danger to other people. The easiest and most usual way of doing this is by advancing the case that treatment has been successful.[1] While some academics have argued that correctional mental health treatments are largely if not completely ineffective (Annis, 1981), the criminal justice and mental health boards at a work-a-day level are in fact almost obliged to acknowledge in some cases the positive effects of various kinds of treatments. Even persons considered extremely disordered on admission to prison or hospital these days stand a good chance of eventual supervised release from institutions (de St Croix, Dry, and Webster, 1988).

This idea, that many severely schizophrenic or mood disordered patients and prisoners do achieve, or are said to achieve, adequate levels of recovery, is worth stressing at the outset. It is a point which might otherwise be lost, and probably would be, were the present chapter to be informed only by a review of the published literature on programme effectiveness with seriously ill forensic patients and prisoners. This literature, taken as a whole, provides remarkably few instances showing how a particular treatment intervention made an appreciable difference to a group of floridly or profoundly mentally disordered offenders or patients. It is therefore necessary to ask whether it is the clinicians who cannot do the job or the researchers who cannot or will not amass disinterested evidence to show what in fact clinicians can and cannot do for schizophrenic, mood disordered, and organically impaired forensic patients and offenders. There are, in other words, two problems here, one of actually doing clinical work and one of assessing the effects of that effort. The former tends to be carried out by psychiatrists, psychologists and other mental health and correctional staff. They rarely have the time or the skill to assess their own efforts with any degree of objectivity. The latter evaluative work is usually done by professional researchers. Because of the difficulties inherent in conducting sound and informative programme evaluation and outcome studies, such scientists often miss or obscure obvious clinical points. Our task is neither to disparage clinicians nor to impugn researchers. It is extremely difficult to comment fairly on present ability to treat seriously mentally ill prisoners and patients. The tasks of *identifying* which kinds of prisoners and patients are apparently in need of treatment, and of figuring out the actual *availability* of current programmes, though not actually simple, are easy by comparison. It is to these two matters we now turn.

POPULATION IDENTIFICATION

For some time we have been studying the characteristics of all Canadian patients

---

[1] Our point is that the mental health and correctional systems are biased in favour of allowing for the positive effects of treatment. Patients and prisoners (and their lawyers) come readily to appreciate that 'treatment is the ticket'. It is often extremely difficult to know whether in fact particular therapeutic interventions did or did not have the effects stipulated. Prisoners and patients may be induced to be deceptive (Rogers, 1988).

held under Warrants of the Lieutenant Governor as a consequence of being found unfit to stand trial or not guilty by reason of insanity (Hodgins, Webster, and Paquet, 1990; Webster, Macfarlane, Hodgins, and Macfarlane, 1990). Such patients currently number about 1100 over Canada at any given time. Since the general Canadian population varies greatly between provinces and territories, the distribution of Warrant patients is also very uneven. Uneven too are the primary psychiatric diagnoses across jurisdictions. Most provinces do not have individuals with primary diagnoses of personality disorder. Yet one such province has about one-quarter of its population in that category. Although this discrepancy can be explained through recourse to historical, legal, and political considerations, its existence makes it difficult to generalize about the characteristics of the Canadian Warrant group as a whole. This much said, the pooled data indicate that some 63% of these patients are considered to be suffering primarily from schizophrenia with a further 11% from 'other psychoses' (Hodgins, Webster, and Paquet, 1990). This diagnostic information may be of some use in treatment planning but, as we argue below, its utility is actually quite limited. As well, the point can be made that the diagnoses have not been applied according to a single diagnostic scheme such as the Diagnostic and Statistical Manual (1987, DSM-III-R) or the International Classification of Diseases (1989, ICD-10, Draft).

Untrustworthy though the diagnostic information may be from patients held in and administered by hospitals, it is even harder to achieve dependable incidence figures from the prison population. Although Teplin (1984) has provided useful information from the jail population, studies of mental disorder in prisons have yielded markedly variable results depending on jurisdictions studied and assessment devices employed. Steadman, Fabisiak, Dvoskin, and Holohean (1987) have published an 8% figure for New York State inmates with serious mental disorder. In addition they estimate that a further 16% require periodic psychiatric help. Maier and Miller (1989) indicate that up to 25% of American inmates have a psychiatric disorder at some time during incarceration. A recent Canadian study bears on this topic (*Forum on Corrections Research*, 1990). The project used the Diagnostic Interview Schedule (DIS) on a random sample of over 2000 inmates serving 'federal time' (i.e. 2 years or longer). The DIS, developed by the National Institute of Mental Health, follows a structured interview format and allows ascription of diagnoses according to the *Diagnostic and Statistical Manual*. Psychotic disorders yielded a lifetime prevalence figure of 10% with depressive disorders at 30%.

AVAILABILITY OF PROGRAMMES

Kerr and Roth (1987), in the United States, have recently published a *Survey of Facilities and Programmes for Mentally Disordered Offenders*. They followed Halleck (1987) in defining mentally disordered offenders as, in their words, 'Alleged and convicted offenders whose adjudication or confinement is handled differently from standard criminal justice processes owing to potential or evident mental disorder' (p. 1). The study was based on 127 questionnaire responses from a variety of institutions across the United States, with an estimated completion rate of 84%. Some site visits were also conducted. Of the institutions, 30 were under correctional auspices, 77 under mental health, and 18 under social services or 'other'. Of particular interest to the present topic are data on availability of and participation rates in various kinds of therapy (Kerr and Roth, 1987, Table 4–11, p. 51). With all institutions combined regardless of funding and administrative source, it is evident that the most available therapy is psychotropic medication (98%) with a median participation rate of 61%. Next in rank comes weekly group therapy available in 90% of facilities with a 60% rate of participation. In third place comes weekly individual therapy available in 88% of institutions and used 34% of the time. Occupational therapy holds fourth place for availability (70%), individual therapy given less than once per week rates fifth (64%), behaviour modification achieves sixth place (63%), and art therapy clocks in seventh (62%). Other approaches were available at 36% (group therapy given less than weekly) down to electroconvulsive therapy (available in 19% of cases but, interestingly, listed with a zero participation rate) and further down to psychoanalysis at 11%. Of considerable interest is the finding that data from the correctional and mental health facilities across treatment categories are more similar than different. The availability figures in some categories are not high as they stand and may be inflated. As Kerr and Roth (1987) say: 'staffing data and observations during site visits suggest that, most commonly, social workers and psychologists supervise ward aides or psychiatric technicians in therapeutic work. In addition, weekly ward meetings are considered group psychotherapy in some facilities' (p. 49). The authors point out, as well, that the 11% psychoanalysis availability figure is probably misleading in that respondents may have lacked understanding of the term or may have tried to inflate the data (p. 52). Kerr and Roth (1987) suggest that, compared to a similar earlier survey in 1967 by Schneidemandel and Kanno (1969), occupational therapy has become less available since the time of their study. If the cross-study comparison can be trusted, the same can be said for the use of electroconvulsive shock which earlier was reportedly available in 34% of institutions. Over time there have apparently been increases in academic, vocational, and recreational programmes.

The site visit information provided by Kerr and Roth (1987) is important. They acknowledge the difficulties entailed in trying to establish therapeutic effectiveness, particularly the matter of distinguishing treatment effects from population effects, and point out that their project was not intended to evaluate programmes. Kerr and Roth suggest that staff members in institutions having a wide range of programmes and heavy emphasis on one-to-one therapy appeared relatively more committed to being treatment professionals (p. 83). They also note that successful treatment was hard to achieve in programmes unable to limit admissions. Unless admissions are controlled, overcrowding can take place and necessary screening for treatability does not occur (p. 84). It is also the case that institutional programmes appear to function better if they have the option of transferring out patients or prisoners who do not wish to participate fully. Kerr and Roth (1987) also make the point that it is important to define the goals of treatment at outset. They found some programmes attempted only 'behavioural stabilization' whereas others worked for 'total restructuring of personality' (p. 84).

A little under half of the institutions surveyed by Kerr and Roth (1977) claimed to have outcome evaluation research in progress. Site visits revealed that these attempts varied appreciably in their size and sophistication. Some institutions had good patient information systems and some were well connected to university research and training programmes. The authors caution: 'Because of variations in legal structure, population mix, resource availability, and public attitudes, to compare the whole of any one program to the whole of another would be a great injustice' (p. 97). Very generally, they conclude: 'Even in the absence of rigorous evaluation, it was possible to observe that the programs whose administrators were supportive and astute in terms of relations with the legislature and oversight authority were the same programs where the most staff excitement was found' (p. 97). They go on to say: 'Staff seemed more professional and committed, and morale was higher. Although no residents were interviewed, it could logically be assumed that they profited from this feeling' (p. 97). They note that many of the institutions have established research departments but: 'Although the structures and procedures exist for the conduct of research, very few facilities had established a feedback loop for utilizing research results to improve actual treatment' (p. 103).

SYSTEMIC CONSIDERATIONS

It is probably fair to say that many forensic psychiatric treatment programmes within corrections should not in fact be required. There is strong evidence that many mentally ill persons are unnecessarily caught up in the criminal justice system (Morrissey and Goldman, 1986). Teplin's (1990) work suggests that the absence of suitable community support for the mentally disordered has obliged the jails to become repositories for the chronically ill. The suggestion, according to this criminalization hypothesis, is that as hospitals gave up institutional programmes with the deinstitutionalization movement, there was a failure to develop substitutes in the community. The criminal justice system remains largely unprepared to provide the necessary resources. What appears to be happening is that those released from the psychiatric hospitals with no place to go, and no practical means to survive in communities unprepared and unwilling to accept them, eventually attract police attention which results in their being drawn into the only system which cannot say no, that is, the criminal justice system (Teplin, 1984). As a result, many of those in jails and prisons today are individuals who previously would have resided in psychiatric hospitals (Maier and Miller, 1989). As Pogrebin and Poole (1987) say: 'By default, arrest becomes the accepted means for dealing with these types of offenders, and distinctions between "mad and bad" offenders become blurred' (p. 120). What has occurred as a result of the deinstitutionalization movement is a shifting of boundaries between the mental health and the criminal justice systems, a 'transinstitutionalization', so to speak, in which mentally ill individuals are shuffled between different types of institutions (Morrissey and Goldman, 1986). Toch (1982) has described the shuttling of 'disturbed disruptive' inmates between correctional and mental health institutions as 'bus therapy'. The idea is that neither system, criminal justice nor mental health, is willing to cope with these highly demanding patients. As a result, 'The inmate fails at being a prisoner as well as at being a patient' (McShane, 1989, p. 417). According to Maier and Miller (1989): 'The central problem lies in the fact that neither the prison system nor the health system wants jurisdiction over the mentally disordered offender. Mentally disordered prisoners fall in a "no-man's land" and are not properly cared for by either prison or psychiatric hospitals' (p. 233). Unfortunately, the widespread reluctance of psychiatric hospitals to accept patients from the courts results in patients being placed in the criminal justice system, a system with little selective choice.

The inspired study by Steadman and Cocozza (1974) will be known to most readers. These authors capitalized on the outcome of a US Supreme Court decision in the case of Johnnie Baxstrom. Baxstrom successfully appealed his detention in a New York State correctional hospital. As a result of the ruling he and 966 others were either released outright or transferred to conditions of lowered security. Steadman and Cocozza saw this as a naturally-occurring study, one which could cast light on the question of the extent to which clinicians are capable of predicting the future violent conduct of their prisoners and patients. All those released were followed over a 4-year period. Since they had been confined on the grounds that they were dangerous, it might have been expected that rates of recidivism, for violent offences especially, would have been high. This is not what was found. The level of reoffending was generally very low.

This result posed a challenge to clinicians. They were quick to point out that in this particular circumstance the decisions to detain were made on grounds more administrative than psychiatric. Wrangles over this were largely laid to rest shortly afterwards by Thornberry and Jacoby (1979) who in Pennyslvania, in the Dixon case, came up with a set of observations surprisingly similar to those of Steadman and Cocozza. In both cases clinicians could be said to over-predict dangerousness, that is, to make too many false-positive errors (Monahan, 1981; Webster and Menzies, 1987). These two studies have been markedly influential legally, administratively, and clinically. An alternative way of viewing the results is that both studies discovered, through legal rather than scientific channels as it turned out, successful treatment programmes for seemingly seriously mentally disordered offenders. The treatment is simple: Release.

The important point to note in these two examples is the creative tension between legal, clinical, and research aims. Notice too, that the release programmes likely succeeded in part because the wrong decisions had been made in the first place. Quite probably some of these persons should never have been incarcerated for so long, if at all. While these projects tell us nothing about the effects of milieu therapy, medications, group work, and the like, all of which can be presumed to have been applied, they do serve to remind us of the necessity of viewing treatment programmes in an administrative, even political, light.

Brief mention can also be made here to the notion of coerced treatment using the British Columbia experience with its ill-fated Heroin Treatment Act (HTA) of 1975 (Boyd, Millard, and Webster, 1985; Webster, 1986). The idea behind the Act was that of obliging heroin addicts to accept compulsory in-patient treatment. Various challenges against the Act were mounted in the courts and by the press and it was eventually rendered powerless. The main problem was that neither the characteristics of the addict nor the treatment programme were ever specified in sufficient detail at outset. Had more pains been taken with definition it would have been shown that such a costly programme was never required in the first place. The experience led Webster (1986) to conclude that, for *any* broad scale forensic treatment programme to be successful, the following are necessary: (i) the problem must be defined and the imperative need for solution propagated; (ii) a remedy must be offered; (iii) legal enforceability must be established if any coercion is to be applied; (iv) funds must be made available; and (v) a suitable patient population must be found. It may well be that by the time the first four conditions have been met the fifth, people to be recipients of treatment, has dissipated. The HTA programme never was required.

TREATABILITY AS PERCEIVED BY CLINICIANS

Treatability is an 'amorphous concept' (Rogers and Webster, 1989). It implies multiple goals which might include partial or complete remission of symptoms, stabilization or maintenance of psychological functioning, reduction or elimination of recidivism and decrease in or prevention of violent conduct (Rogers and Webster, 1989). Treatability has to do with decision-making and judgement (Webster, Menzies, and Jackson, 1982). Clinicians, judges, and members of review boards, all of whom may have markedly different agendas, have to make projections as to how individual patients and prisoners may or may not benefit from particular kinds of treatment. Key decision-makers often have little idea of the actual rather than intended effects of different therapeutic approaches. As well, they may be quite wrong in supposing that the seemingly necessary programme is actually available in prison, hospital, or community. It can even be that experts are paraded by legal officials in courts and in boards to make an individual's treatment prospects seem unreasonably positive on the one side or hopeless on the other. While the adversarial approach can doubtless induce procedural fairness at trial and under other related circumstances, there can also be little question that it sometimes obscures the vital issue of which kind of treatment approach ought to be applied to whom, for how long and under what circumstances. This is only to point out that the clinical treatment venture often gets off to a bad, or even unnecessary, start.

Clinicians themselves have a difficult time agreeing about what needs to be done. Perhaps the clearest example of this is shown in a paper by Quinsey and Maguire (1983). These authors had clinicians in various disciplines complete a form on some 200 consecutive forensic psychiatric evaluations. The clinicians could choose from a wide range of possible treatments. Inter-clinician agreement was, however, very low. This is all the more interesting because the clinicians completed their forms after, not before, team discussion. The only area in which acceptable agreement was found concerned the use of psychoactive medication for psychotic patients. Yet it should be realized that the study did not attempt to explore what the reliabilities might have been among doctors had they been asked to suggest specific types of medication at specific doses.

Jackson (1985) has also contributed to the literature on treatability. She gave a series of written forensic cases to mental health professionals, judges and laypersons. Considerable variability was found within and between groups. Social workers tended to be most optimistic and nurses most pessimistic. Patients who were portrayed as committing the most serious offences were seen as most in need of treatment. A similar finding has been made by Ashford (1988) who completed a retrospective study of some 100 pre-sentence drug offenders. Through the use of discriminant analysis, he tried to find out which variables would best predict the clinicians' evaluation of treatability. What he discovered was that the clinicians were most influenced by factors such as marital status, prior criminal history, and personality characteristics; and least by treatment variables like drug history, motivation, diagnosis, prior response to treatment, and the like. Is it any wonder that forensic psychiatric and psychological treatment is so difficult to apply and evaluate when there is so little in the way of workable and tested criteria for use in deciding entry and exit from therapy programmes?

ACCEPTABILITY OF PARTICULAR TREATMENTS TO PATIENTS AND PRISONERS

We do not doubt that there are in fact many treatments which can be used to help seriously mentally disordered prisoners and patients. Pessimistic views to the contrary (Martinson, 1974, 1976), there is ample evidence to suggest that the right treatment applied with the right person at the right time can yield markedly beneficial effects (Gendreau and Ross, 1987). The difficulty is that secure psychiatric hospitals and prison hospitals all too frequently develop a 'life of their own' and become immune to external influence from the literature and other sources. As well, administrators and clinicians may expend too little effort in determining what needs to be done at the initial assessment stage. Unless the match of patient-prisoner to programme is correct, and kept in line, it seems almost self-evident that failure can be expected. The 'theory' needs to be kept alive and adjusted as therapy proceeds. For therapy to be successful with prisoners and patients who are or were seriously mentally disturbed it is most usually necessary that these individuals have an outlook towards therapy roughly congruent with that being offered by the staff. They must accept treatment. If a man, non-psychotic, considers himself a sick person, one not to be held liable for his crime, it may well be that he will fare poorly in a programme which emphasizes the development of personal responsibility. If such a man sees himself as responsible for his past acts it may be that he will benefit little from the solicitous attentions of those who see him as suffering from a 'mental disease'. Chances of benefit are greatest when the clinician's perceptions coincide with the patient's perceptions. Finding the necessary middle ground may be the first important step in therapy. Patients entering 'ordinary', non-institutional, non-forensic, therapy usually select their therapists with an eye toward ensuring basic compatibility so far as fundamental values are concerned. They can also often determine which of their problems they will attend to and which they will not. These are luxuries frequently denied the forensic patient or prisoner. The usual standards for consent to treatment do not always apply to forensic patients. Not infrequently, the range of options open to them is limited. Only by pursuing a course actually unwanted can they hope to provide a successful case to the review board, tribunal, or other authority.

IDENTIFICATION OF MEASURABLE OBJECTIVES

Rice, Harris, Quinsey, and Cyr (1990) have recently published a thorough review of the literature as it relates to programme planning for forensic psychiatric patients in secure psychiatric facilities. Most of their conclusions would apply to psychiatric units administered by correctional authorities. Although their survey identifies few studies methodologically tight enough to show the unambiguous benefits of one approach to treatment over another, they nonetheless conclude that knowledge is advancing strongly in this important area and that there is encouraging evidence for several therapeutic interventions (p. 215).[2]

A particular strength of the Rice *et al.* (1990) review is that it takes account of the administrative, political, and research problems in instituting programmes of care and treatment of seriously mentally disordered offenders. Some patients are in hospital or in a psychiatric unit of a prison not so much because their illness is beyond remedy but because their crime militates against release or transfer to community. The hospital may have to receive and retain individuals for whom it is unable to develop treatment plans. Another difficulty is that secure hospitals and prison psychiatric units are often located in out-of-the way places. This means that it becomes hard to integrate families into therapy and that it is difficult to help the patient or prisoner make gradual adjustments to ordinary life in his or her own family and town. A major problem in special hospital units is that treatment efforts can easily be marred by high security requirements. Staff become convinced that the primary task is not one of treatment but one of maintaining security and good order. Some staff will even argue that the secure hospital unit should be perceived to be a 'tough place'. They see the unit as having a 'therapeutic' influence in so far as its forbidding nature discourages prisoners and patients from penetrating to the 'core'. The obstacles to effective treatment implementation, both those mentioned by Rice *et al.* (1990) and others which could be raised (Hucker and Webster, 1991), need not be rehearsed here further except to point out that treatments are often insufficiently tailored to the requirements of individual patients. Programmes are frequently erected on

---

[2] The present authors urge readers to consult the excellent prior review of Rice *et al.* (1990). We acknowledge our indebtedness to this paper.

general principles, themselves rarely articulated in necessary detail, and applied to prisoners and patients without it ever being clear which elements of therapy are expected to accomplish which ends. It is certainly the case that the activities of clinicians, as they try to reach decisions on treatability (Quinsey and Maguire, 1983) and dangerousness (Menzies, 1989; Pfohl, 1979) are of as much scientific interest as are the effects of treatment procedures themselves. Rice *et al.* (1990) argue that treatment effectiveness is hard to gauge unless clinicians are encouraged to define the treatment issues at outset and to construct case-specific interventions.

The approach favoured by Rice *et al.* (1990) is called Programme Development Evaluation (PDE) and is derived from Gottfredson (1984). They refer to this as an 'incremental' method meaning that the job of the clinician-researcher is to identify the issues and to establish measurable objectives. Their idea, similar to that of Kerr and Roth (1987) noted earlier, is that the institution or programme should be able to learn from errors, that some kind of 'cybernetic' process is needed. Cybernetics gets across the idea that new information gained in the treatment of a patient or group of patients should be used to readjust programme aims. The basic principle can be applied at the level of the individual or the institution. When applied to the latter it becomes possible to see treatment in the light of quality control. In PDE, particular emphasis is placed on the identification of problems because, with such analysis having been completed in the first place, treatment plans usually evolve quite naturally and easily.

What then is the 'problem' and how is it to be identified? Rice *et al.* (1990) point out that, usually, secure hospitals do not in fact have, in the record, clear statements about what needs to be done for and with the patient or prisoner. A diagnosis of schizophrenia by itself is not necessarily a very helpful piece of information. What is needed are fairly precise indications of strengths and deficits on a large number of items. To this end Quinsey, Cyr, and Lavalle (1988) developed a Patient Problem Survey (PPS). The Survey deals with problems in community adjustment and with difficulties observed in the institution. It has been tested at two secure forensic psychiatric institutions, the Philippe Pinel Institute in Montreal and the Oak Ridge Division of the Penetanguishene Mental Health Centre in Ontario. The device contains subscales to cover positive schizophrenic symptoms, criminal lifestyle, life skill deficits, social withdrawal, institutional management problems, depression, and substance abuse. Items are detailed. Under inappropriate social behaviour, for example, the authors include assaultiveness, threats, pro-criminal statements, insulting, social withdrawal, poor assertion, dependence, shyness, lack of consideration, impulsivity, poor manners, and being easily led by others. With scores tallied for a large sample of Oak Ridge patients, Quinsey, Cyr, and Lavalle (1988) were able to use cluster analysis techniques to determine the most economical solution in terms of types of profile. They yielded eventually seven types: good citizens, social isolates, personality disorders, institutional management problems, institutionalized psychotics, psychotics, and developmentally handicapped. Essentially these same types were found in the Pinel sample.

The scores from the PPS led the Oak Ridge research group to suggest new groupings of patients. Although seven distinct programmes could not be arranged for practical reasons, it was possible to organize three units to do the job with two wards in each unit. The units were social management, rehabilitation, and behaviour therapy. Rice *et al.* (1990) point out that this shift in programme emphasis subsequently meant marked alteration in the functioning of the admissions ward. Staff there had to broaden their base of evaluation and, because traditional tests would not suffice, find or devise instruments to make the necessary assessments. Rice *et al.* (1990) offer readers suggestions concerning a number of scales which measure management problems, level of functioning, social withdrawal, and schizophrenic symptomatology. They are most inclined towards scales which show some prospect for indexing change as a result of treatment or programmes. They make the point that conventional psychiatric diagnostic criteria by themselves, being intended to emphasize stability of condition, are not likely to be very helpful markers of change.

COMPARABILITY

In the mid 1960s through to the mid 1970s the Oak Ridge Division of the Penetanguishene Mental Health Centre in Ontario conducted a large-scale programme to treat psychopaths. Most of the men at Oak Ridge had been found not guilty by reason of insanity after committing murder or serious assaults; many were diagnosed as primarily personality disordered. The programme leaders deliberately selected men who had strong psychopathic tendencies. Patients lived together in close physical contact and the treatment was largely coerced. Basic principles of conduct were established and taught (Barker and Mason, 1968). The actual day-to-day teaching was left largely in the hands of specially-selected and trained patients. These patients had an unusual degree of control over the lives of their peers. The project came to enjoy an international reputation as being effective in the treatment of psychopaths.

Since the main subjects of the study were psychopaths it might seem that this project could be more suitably discussed elsewhere in the present volume. There are two reasons why it is included here. First, the project allowed a comparative design by including a number of patients whose principal diagnosis was schizophrenia. It was expected that these patients would benefit from the intensive ministrations of their non-schizophrenic counterparts. Medication levels were deliberately reduced for the schizophrenic patients. Second, the new work on this now defunct project shows what can be done on a retrospective basis provided that good clinical records have been kept. Several years after the project was folded, Harris, Rice, and Cormier (1989) decided to conduct a follow-up study of the former patients. This entailed making retrospective diagnoses from standards that were unavailable at the time of the study. The researchers used Hare's (1980) Psychopathy Checklist against the files and discovered that an appreciable portion of the sample would indeed have met the criteria for a diagnosis of psychopathy. These could then be matched against similar patients admitted to Oak Ridge for assessment, not treatment, during the equivalent period. Some years later all patients, treated and untreated, psychopaths and schizophrenics, were followed via police records, parole reports, and the like. The most striking finding from this painstaking effort was that, seemingly, the project failed to reduce violent recidivism in psychopathic patients. This ran to a level of 77% over the 10 year follow-up period. If anything, treatment increased violent offending relative to untreated controls. So far as this chapter is concerned, what is important is the *incidental finding* that the schizophrenic patients showed decreased tendencies to reoffend as a result of treatment. It would seem that forensic psychiatric schizophrenic patients can benefit from intense sustained social interventions. The findings of Harris, Rice, and Cormier (1989) suggest that it may be a mistake to place more-or-less exclusive reliance on medications, that there remains a role for other organized therapeutic endeavours. There is in fact ample evidence to suggest that schizophrenic patients in the community fare much better when treated with drugs in addition to family work and visits from a nurse than when simply medicated (Hogarty, Anderson, Reiss, Kornblith, Greenwald, Javna, and Madonia, 1986).

Bailey and MacCulloch (1992b) have also recently reported the comparable treatment success rates of psychopathic versus seriously mentally disordered patients. They examined the fate of the first 106 male patients discharged from Park Lane Hospital in Liverpool. Of these, 54% of the total were classified as mentally ill and 45% as psychopathic. The majority (75%) of the mentally ill group were diagnosed as suffering from paranoid schizophrenia (Bailey and MacCulloch, 1992a). Patients in both groups had been in the community for some 6 years on average. They were released either absolutely or conditionally. Over one-third, 37% reoffended after being discharged. The bulk of those reconvicted were in the psychopathic group (55%) rather than the mentally ill group (21%). The authors also noted that those discharged conditionally with Home Office or Tribunal conditions had a much lower reconviction rate (27%) than those discharged absolutely (63%). The best risks were those patients deemed mentally ill and under supervision during follow up (11% failure); the worst risks were those diagnosed psychopathic and given absolute discharges (79%). Since ex-patients are probably at increased risk for rearrest and reconviction following release from hospital, it can also be asked if the general findings of Bailey and MacCulloch hold if the analysis is restricted to serious offences only. With such offences defined to include arson, they found the same general pattern. This time the mentally ill, conditionally discharged, patients committed only 4% of the offences while the absolutely discharged psychopathic patients accounted for 36% of the total offences committed. Bailey and MacCulloch (1992b) also demonstrate that if the mentally ill patients do reoffend they are especially likely to do so in the first 3 years. Once the first 3 years had passed the cumulative reconviction curve was virtually flat. This was in contrast to the psychopathic group which continued to reoffend throughout the full follow-up period.

The data of Bailey and MacCulloch (1992b) are similar to those of Harris, Rice, and Cormier (1989) in that both studies contrast psychopathic patients with seriously mentally disordered patients. The strength of the Harris, Rice, and Cormier study is that it provides a wealth of detail about the nature of the pre-release treatment programme. Yet these authors have little information about living conditions after release from the programme. While Bailey and MacCulloch similarly fail to offer data concerning post-release circumstances, they are able to contrast the absolute versus conditional discharges. That the conditionally released patients fared appreciably better than their absolutely discharged counterparts may in part be accounted for by the fact that those who committed the most serious index offences were the ones most likely to attract conditions (i.e. were the 'harder cases', the ones most likely to have murdered or carried out sexual assaults). While this may be the most obvious explanation, Bailey and MacCulloch (1992b) point out that part of the relative success of the conditionally discharged patients may be related to the fact that they received compulsory supervision in the community. These patients had to see both a parole officer and a mental health worker on a regular basis. Although it is not possible to apportion the relative sizes of the supervision and seriousness of crime effects because of the inherent confound, it is nonetheless the case that supervision is probably a critical factor in the rehabilitation of patients earlier deemed to be seriously mentally disordered. However this may be, both of these recent studies are important because of the light they cast on treatment effectiveness with schizophrenic and other such patients.

CONNECTIONS BETWEEN SYSTEMS: CASE ILLUSTRATION

In this chapter we are attempting to cover the provision of mental health treatment services in both prisons and hospitals. This is a large undertaking. Yet in fact it is important to consider both systems simultaneously. Patients become prisoners and prisoners become patients to an extent that is sometimes surprising (Menzies, 1987; Menzies and Webster, 1987; Toch, 1982). The following case illustrates: (i) how a person with personality disorder at one time can later become floridly psychiatrically ill; (ii) how under common circumstances, responsibility for a person moves back and forth between correctional and mental health authorities, sometimes with eventual premature termination.

Allan was aged 18 years when charged with sexual assault. He had been in Canada for some 4 years at the time of the offence. His upbringing in the Caribbean had been harsh and he himself had been sexually assaulted as a child. Shortly after arrival in Canada he had been placed in a group home but was again living with his family when charged. The sexual assault was committed on a stranger and a weapon was later found at the scene. He had had previous satisfactory sexual relations with girlfriends and had such a friend at the time of the incident. According to his own report, he was at times overwhelmed with an impulse to 'touch and run', and confessed that he had done this many times prior to being caught.

After sentencing he was removed to a federal penitentiary under protective custody. There for some several months he participated in a well-structured treatment programme for sex offenders. In due course he was paroled and allowed to return to his family in another city. His parole officer identified Allan as possibly mentally unstable and possibly risky. A psychologist was asked to assist him on an out-patient basis at weekly intervals. Allan was seen regularly over a period of a year. The interviews often included members of his family and his girlfriend. For a few weeks he participated in a government-sponsored job training and preparation programme but no job materialized. The treatment sessions centred on improving his self-perception and increasing his self-control. Normally intelligent and able to converse rationally, at one point his associations loosened quite remarkably. Family members were alarmed when he went, without warning, and spent a whole night walking to another town. He felt that in doing this he was obeying God. His thinking included much religiosity. This necessitated a voluntary in-patient admission. Because of his hostile manner on the secure unit he had to be certified and given anti-psychotic medication. After a few days he was able to convince his family that he was being badly treated and he signed out against medical advice. Because his condition remained unstable and worrisome, probably prodromal for schizophrenia, the psychologist and parole officer took to making home visits. After he had smashed up his room, his parents had him admitted to another hospital. With medication, his condition resolved after a few days and he was again discharged. Nevertheless, Allan refused to take the drugs once at home and his adjustment to his family and his girlfriend became very poor. About 9 months after discharge from prison his parole ended. Since his treatment was tied to parole considerations, this leaves Allan 'in the community'. He remains living at home without income or prospects. He needs, at a minimum, some more education, a job, a better living arrangement, continued counselling, and prompt psychiatric intervention when in crisis.

What will happen to Allan? After his original arrest he was assessed pre-trial as an in-patient at the Metropolitan Toronto Forensic Service (METFORS). From an earlier 6-year follow-up of some 200 METFORS patients (McMain, Webster, and Menzies, 1989), we see that he has already joined that half of the sample which receives additional psychiatric admissions. Since the 51% who were re-admitted at least once over the 6 years were in fact admitted three times on average, it is likely that he will achieve another admission during the 6-year post-assessment period. It is also possible to project from the sample that, although it has not yet occurred, further involvement with the law is likely. The METFORS sample showed that 158 persons incurred 702 terms of imprisonment (i.e. 4.4 prison terms per person).

Probably the biggest single obstacle facing mentally disordered prisoner-patients is the disjunction between health and correctional systems. Mental health officials often resist accepting patients into half-way houses, day-treatment programmes, and the like, if they have criminal records. What they so frequently lack, as well as a facility which will house them (Easton and Howard, 1987), is a mental health worker who will 'stand by them through thick and thin'. It comes as a surprise to see examples of what can be accomplished if only the clinician is willing to form a sustained partnership. Ryan (1988) describes how one psychologist seemingly kept a highly institutionalized man out of jail through constant attention to his client's financial, housing, and employment worries.

BOARDS AND TRIBUNALS AS TREATMENT AGENCIES

The examples cited above call attention to the function of mental hospitals and penitentiaries. Both serve mainly to protect the public from that which is foreign or frightening (Mohelsky, 1982). The separation of prisoners and forensic psychiatric patients from the rest of society enables the general population to presume that it is safe from the hands of those especially apt to disturb the prevailing order or even plunge it into adversity. These days it is presumed that, at least in a cloudy way, treatment in hospitals and prisons plays a part in rendering dangerous and violent people more tractable and congenial. This assumption guides the work of board members who review the progress of forensic patients and who oversee the release of prison inmates via parole boards. Patients are accountable to such boards which usually contain a mix of lay and mental health opinion and often include lawyers and judges. They are viewed as being in existence in order to check that treatment or rehabilitation has indeed taken place. But it needs also to be recognized that in many instances the boards *are* the main treatment. It is not easy, either administratively or from a research point of view, to separate the Boards' activities into those which monitor change and those which induce change. Intensive preparation for board hearings is usual. Most prisoners and forensic psychiatric patients work hard, often with legal assistance, to be able to demonstrate how they have altered since the last review. So an organization engineered to make decisions often becomes a quite critical part of the treatment itself.

How can the board be sure in a particular case that some specific treatment has in fact been responsible for psychological or behavioural change? It has already been said that prisoners and patients are under pressure to convince the board or tribunal that they are now recovered from mental illness and safe to rejoin society. But in fact it becomes very difficult to determine whether the necessary 'fundamental change' has occurred, or if instead the individual managed, perhaps via the 'rhetoric of treatment', to 'look good' (Sullivan, 1980). Viewed from the worst angle, the prisoner or patient may have managed to 'con' the authorities and may in fact have every intention, appearances to the contrary, of re-entering a criminal life at the first opportunity. This means that clinicians and researchers, in endeavouring to chart the actual progress of patients and prisoners, must be attentive to ways of checking deception and dissimulation (Rogers, 1988). It is often singularly difficult to distinguish the 'real' positive effects of psychiatric and psychological treatments from 'changes' put on like a coat for the occasion. It needs also to be added for balance, and to do justice to the complexities involved in assessing treatment outcome, that the superficial or shammed change may in some instances be a necessary precursor for more solid and permanent alterations in mental stability or character. The clinicians and even the boards may sometimes be doing their charges no harm by inducing them to 'play a part', at least as a first step.[3]

---

[3] There is also to be considered the case in which a forensic psychiatric patient or prisoner 'recovers' as a result of procedures which most clinicians would consider extraneous. A good example is given by Glasberg and Wayne (1981). They describe a man held in a maximum secure psychiatric facility on grounds of being not guilty by reason of insanity. The record in this case draws attention to the turning point in treatment as being the work of a visiting relative who offered incantations over him.

The foregoing raises awkward definitional issues. What is treatment? What is a treatment programme? Does change, of the sort that might be convincing to a board, have to be an 'interior' psychological event or will 'mere conformity' with rules suffice? To what extent, in constructing a treatment programme, is it wise and necessary to take into account the prisoner or patients' objectives and views as well as those of senior clinicians and researchers?

PHARMACOLOGICAL APPROACHES

From the Kerr and Roth (1987) review discussed above it is evident that at the present time medication places highest on a list of possible therapeutic approaches. The evidence over the past quarter century or more is incontrovertible that the positive symptoms of schizophrenia can often be held in check through the use of phenothiazines and other medications (Andreasen and Black, 1991). There is as well, strong support, though not from the forensic psychiatric literature *per se*, that the tricyclics play an important role in the treatment of depression (Andreasen and Black, 1991). Although it is now well understood that it frequently takes as much skill (and much more time) to convince a patient or prisoner to accept medication as to administer it (Gutheil and Appelbaum, 1982; Marder, Mebane, Chien, Winslade, Swann, and Van Putten, 1983), there can be no question that medication, along with electroconvulsive therapy in cases of severe depression (Andreasen and Black, 1991), is a strong weapon in the armamentum. There is of course a large literature with direct bearing on this matter.

One trouble with drug treatments is that their very success with some patients frequently induces expectations among staff members that they will be similarly and necessarily effective with others. In fact there usually is, in most secure mental and prison hospitals, a core of persons who receive few, if any, positive effects of medication. If these 'non-responders' had in fact been 'responders' they might well have been released or transferred years ago. As it is, they stay and tax the energies of medical and other staff. The line staff, faced daily with other encouraging outcomes from medication, become understandably puzzled that the prisoner or patient has not improved. Under pressure to relieve difficult matters, the physicians sometimes feel constrained to alter medications before the drugs have an opportunity to achieve maximum effectiveness. Doses are varied up and down. Harris (1989) has drawn attention to the sometimes 'doomed search' for the right drug in the right dose and he points out that such activity detracts from the effort to find alternative ways of achieving symptom relief and of solving institutional management problems. Certainly the evidence is very clear that medications, when they work, achieve their maximum effectiveness when combined with other kinds of therapeutic and supportive assistance (Drake and Sederer, 1986; Hogarty, Goldberg, and Schooler, 1974; Liberman, Mueser, and Wallace, 1986; Linn, Caffey, Klett, Hogarty, and Lamb, 1979).

BEHAVIOURAL MANAGEMENT

In the late 1950s and early 1960s researcher-clinicians from the radical behaviourist tradition tried to demonstrate that psychiatric symptoms were simply responses conditioned, often unwittingly, by ward staff (Ayllon and Haughton, 1962; Ayllon and Michael, 1959). It was thought that bizarre-seeming, schizophrenic behaviour, like broom-holding or towel-hoarding, had been previously strengthened by adventitious reinforcement. Certainly there was profound optimism that such maladaptive behaviours could be weakened through extinction and punishment procedures, and that they could be replaced by differential reinforcement of other, more adaptive, behaviours. These principles were extended to the modification of behaviour within classrooms (Barrish, Saunders, and Wolf, 1969), hospital wards (Ayllon and Azrin, 1968), and juvenile detention centres (Cohen, Filipczak, and Bis, 1970). Although they are not perhaps as formally evident in institutions or in community corrections (cf. Erickson, Crow, Zurcher, and Connett, 1973) as they were a quarter century ago, they do of course continue to act as the backbone of most ward programmes. Twenty or so people living in a hospital or prison unit require a set of rules for safe and orderly living and these have to be backed by sanctions and rewards. Yet Rice *et al.* (1990) are correct to point out that the token economy does not today enjoy the centrality which it probably deserves. There is, as we have said, a great deal of evidence to support the effectiveness of these schemes (Paul and Lentz, 1977).

That the token economy has declined in acceptance is probably due to many reasons. There has been widespread recognition that the effects may not always or easily generalize from ward to life on the street. Its apparent early over-success may have later induced disappointment in programme leaders and administrators. Members of the institutional hierarchy have sometimes been loath to relinquish control over the day-to-day functioning of the wards (Rice *et al.*, 1990). Line staff are often reluctant to give over control to a 'programme' and to retain crispness of conception through sticking to agreed-upon definitions of behaviour. Another problem for the would-be token-economy manager is that the range of reinforcers is quite limited in prisons and hospitals. Patients in the 1990s are expected to receive minor 'necessaries' as a 'right' and, properly, it is deemed inhumane to take away basic food and bedding. Some mentally disordered patients and prisoners would be willing to work hard for unescorted leaves, conjugal visits, and the like. Yet these privileges are but rarely seen on the menu. Managers of token-economy units also have to face the fact that senior administrators, when made aware of some apparently serious difficulty within the token economy project, are usually anxious to resort to 'traditional methods' at the first opportunity (i.e. to override the established and agreed-upon contingency management plan). Yet token economies and behavioural contracting programmes generally remain powerful clinical devices. Although they do not solve all behavioural management tasks, and should not be expected to do so, they continue to be an important means of providing support and much-needed structure for seriously mentally disturbed persons (Andreason and Black, 1991).

A particularly compelling recent example is given by Foxx, McMorrow, Bittle, and Fenlon (1985). These investigators showed how the social skills of chronic schizophrenic in-patients could be enhanced through the use of a modified commercially available card game. Quinsey and Varney (1977) had earlier published such an approach.

It is important to realize that medication most usually has to be combined with attempts, within or outside a token economy, to manage disruptive behaviour and to improve conversational skills. As Rice *et al.* (1990) put it:

> Careful assessment, probably including direct behavioral observation, is required due to the unreliability of routine staff reports of such behaviors. Drugs and restrictive or punitive management strategies alone are unlikely to be successful. Instead, careful behavioral consequation of problem behaviors and the on-ward reinforcement of incompatible prosocial behaviors will be required. Staff training in verbal calming and defusing skills combined with fair and reasonable management policies are probably essential. It is also necessary to ensure that there are effective prosocial models present in the institutional environment. (p. 188)

ADMINISTRATIVE TECHNOLOGY

Rice *et al.* (1990) have argued with force that there is plenty of evidence to suggest that severely mentally ill patients and prisoners can be treated with greater success than is generally realized or published. They point to drug and non-drug treatments, often in combination, which can reduce both positive and negative symptoms of schizophrenia (cf, Liberman, 1988). But they also note that to administer such treatments effectively it is absolutely necessary that institutional administration plan carefully and control the activities of staff at all levels. It is much easier to administer drug treatments than non-drug treatments. As Rice *et al.* conclude: 'Optimal treatment of the chronically mentally ill, especially those in secure *treatment* settings, probably awaits the implementation of advances in *administrative* technology' (p. 197, emphasis added).

CONCLUDING COMMENT

Much good sense has been written in recent years on the treatment of severely mentally disordered offenders and patients (e.g. Toch and Adams, 1989). Although the specific effectiveness of most generally-available treatment programmes is unknown, it is fair to say that several strong methods are at hand and also that the means to evaluate these ventures are available. Most conspicuous is the present lack of administrative structures within which to develop researchable programmes which are neither strictly within correctional agencies nor solely from mental health departments. It is always important to be able to *identify* the issue (e.g. Heller, Traylor, Ehrlich, and Lester, 1984). Only with the requirements known is it wise to ensure that programmes are to be made *available*. But before programmes are actually launched it is well to question thoroughly whether they are in fact *required*. Some firm opinion needs to be reached as to which prisoners and patients are *treatable* and with which means. The programmes must be designed with an eye to their *acceptability* by patients and by staff. New projects have to be based on carefully *defined* and achievable aims. Because severely mentally ill patients and prisoners tend to suffer from a variety of difficulties simultaneously, and because these tend to change over time, knowledge of a conventional primary diagnosis is of restricted use in planning (Abram, 1990). Programmes, once launched, have to be evaluated carefully, usually over time and usually with the inclusion of *comparison* groups (Roesch and Corrado, 1979). Administrators have the difficult task of ensuring that programmes are *interlocked* between mental health, correctional, housing, welfare, education, immigration and other authorities (cf. Greene, 1989; Wardlaw, 1983). Mentally disordered patients and prisoners are ordinarily held *accountable* to clinicians, boards, and tribunals. This accountability through supervision would seem to be a vital component in treatment. However, rates of failure and success are seldom tabulated as a matter of routine. One of the main approaches to treatment is by way of *mediciation*. Yet drugs are not often tested against specific behavioural indices let alone applied under blind conditions. Social learning theory continues to provide the most generally applicable and theoretically well grounded treatment model. *Reinforcement* principles are underused despite the fact that they can be applied to advantage (MacKain and Streveler, 1990). The largest difficulty at present in the treatment of seriously disturbed patients and prisoners comes not from lack of technical knowledge but from inability to coordinate, monitor, and generally *administer* sub-components within mental health and correctional systems.

REFERENCES

Abram, K. M. (1990). The problem of co-occurring disorders among jail detainees. *Law and Human Behavior*, **14**, 333–45.

American Psychiatric Association (1987). *Diagnostic and Statistical Manual of Mental Disorders* (3rd edn rev.). Washington, DC: Author.

Andreasen, N. C., and Black, D. W. (1991). *Introductory Textbook of Psychiatry*. Washington, DC: American Psychiatric Press.

Annis, H. M. (1981). Treatment in corrections: Martinson was right. *Canadian Psychology*, **22**, 321–6.

Applebaum, P. S., and Gutheil, T. G. (1980). Drug refusal: A study of psychiatric inpatients. *American Journal of Psychiatry*, **137**, 340–6.

Ashford, J. B. (1988). Factors used in treatment discriminations used in Ohio drug legislation. *Behavioural Sciences and the Law*, **6**, 139–49.

Ayllon, T., and Azrin, N. (1968). *The Token Economy: A Motivational System for Therapy and Rehabilitation*. Englewood Cliffs, NJ: Prentice-Hall.

Ayllon, T., and Haughton, E. (1962). Control of behavior of schizophrenic patients by food. *Journal of Experimental Analysis of Behavior*, **5**, 343–52.

Ayllon, T., and Michael, J. (1959). The psychiatric nurse as a behavioral engineer. *Journal of Experimental Analysis of Behavior*, **2**, 323–34.

Bailey, J., and MacCulloch, M. J. (1992a). Characteristics of 112 cases discharged directly to the community from a new Special Hospital and some comparisons of performance. *Journal of Forensic Psychiatry*, **3**, 91–112.

Bailey, J., and MacCulloch, M. J., (1992b). Patterns of reoffending in patients discharged directly to the community from a Special Hospital: Implications for aftercare. *Journal of Forensic Psychiatry*, **3**, 445–461.

Barker, E. T., and Mason, M. H. (1968). Buber behind bars. *Canadian Psychological Association Journal*, **13**, 61–72.

Barrish, H. H., Saunders, M., and Wolf, M. M. (1969). Good behavior game: Effects of individual contingencies on disruptive behavior in a classroom. *Journal of Applied Behavior Analysis*, **2**, 119–24.

Boyd, N., Millard, C., and Webster, C. D. (1985). Heroin 'treatment' in British Columbia 1976–1984: Thesis, antithesis, and synthesis? *Canadian Journal of Criminology*, **27**, 195–208.

Cohen, H. L., Filipczak, J., and Bis, J. (1970). A study of contingencies applicable to special education: Case 1, In R. Ulrich, T. Stachnik, and J. Mabry (eds). *Control of Human Behavior: From Cure to Prevention*, vol. 2. Glenview, Ill: Scott, Foresman, pp. 51–69.

de St Croix, S., Dry, R., and Webster, C. D. (1988). Patients on Warrants of the Lieutenant Governor in Alberta: A statistical summary with comments on treatment and release procedures. *Canadian Journal of Psychiatry*, **33**, 14–20.

Drake, R. E., and Sederer, L. I. (1986). Inpatient psychosocial treatment of chronic schizophrenia. *Hospital and Community Psychiatry*, **37**, 897–901.

Easton, R., and Howard, W. (1987). Specialized halfway house for male forensic patients: Five year experience. *Canada's Mental Health*, March, 17–18.

Erickson, R., Crow, W., Zurcher, L., and Connett, A. (1973). *Paroled but not Free: Ex-offenders Look at What they Need to Make it on the Outside*. New York: Behavioral Publications.

Forum on Corrections Research (1990). A mental health profile of federally sentenced offenders. Ottawa, Correctional Service, Canada, **1**, 7.

Foxx, R. M., McMorrow, M. J., Bittle, R. G., and Fenlon, S.J. (1985). Teaching social skills to psychiatric inpatients. *Behaviour Research and Therapy*, **23**, 531–7.

Gendreau, P., and Ross, R. (1987). Revivification of rehabilitation: Evidence from the 1980s. *Justice Quarterly*, **4**, 349–407.

Glasberg, R., and Wayne, I. (1981). The beginnings of a new story: Post-release adjustment of men found not guilty by reason of insanity. In S. J. Hucker, C. D. Webster, and M. H. Ben-Aron (eds). *Mental Disorder and Criminal Responsibility*. Toronto: Butterworth.

Gottfredson, G. D. (1984). A theory-ridden approach to program evaluation: A method for stimulating researcher-implementer collaboration. *American Psychologist*, **39**, 1101–12.

Greene, R. T. (1989). A comprehensive mental health care system for prison inmates: Retrospective look at New York's ten year experience. *International Journal of Law and Psychiatry*, **11**, 381–9.

Gutheil, T. G., and Appelbaum, P. S. (1982). *Clinical Handbook of Psychiatry and the Law*. Toronto: McGraw-Hill, ch. 3, pp. 76–139.

Halleck, S. (1987). The mentally disordered offender. Rockville, MA: *National Institute of Mental Health*, DHHS Pub # (ADM) pp. 86–147.

Hare, R.D. (1980). A research scale for the assessment of psychopathy in criminal populations. *Personality and Individual Differences*, **1**, 111–17.

Harris, G. T. (1989). The relationship between neuroleptic drug dose and the performance of psychiatric patients in a maximum security token economy program. *Journal of Behaviour Therapy and Experimental Psychiatry*, **20**, 57–67.

Harris, G. T., Rice, M. E., and Cormier, C. A. (1989). Violent recidivism among psychopaths and nonpsychopaths treated in a therapeutic community. Mental Health Centre, Penetanguishene, Research Report, vol. 6, no. 1.

Heller, M. S., Traylor, W. H., Ehrlich, S. A., and Lester, D. (1984). A clinical evaluation of maximum security patients by staff and independent psychiatric consultants, *Bulletin of the American Academy of Psychiatry and the Law*, **12**, 85–92.

Hodgins, S., Webster, C. D., and Paquet, J. (1990). Canadian database: Patients held on Lieutenant Governors' Warrants. vol. 2. Ottawa: Department of Justice, Canada.

Hogarty, G. E., Anderson, C. M., Reiss, D. J., Kornblith, S. J., Greenwald, D. P., Javna, C. D., and Madonia, M. J. (1986). Family psychoeducation, social skills training, and maintenance chemotherapy in the aftercare treatment of schizophrenia. *Archives of General Psychiatry*, **43**, 633–42.

Hogarty, G. E., Goldberg, S. C., and Schooler, N. (1974). Drug and sociotherapy in the aftercare of schizophrenic patients. Two-year relapse rates. *Archives of General Psychiatry*, **31**, 603–8.

Hucker, S. J., and Webster, C. D. (1991). Security and psychiatry. In E. Persad, S. S. Kazarian, and L. W. Joseph (eds) *The Mental Hospital in the Twenty-first Century*. Toronto: Wall & Emerson.

Jackson, M. A. (1985, October). Understanding the concepts of need for treatment/ treatability. Paper presented at the American Academy of Psychiatry and Law, Albuquerque, NM.

Jemelka, R. E., Trupin, E., and Chiles, J. A. (1989). The mentally ill in prisons: A review. *Hospital and Community Psychiatry*, **40**, 481–91.

Kerr, C. A., and Roth, J. A. (1987). *Survey of Facilities and Programs for Mentally Disordered Offenders*. National Institute of Mental Health, US Department of Health and Human Services. DHHS Publication No (Adm) 86-1493.

Liberman, R. P. (ed.) (1988). *Psychiatric Rehabilitation of Chronic Mental Patients*. Washington, DC: American Psychiatric Press.

Liberman, R. P., Mueser, K. T., and Wallace, C. J. (1986). Social skills training for schizophrenic individuals at risk for relapse. *American Journal of Psychiatry*, **143**, 523–6.

Linn, M. W., Caffey, E. M., Klett, J., Hogarty, G. E., and Lamb, R. (1979). Day treatment and psychotropic drugs in the aftercare of schizophrenic patients. *Archives of General Psychiatry*, **36**, 1055–66.

MacKain, S. J., and Streveler, A. (1990). Social and independent living skills for psychiatric patients in a prison setting. *Behavior Modification*, **14**, 490–518.

Maier, G. J., and Miller, R. D. (1989). Models of mental health service delivery to correctional institutions. In R. Rosner and R. B. Harmon (eds), *Correctional Psychiatry: Critical Issues in American Psychiatry and the Law*, New York: Plenum, pp. 231–41.

Marder, S. R., Mebane, A., Chien, C., Winslade, W. J., Swann, E., and Van Putten, T. (1983). A comparison of patients who refuse and consent to neuroleptic treatment. *American Journal of Psychiatry*, **40**, 470–2.

Martinson R. (1974). What works? Questions and answers about prison reform. *The Public Interest*, **35**, 22–54.

Martinson, R. (1976). California research at the crossroads. *Crime and Delinquency*, **22**, 180–91.

McMain, S., Webster, C. D., and Menzies, R. J. (1989). The post-assessment careers of mentally disordered offenders. *International Journal of Law and Psychiatry*, **12**, 189–201.

McShane, M. D. (1989). The bus stop revisited: Discipline and psychiatric patients in prison. *Journal of Psychiatry and Law*, **17**, 413–33.

Menzies, R. J. (1987). Cycles of control: The transcarceral careers of forensic patients. *International Journal of Law and Psychiatry*, **10**, 233–49.

Menzies, R. J. (1989). *Survival of the Sanest: Order and Disorder in a Pre-trial Psychiatric Clinic*. Toronto: University of Toronto Press.

Menzies, R. J., and Webster, C. D. (1987). Where they go and what they do: The longitudinal careers of forensic patients in the medicolegal context. *Canadian Journal of Criminology*, **29**, 275–93.

Mohelsky, H. (1982). The mental hospital and its environment. *Canadian Journal of Psychiatry*, **27**, 478–81.

Monahan, J. (1981). *Predicting Violent Behavior: An Assessment of Clinical Techniques*. Beverly Hills, CA: Sage.

Morrissey, J. P., and Goldman, H. H. (1986). Care and treatment of the mentally ill, in the United States: Historical development and reforms. *Annals, AAPSS*, **484**, 12–27.

Paul, G. L., and Lentz, R. J. (1977). *Psychosocial Treatment of Chronic Mental Patients: Milieui versus Social Learning Programs*. Cambridge, MA: Harvard University Press.

Pfohl, S. (1979). *Predicting Dangerousness: The Social Construction of Psychiatric Reality*. Lexington, Mass: D. C. Heath.

Pogrebin, M. R., and Poole, E. D. (1987). Deinstitutionalization and increased arrest rates among the mentally disordered. *Journal of Psychiatry and Law*, **15**, 117–27.

Quinsey, V. L. (1981). The long-term management of the mentally disordered offender. In S. J. Hucker, C. D. Webster, and M. Ben-Aron (eds), *Mental Disorder and Criminal Responsibility*. Toronto: Butterworth, pp. 137–55.

Quinsey, V. L., Cyr, M., and Lavalle, Y. J. (1988). Treatment opportunities in a maximum security psychiatric hospital: A problem survey. *International Journal of Law and Psychiatry*, **11**, 179–94.

Quinsey, V. L., and Maguire, A. (1983). Offenders remanded for a psychiatric examination: Perceived treatability and disposition. *International Journal of Law and Psychiatry*, **6**, 193–205.

Quinsey, V. L., and Marshall, W. L. (1983). Procedures for reducing inappropriate sexual arousal: An evaluation review. In J. G. Greer and I. R. Stuart (eds), *The Sexual Aggressor: Current Perspectives on Treatment*. New York: Van Nostrand Reinhold, pp. 267–89.

Quinsey, V. L., and Varney, G. W. (1977). Social skills game: A general method for the modelling and practice of adaptive behaviors. *Behavior Therapy*, **8**, 278–81.

Rice, M. E., Harris, G. T., Quinsey, V. L., and Cyr, M. (1990). Planning treatment programs in secure psychiatric facilities. In D. N. Weisstub (ed.), *Law and Mental Health: International Perspectives*, vol. 5, New York: Pergamon Press, pp. 162–230.

Roesch, R., and Corrado, R. R. (1979). The policy implications of evaluation research: Some issues raised by the Fishman study of rehabilitation and diversion services. *Journal of Criminal Law and Criminology*, **70**, 530–41.

Rogers, R. (ed.) (1988). *Clinical Assessment of Malingering and Deception*. New York: Guildford.

Rogers, R., and Webster, C. D. (1989). Assessing treatability in mentally disordered offenders. *Law and Human Behavior*, **13**, 19–27.

Ryan, L. (1988). Harry and the bus: Assisting one mentally disordered offender over the long range. Unpublished Working Paper No. 101, Metropolitan Toronto Forensic Service, Clarke Institute of Psychiatry.

Schneidemandel, P. L., and Kanno, C. K. (1969). The mentally ill offender: A survey of treatment programs. Washington, DC: The Joint Information Service of the American Psychiatric Association and the National Association for Mental Health.

Steadman, H. J., and Cocozza, J. J. (1974). *Careers of the Criminally Insane*. Lexington, MA: Lexington Books.

Steadman, H. J., Fabisiak, M. A., Dvoskin, J., and Holohean, E. J. (1987). A survey of mental disability among state prison inmates. *Hospital and Community Psychiatry*, **38**, 1086–91.

Sullivan, D. (1980). *The Mask of Love: Corrections in America: Toward a Mutual Aid Alternative*. London: National University Publications, Kennikat Press.

Teplin, L. A. (ed.) (1984). *Mental Health and Criminal Justice*. Beverly Hills, CA: Sage.

Teplin, L. A. (1990). The prevalence of severe mental disorder among male urban jail detainees: Comparison with the epidemiologic catchment area program. *American Journal of Public Health*, **80**, 663–9.

Thornberry, T.P., and Jacoby, J. E. (1979). *The Criminally Insane: A Community Follow-up of Mentally Ill Offenders*. Chicago: University of Chicago Press.

Toch, H. (1982). The disturbed disruptive inmate: Where does the bus stop? *Journal of Psychiatry and Law*, Fall, 327–49.

Toch, H., and Adams, K. (1989). *The Disturbed Violent Offender*, New Haven: Yale University Press.

Wardlaw, G. (1983). Models for the custody of mentally disordered offenders. *International Journal of Law and Psychiatry*, **6**, 159–76.

Webster, C. D. (1986). Compulsory treatment of narcotic addiction. *International Journal of Law and Psychiatry*, **8**, 133–59.

Webster, C. D., Macfarlane, P. D., Hodgins, S., and Macfarlane, E. (1990). Schizophrenia and violence: Observations based on Canadian Warrants of the Lieutenant Governor. Paper presented at the American Academy of Psychiatry and the Law, San Diego, CA.

Webster, C. D., and Menzies, R. J. (1987). The clinical prediction of dangerousness. In D. N. Weisstub (ed.), *International Yearbook of Law and Mental Health*, vol. 3, New York: Pergamon.

Webster, C. D. Menzies, R. J., and Jackson, M. A. (1982). *Clinical Assessment before Trial: Legal Issues and Mental Disorder*. Toronto: Butterworth.

World Health Organization (1989). Tenth Revision of the *International Classification of Diseases*, 1989 Draft of Chapter V (F): Mental and Behavioural Disorders. Geneva.

5

Crime and Mental Retardation: A Review

KENNETH DAY
Northgate Hospital, Morpeth, Northumberland, UK

INTRODUCTION

It was widely held in the first quarter of the twentieth century that mental handicap was a major causative factor in crime. Writing in 1920 the American psychologist, Goddard, stated that 'it is no longer to be denied that the greatest single cause of delinquency and crime is low grade mentality, much of it within the limits of feeble-mindedness'. Similar views prevailed in the United Kingdom (Goring, 1913) and gave rise to the first comprehensive piece of legislation for the mentally handicapped—The Mental Deficiency Act, 1913, which included the concept of the Moral Defective who 'from an early age displayed some permanent mental defect coupled with strong, vicious or criminal propensities on which punishment had little or no effect'. These early views were based upon surveys of criminal populations using intelligence tests which had a high verbal bias and were more a measure of educational under-achievement than innate low intelligence. Subsequent studies have demonstrated a much more limited negative correlation with, on average, only an 8 IQ point difference between delinquent and non-delinquent populations and a very low prevalence of frank mental handicap (Hirschi and Hindelgang, 1977; McGarvey, Gabriele, Bentler, and Mednick, 1981; Moffit, Gabriele, Mednick, and Schulsinger, 1981; Reichel, 1987; Sutherland, 1931; West and Farrington, 1973; Woodward, 1954). Nevertheless the small number of mentally handicapped people who do fall foul of the law require special consideration because of the distinctive nature of their offending and their particular management and treatment needs.

Clinical Approaches to the Mentally Disordered Offender
Edited by K. Howells and C. R. Hollin © 1993 John Wiley & Sons Ltd

SEX CHROMOSOME ABNORMALITIES, CRIME AND MENTAL HANDICAP

An association between mental handicap, criminality and additional sex chromosomes was first postulated when Jacobs, Brunton, Melville, Brittain, and McClemont (1965) and Jacobs, Price, Brown, Brittain, and Whatmore (1968) found a greater than expected number of males with the XYY complement in the Scottish State Hospital, Carstairs, the majority of whom were 'high grade defectives'. Surveys of maximum secure hospitals, (Casey, Segal, Street, and Blank 1966; Casey, Blank, Mobley, Kohn, Street, McDougall, Gooder, and Platts, 1971) and mental handicap hospitals (Aitken, Brunton, Jacobs, Price, and MacColl 1971; Akesson, Forssman, Wahlstrom, and Wallin, 1974; Hunter, 1977; Newton, Jacobs, Price, Woodcock, and Frazer, 1972) followed and appeared to confirm this, suggesting that the possession of an additional sex chromosome predisposed males to mental handicap and to socially deviant behaviour and offending. From these early studies emerged a picture of the XYY male as an individual functioning in the mild to borderline mental handicap range, well above average in height, with a history of disturbed and antisocial behaviour including offending beginning in the early teens and without any apparent sociocultural factors predisposing to crime in his background and environment. A high frequency of physical aggression including murder and serious and aggressive sexual offences was also reported (Court-Brown, 1968; Daly, 1969; Melnyk, Derencseny, Vanasek, Rucci, and Thompson, 1969; Nielsen, 1970; Wiener, Sutherland, Bartholomew, and Hudson, 1968).

In the debate surrounding these findings attention was drawn to the lack of adequate prevalence data for the XYY genotype in the general population, the highly selective nature of the groups studied and the lack of use of XY controls (Witkin, Mednick, Schulsinger, Bakkestrom, Christiansen, et al., 1976). A number of commentators (Hook, 1973; Hunter, 1977; McGuffin, 1984; Pitcher, 1975) cautioned against over-interpretation, pointing to the large numbers of males with the XYY genotype who are intellectually normal and show no anti-social behaviour. Hunter (1977) opined that the combination of above average height, large stature, behaviour disturbance and low intelligence led to a greater likelihood of hospitalisation. At least one study of the families of XYY males (Casey, 1970) revealed a high frequency of criminal offences in other family members—in contrast to earlier findings which had suggested that the XYY male was something of a 'black sheep' within an otherwise normal and stable family. Later studies, while verifying the findings in respect of height and intelligence, have confirmed the wisdom of this caution.

In a large-scale study of 4139 Danish males 184 cm or over in height, living in Copenhagen in 1944–7, Witkin et al. (1976) identified 12 with the XYY genotype, a prevalence rate of 2.9 per thousand compared to 1.5 per thousand live male births. Compared to those with the normal XY complement the XYY men had a higher mean rate of criminal convictions (a finding which continued to hold true after adjustment for backgrounds had been made), were significantly taller and obtained significantly lower scores on intelligence testing, but there were no differences in respect of crimes involving aggression or parental socioeconomic status. They concluded from their findings that the personal variables of tallness, intelligence and educational grade and the social variables of parental and family background bore a closer relationship to the possibility of conviction than genotypic abnormalities.

Prospective studies of neonates with identified X and Y aneuploidy followed up to adolescence and early adulthood have all found the boys to be taller than normal but have produced conflicting results in relation to cognitive skills and behaviour problems (Netley, 1986). Ratcliffe, Murray, and Tague (1986), for example, found a slightly raised incidence of learning difficulties and cognitive deficit in XYY boys compared to controls, and a higher frequency of behaviour problems as evidenced by frequency of psychiatric referral in a 12-year follow-up of 18 XYY boys. On the other hand, Leonard and Sparrow (1986) in an evaluation at 17–18 years of 11 boys with sex chromosome aneuploidy found that those with the XYY karyotype showed variable cognitive development but no severe or unusual aggressive or delinquent tendencies compared to their siblings and a control group.

A higher than expected prevalence of Klinefelter's syndrome (XXY) has also been found in tall men (Phillip, Lundstrom, and Hirschhorn, 1976), criminal offenders (Nielsen, 1970; Nielsen and Henricken, 1972; Schroder, De La Chapelle et al., 1981) and the mentally handicapped (Akesson et al., 1974; Hunter, 1969). Aggression (Sourial and Fenton, 1988) and chronic fire-setting behaviour (Miller and Sulkes, 1988) have also been described in association with the syndrome. Witkin et al. (1976) found that the XXYs in their study showed an elevated crime rate compared to the XYs but this was not maintained when background variables were controlled; there were no differences in the frequency of violent crime. The XXYs had substantially lower mean scores on intelligence scales and were taller. Prospective studies of affected neonates have produced the same conflicting results in respect of behaviour problems as in the XYY syndrome (Ratcliffe and Paul, 1986). A significant reduction in aggression and fire-setting behaviour has been reported following Testosterone treatment (Miller and Sulkes, 1988; Sourial and Fenton, 1988). Studies of the Fragile X Syndrome have so far not revealed any association with criminality or antisocial behaviour.

PREVALENCE OF OFFENDING IN THE MENTALLY HANDICAPPED

In a survey of 22 000 mentally handicapped people known to the Danish services on a census day in 1973, Svendsen and Werner (1977) found 290 to be subject to a penal court decision—a point prevalence of little over 1%. A recent study of mentally retarded criminal offenders in Denmark (Lund, 1990) identified only 91 patients serving statutory care orders under the Danish penal code on the census day in 1984—a point prevalence of less than 0.5%. Lund concluded that this apparently dramatic decrease since the 1973 census was less a reflection of a genuine reduction in criminal activity and more a reflection of shorter sentences

Table 5.1 Prevalence of mentally handicapped offenders in court cohorts and remanded and convicted males

Author	Location	Sample	Instrument	Mentally handicapped (%)
Glueck (1918)	Sing Sing Prison, USA	608 consecutive receptions	Clinical interview	28 'Intelligence of a 12 year old American child or below'
Bromberg and Thompson (1937)	Court of General Sessions, New York County, USA	9958 examinations 1932–1935	WAIS	2.4
Thompson (1937)	Court of General Sessions, New York County, USA	1380 recidivists	WAIS	2.6
East, Stocks, and Young (1942)	Wormwood Scrubs Prison, UK	3366 convicted youths	Colombian Group Test followed by Merrill Intelligence Test	3.5
Roper (1950, 1951)	Wakefield Prison, UK	1100 consecutive sentences	Clinical interview Ravens Matrices	45 subnormal and borderline subnormal
Levy (1954)	Washington State Penitentiary, USA	1610 inmates	Group screening tests followed by Wechsler Bellevue Intelligence Scale	1 (IQ less than 70)
Messinger and Apfelburg (1961)	Court of General Sessions, New York County, USA	Psychiatric clinics 57 000 Felons 1932–1953	WAIS	2.5
Gibbens (1963)	England	200 Borstal Boys	Ravens Matrices	3
Robinson, Patten, and Kerr (1965)	Belfast Prison, Northern Ireland	566 consecutive sentences	Clinical interview Case records	24
Bluglass (1966)	Perth Prison, Scotland	300—every 4th reception	Clinical interview Mill Hill and Ravens Matrices	2.6 subnormal 11.6 borderline

Study	Location	Sample	Method	Rate
Gibbens (1966)	Pentonville Prison Eastchurch Open Prison, UK	Not known	Not known	6 9
Brown and Courtless (1968)	5 State Penitentiaries, USA	Not given	WAIS	7 MR (IQ 69) 0.8 borderline (IQ 70–74)
Brown and Courtless (1968)	USA National Survey	Weighted average of rates in all States	Range IQ tests and test procedures (75% WAIS)	9.5 (range 2.6 to 24.3)
Haskins and Friel (1973)	USA	National surveys	Not known	4.1
Faulk (1976)	Winchester Prison, UK	72 consecutive releases	Clinical interview	5.5
Guze (1976)	Missouri Probation Board, USA	223 parolees and flat timers	Clinical interview Feighners Criteria	1
Jones (1976)	Tennessee State Penitentiary, USA	1040 prison population	Case notes DSM II	2.3
Bowden (1978)	Brixton Prison, UK	126 remands into custody for medical reports—every 5th referral	ICD 9 (2 independent raters)	2
MacEachron (1979)	State Penal Institutions USA, Maine, Massachusetts	690—all tested 3248—tested proportion unknown	Most recent IQ test score—various tests	2.3 0.6
Taylor and Gunn (1984)	Brixton Prison, UK	1241 remanded males	ICD 9	0.9
Home Office and DHSS (1987)	Census of mentally disordered offenders by prison medical officers, England and Wales	1497 sentenced males and females	Clinical interview and case notes	5
Gunn, Maden, and Swinton (1991)	Sentenced prisoners England and Wales	2250 males and females stratified sample	ICD 9 Reading test Case records	0.9

and a reduction in the number of borderline retarded persons receiving such sentences—the implication being that they had been dealt with within the normal penal system. There was a decrease in crimes of property and an increase in sex offences, violence and arson amongst those convicted in 1984.

Lifespan figures are naturally higher. Dyggve and Kodahl (1979) reported that 31 (3%) of 942 mentally retarded persons registered in the Danish county of West Zealand in 1973 whom they examined had a history of conviction for a criminal offence. Gostason (1985), in an in-depth study of a sample of 122 mentally retarded people resident in the Swedish county of Koppaberg, found an overall offence rate of 4.9% for the mentally retarded compared to 25% in a non-handicapped control group. This difference was entirely accounted for by the high frequency of traffic offences of all types amongst the controls: there were no significant differences between the mentally retarded and non-retarded controls in respect of other types of criminal offences. In a study of a mentally handicapped population in one United Kingdom city followed up from childhood, Richardson, Katz, Koller, McLaren, and Rubinstein (1979) found that 14% of the 190 who had survived to the age of 22 years showed evidence of antisocial behaviour defined as delinquent behaviour leading to fines or imprisonment; included in this figure, however, was an unspecified number of cases where offences had occurred in childhood without legal action.

The contribution of the mentally handicapped to the criminal statistics is small. In two large-scale court cohort studies from America (Bromberg and Thompson, 1937; Messinger and Apfelberg, 1961), employing the Wechsler Adult Intelligence Scale (WAIS) administered by a trained psychologist, it was found the mentally handicapped comprised 2.4% and 2.5% respectively of the criminal population. Studies of prison and other criminal populations employing standardised intelligence tests arrive at similar figures. In a recently completed study of a stratified sample of sentenced prisoners, Gunn, Maden, and Swinton (1991) found a prevalence of 0.9%. Those relying primarily on clinical interviews or an acceptance of the diagnosis of others have, not surprisingly, produced widely ranging figures (Table 5.1).

Although the prevalence of offending in the mentally handicapped appears to have remained unchanged over the years, some increase is to be anticipated in the coming years as implementation of Care in the Community policies exposes more mentally handicapped people to greater temptations and opportunities for offending and the 'hidden offences' which occur regularly in institutions become more visible. A hint of this is provided by Lund's (1990) finding of a significant increase in mildly retarded offenders receiving first sentences in 1984 compared to 1973.

THE PSYCHOPATHOLOGY OF OFFENDING IN THE MENTALLY HANDICAPPED

The bulk of offences committed by the mentally handicapped are carried out by youths functioning in the mild to borderline mental handicap range of intelligence. Female offenders are uncommon and differ significantly from male offenders; they are considered later in a separate section. The contribution of the severely mentally handicapped is small but tends to be over-represented in official statistics because legal classifications under the Mental Health Acts do not always coincide with the clinical classification. Thus, while 19% of mentally handicapped people on hospital orders studied by Walker and McCabe (1973) and Gibbens and Robertson (1983a, b) were classified as 'severely subnormal', Parker (1974) in a survey of Special Hospital patients found that two-thirds so classified had IQs above 50. Consequently, the histories of 'severely subnormal' offenders differ little from the 'subnormal offenders' (Gibbens and Robertson, 1983a).

Psychosocial deprivation, low socioeconomic class, a family history of criminality, cerebral abnormality, minor physical imperfections and a history of behaviour disorder as a child, all implicated in delinquency and adult crime generally (Gunn and Fenton, 1969; McCord, 1979; West and Farrington, 1973, 1977) are found commonly in mentally handicapped offender populations (Table 5.2). Contamination by criminal family members or peers, gullibility, lack of self-control are common features and sometimes offending may be motivated by status seeking (Day, 1990a). According to Eysenck (1977) criminality and anti-social behaviour are causally related to certain inborn temperamental traits, namely high psychoticism, high extroversion and high neuroticism. Evidence in support of this theory has been reviewed by Farrington, Biron, and Le Blanc (1982) and Eysenck and Gudjonsson (1989). There is no research which examines Eysenck's theory of criminality in mentally handicapped populations.

Richardson, Koller, and Katz (1985) and Koller, Richardson, and Katz (1983) demonstrated a significant linear link between unstable upbringing and the presence of behaviour disturbance including sexual misconduct, arson and other offences in a cohort of 156 mildly mentally retarded children followed up from infancy to the age of 22 years. Lund (1990) found a much higher prevalence of behaviour disorders in a group of mentally retarded offenders than a randomly selected group of mentally retarded non-offenders and a statistically significant association between behaviour disorder, institutional care before five years of age, low socioeconomic status and a history of retardation in one or both parents and criminal behaviour: the most important predictor of subsequent criminal activity being behaviour disorder. Using adjusted and raw OR values Lund calculated that if a mentally handicapped person had a father who was also mentally handicapped, was institutionalised before the age of five years and developed a behaviour disorder, his risk of being charged with a criminal offence would be 97%.

Information on the association between mental illness and criminal behaviour in the mentally handicapped is scant and warrants further investigation. A number of studies report relatively high frequencies of psychotic disorder in mentally handicapped offender populations (Day, 1988; Isweran and Bardsley, 1987; Tutt, 1971), while others report no significant differences from mentally handicapped controls and the general population (Lund, 1990). Day (in press) found mental illness to be the causative factor in 3 of 197 sexual incidents committed by 47 mentally handicapped males; two cases of minor

Table 5.2 Characteristics of mentally handicapped offenders—principal studies

Author	Kugel, Trembath, and Sagar (1968)	Tutt (1971)	Craft (1984)	Denkowski and Denkowski (1985)	Day (1988)	Lund (1990)
Population	67 males committed to state institution for mentally retarded	44 males admitted to mental handicap hospital	209 males admitted to mental handicap hospital	65 males placed in a community residential programme for MR offenders	20 males admitted to mental handicap hospital unit	91 predominantly males on statutory care orders Denmark
Intelligence level	Av. IQ 60	Av. IQ 80	Av. IQ 83	Av. IQ 54	Av. IQ 65	89% Mild MR 9% Mod/Sev MR
Family	81% broken homes 50% low income	52% broken homes 77% social class V 9% chronically unemployed	46% grossly deprived upbringing 18% high degree home disturbance	55% one-parent family 17% neither natural parent at home 53% families receiving welfare benefit 47% alcoholism 18% serious mental illness 31% PH neglect/physical abuse	50% severe psychosocial deprivation 10% mental handicap 20% serious mental illness 85% poor urban environment 60% high delinq. area 50% FH crim/delinq.	34% parents separated before age 5 yrs 60% social class V 20% one or both parents retarded

Institutional care as child	—	—	—	38% beyond parental control	90% at least one residential placement 75% multiple	37.5% institutional placement before 5 yrs 26% 3 placements before 7 years
Behaviour disorder	42%	87%	—	66% 23/65 physical aggression	83% from early childhood	87.5% social aggression
Cerebral abnormality	25% brain damage	9% epileptic	14% brain damage 9% epileptic	—	30% brain damage 15% epileptic	—
Sex chromosome some abnormality	—	2.27% (1 case) XYY	—	—	10% (2 cases) XYY	3.3% (3 cases) type not specified
Minor physical imperfections	—	—	—	—	55%	—

indecent assault associated with hypomania and one case of serious indecent assault due to arteriosclerotic dementia in a 63-year-old man of previously blameless character. In Aspergers syndrome criminal behaviour may occur as a reaction to disturbed routine or as a consequence of morbid obsessional behaviour or the misinterpretation of social cues (Tantam, personal communication).

The high frequency of brain damage and epilepsy reported in most studies of menially handicapped offenders is generally thought to contribute to criminal behaviour by impairing social learning and reducing impulse control. Lund (1990), however, found no statistically significant association between epilepsy and brain damage and criminal behaviour or behaviour disorder, although both pre- and post-natal brain damage were more frequent in the offender group. In their studies Richardson, Koller, and Katz (1985) similarly found no evidence to support the hypothesis that CNS impairment is a contributory factor to behaviour disturbance in adulthood. Commenting on this finding, which was based on clinical and neurological examinations carried out in 1962, they speculate whether the use of modern neurological investigative techniques would have produced the same results. More work is clearly needed in this area.

Physical disabilities like an unusual appearance or limp, which mark out the individual, or stammering or deafness which impair social integration, were present in over half of the mentally handicapped offenders studied by Day (1988). No other study has addressed this issue in the mentally handicapped but a higher than normal prevalence of minor auditory and visual defects and other physical imperfections has been repeatedly reported in studies of non-handicapped delinquents (Gibbens, 1963; Stott, 1962; West and Farrington, 1977). Maberly (1950) has suggested that such physical defects act to alienate the individual from society and impede social integration and that criminal behaviour may arise as a compensation for feelings of inferiority. Hunter (1979) has drawn attention to the barriers to socialisation caused by minor speech defects.

Mentally handicapped offenders have many features in common with non-handicapped offenders (West and Farrington, 1973, 1977) but differ significantly from mentally ill and psychopathic offenders (Murray, Briggs, and Davis, 1992; Robertson, 1981, 1982). In Gibbens and Robertson's (1983a, b) study of male hospital order patients, 50% of the mentally ill group first offended between the ages of 20 and 35 years, 25% were first convicted under the age of 20 years, and only 16% had a juvenile conviction while 73% of the mentally handicapped were first convicted in their teens, only 9% were first convicted after the age of 30 years and 50% had juvenile offences recorded against them. In the same study, 80% of the mentally ill had received psychiatric in-patient care prior to conviction, compared to only 50% of the mentally handicapped and the mentally ill offenders who showed a higher frequency of violence, were detained for shorter periods and committed fewer serious crimes in the follow-up period. The schizophrenics in Walker and McCabe's (1973) study had a higher mean age at first conviction while the offending history of the subnormals and psychopaths began in their teens.

Table 5.3   Patterns of offending in the mentally handicapped males

Author	Population studied	Offences (%)				
		Property	Sex	Arson	Violence	Other
Morris (1948)	63 subnormal and severely subnormal males, Norfolk, UK	38	42.8	4.8	6.3	4.8
Kugel, Trembath, and Sagar (1968)	67 committals to institutions for mentally retarded, USA Mean IQ 60	26	22	11	4	–
Shapiro (1969)	154 admissions to mental handicap hospital, UK Average IQ 83	88	33	2	–	–
Tutt (1969)	44 admissions to mental handicap hospital, UK Mean IQ 80	73	16	2.3	–	8.3
Walker and McCabe (1973)	330 hospital order patients, England and Wales, subnormal and severely subnormal	52	28	4.8	4.5	28.7
Svendsen and Werner (1977)	290 all offenders known to Danish mental retardation service 1973	60	25	15		–
Gibbens and Robertson (1983a)	Post-discharge offences. 15-year follow-up 170 subnormal and severely subnormal male hospital order patients	59	13	2	10	16
Craft (1984)	209 admissions to three mental handicap units Average IQ 83	25	12	7	15	–
Day (1990)	72 Admissions to mental handicap offender unit 1974–1990	24	46	8	24	–
Lund (1990)	65 mentally retarded criminal offenders serving care orders Denmark 1984— Sentence on census day	19.8	12.5	26.4	11	–
Home Office (1990)	208 mentally impaired and severely mentally impaired patients detained under MHA 1983 in 1988	7.7	31.7	20.6	38.9	0.5
Criminal statistics UK (1979)	General population indictable offences	78	0.9	<1	3.4	17

OFFENCE PATTERN

The commonest offences committed by the mentally handicapped are property and technical offences, sex offences and arson are over-represented, and there is a low incidence of personal violence, although the latter comprise a significant percentage of admissions to special units and hospitals for mentally handicapped offenders (Table 5.3). The incidence of sex offences is four to six times (Milner, 1949; Tutt, 1971; Walker and McCabe, 1973) that in the general population—an over-representation which should not surprise when society's attitude to the sexuality of the mentally handicapped is considered and the nature of sex offending in the mentally handicapped is examined. Koller, Richardson, Katz, and McLaren (1982), in their follow-up study of mentally handicapped children to age 22 years found that 12.5% of the males had been involved in sexual misconduct compared to 1% of the matched controls. Higher detection and prosecution rates have been advanced as an explanation (Murphy, Coleman, and Haynes, 1983; Schilling and Schinke, 1988) but this is not supported by the findings of a recent study (Day, in press) in which only 60% of 191 sexual incidents committed by 47 mentally handicapped men were reported to the police and only a half of these were proceeded against—figures comparable to those for non-detection and non-prosecution in other major studies of sex crimes.

Arson is another offence which appears to be particularly associated with mental handicap. Nearly 50% of 1300 arsonists studied in the USA by Lewis and Yarnell (1951) were classified as mentally handicapped. 'Subnormal' patients who made up one third of Walker and McCabe's Hospital Order patients (1973) were responsible for nearly half of the cases of arson committed by the group as a whole. Over 20% of convicted French arsonists studied by Yesevage, Benezech, Ceccaldi, Bourgeois, and Addad (1983) were found to be mentally handicapped and a figure of 14.7% was reported by Bradford (1982) in a study of 34 Canadian arsonists referred for forensic examination. In a survey of 54 fire setters in South West Ireland (O'Sullivan and Kelleher, 1987), 7% were diagnosed as mentally handicapped.

RECIDIVISM

Follow-up studies of mentally handicapped patients institutionalised following a conviction show high rates of reconviction during the follow-up period (Table 5.4). The risk is highest during the year immediately following discharge (Day, 1988; Gibbens and Robertson, 1983a; Tong and Mackay, 1969; Walker and McCabe, 1974). A history of convictions prior to the index offence substantially increases the chances of further convictions (Day, 1988; Payne, McCabe, and Walker, 1974) and is the best single predictor of the likelihood of reconviction (Gibbens and Robertson, 1983a, b). Property offenders have a substantially greater chance of reconviction than offenders against the person (Day, 1988; McCabe, and Walker 1974; Tong and Mackay, 1969). Day (1988) has suggested that offences against the person are essentially problems of poor self-control

Table 5.4   Reconviction rates in mentally handicapped offenders

Author	Sample	Follow-up Period (years)	Reconvicted (%)
Wildenskov (1962)	47 convicted males of borderline IQ placed in the Danish Mental Deficiency Service	20	51
Tong and Mackay (1969)	423 male Rampton Hospital patients	1–12	40
Craft (1969)	250 male mixed subnormal and psychopathic patients admitted to three special units. Av. IQ 83	3–5	49
Walker and McCabe (1973)	370 subnormal and severely subnormal hospital order patients. Both sexes	1	39
Gibbens and Robertson (1983a)	250 subnormal male hospital order patients	15	68 (41% three times or more)
Craft (1984)	209 predominantly subnormal patients admitted to a special treatment unit	20	42
Day (1988)	20 males admitted to specialised hospital unit Av. IQ 62	3–5	55 (40% two to four times)
Lund (1990)	83 mainly male mentally retarded patients on statutory care orders Denmark	10	72

and immaturity with the potential to respond to treatment, while property offences are more a function of lifestyle and sub-cultural influences to which the offender frequently returns. Sex offenders, both non-handicapped and mentally handicapped, display a low but persistent tendency to repeat sex offences (Day, in press; Soothill and Gibbens, 1978).

Individual mentally handicapped offenders tend to commit a wide range of offences. Kugel, Trembath, and Sagar (1968) reported that most of the 142 male and female patients committed to a state institution for the mentally retarded in Rhode Island were charged with a variety of often three or four different offences. The 83 males in the study were convicted of a total of 2206 offences ranging through sex offences, larceny, vandalism, fire setting, truancy and alcoholism. This tendency is more pronounced in offenders against the person. In a 3–5 year follow-up of 20 male mentally handicapped offenders, Day (1988) found that of the sex offenders 75% had previous and 50% subsequent convictions for offences other than sex offences compared to only 17% of the property offenders although the latter had twice the reconviction rate. Lund

(1990) also found that property offenders tended to continue to commit property offences whereas only one-quarter of those who had committed arson, violence or sex offences repeated such crimes, the majority subsequently committing property offences. A similar finding has been reported in non-handicapped offenders (McClintock, 1963; West and Farrington, 1977).

Reconviction for serious offences is uncommon. Tong and Mackay (1969) in their 1–12 year follow-up of 423 Rampton patients found that the prevalence of violent offences had fallen from a pre-admission rate of 39% to 11% and hetero-sexual offences from 13.5% to 7%, while property offences had risen by 10%. Only 3–4% of offences committed by 250 mentally handicapped male hospital order patients followed up over 15 years by Gibbens and Robertson (1983a, b) were serious in nature. Craft (1984) similarly found that only 12 of 324 recon-victions in a 20-year follow-up of 88 male offenders were for murder, grievous bodily harm, rape or arson. Lund (1990), however, found that 19 (26%) of his cohort of 83 mentally handicapped offenders had committed serious offences including arson or sexual crimes during a 10-year follow-up period. He also found that the frequency of recidivism was significantly increased in those with a past history of behaviour disorder and that recidivism for violent and sexual offences was found only in this group.

Reconviction rates alone paint an over-gloomy picture of prognosis. Global assessments utilising a range of social measures indicate a rather better outcome. Craft (1969, 1984) in two separate studies found that between one-third and one-half of the offenders he studied were living successfully in the community and employed on follow-up at 3–5 years and at 20 years. Using a range of social criteria Day (1988) found that 30% of 20 ex-hospitalised patients followed-up for 3–5 years rated as well adjusted, and 40% as reasonably well adjusted at last contact, and that only 15% had been rehospitalised as a result of reconviction.

Duration of institutional care and quality of aftercare crucially affect prog-nosis. Tong and Mackay (1969) and Walker and McCabe (1973) both found that a shorter duration of institutional care was associated with a greater likelihood of reconviction and rehospitalisation or imprisonment. A positive correlation between a length of stay of over two years and better outcome was reported by Day (1988). Craft (1984) found that only 11% of the men placed in sheltered lodgings, employed and supervised were reconvicted during a 20-year follow-up, as opposed to 44% of those living unsupervised in the community. Day (1988) reported a positive correlation between good outcome and stable residential placement, regular daytime occupation and regular supervision and support. Good aftercare was associated with a more advantageous outcome at one year follow-up in Walker and McCabe's study (1973).

MENTALLY HANDICAPPED SEX OFFENDERS

The overall pattern of sex offending in the mentally handicapped is similar to that in the non-handicapped (Table 5.5). Offences involving physical aggression are unusual. In an analysis of 161 sex offenders on hospital orders, of whom 60%

were classified as 'subnormal' Walker and McCabe (1973) concluded that only 9% of offences involved seriously bodily harm, violence or death, in 17% the victim was likely to be shocked, and in 65% of cases the offence was trivial or the victim was unlikely to have been offended. Although one-quarter of the heterosexual and one-third of the homosexual offences committed by 47 male mentally handicapped sex offenders studied by Day (in press) were classified as serious in nature, physical violence and injury to the victim were extremely uncommon.

Recidivism is common. Half of the mentally handicapped sex offenders in a Rampton cohort of 200 men studied by Milner (1949) had a record of more than one sex offence and one in five of the 67 mentally handicapped patients in the Cambridge study of convicted sex offenders (Radzinowicz, 1957) had at least one previous conviction for a sex offence and one in three were reconvicted after release. Mein (1957), in a survey of 83 mentally handicapped sex offenders admitted to Harperbury Hospital, found that 45% had committed sex offences prior to admission, 20% of those allowed out on licence had repeated their offences and 10% of those discharged displayed further sexual misconduct. Of the patients in Day's study, 85% were involved in more than one sexual incident, and 38% had received one conviction, 17% two, and 17% three or more convictions for sex offences during an average period of 10.3 years (range 1–22 years). Prognosis appears to be more favourable with appropriate treatment (Day, 1988).

Mentally handicapped sex offenders show far less specificity in relation to offence type and victim characteristics than their non-handicapped counterparts, the victim's age and sex being largely a matter of circumstance and opportunity rather than an indication of a particular sexual preference or orientation. Two-thirds of the mentally handicapped sex offenders in Day's study had committed more than one type of sex offence; 20% had committed both homosexual and heterosexual offences and 50% offences against both children and adults. Gilby, Woolf, and Goldberg (1989) similarly found that mentally retarded adolescents were less discriminating in their sex play than non-retarded adolescents, showing evidence of both homosexual and heterosexual activity and that the spread of victim characteristics was much greater.

There are certain other differences from non-handicapped sex offenders. The mentally handicapped are far more likely to commit heterosexual offences against adult victims and much less likely to know their victims (Day, in press; Gilby, Woolf, and Goldberg, 1989). Such offences rarely occur in the context of an established or developing relationship—a reflection of the general lack of opportunities for and discouragement of sexual relationships between mentally handicapped people which is only just beginning to change. Alcohol is rarely a predisposing factor (Day, in press) while in the non-handicapped it is reported to be a significant factor in one-third to two-thirds of heterosexual offences (Gebhard, Gagnon, Pomeroy, and Christenson, 1965). Mentally handicapped indecent exposers are far more likely to know their victims and to expose from their own home (Day, in press) than non-handicapped exposers and rarely display the characteristic patterning (Bluglass, 1980; Rooth, 1971), suggesting that indecent exposure in the mentally handicapped is usually a crude expression of

Table 5.5 Sexual incidents/offences committed by mentally handicapped men compared to sex offending in the general population

	Day (in press) 47 male mentally handicapped offenders admitted to a mental handicap hospital unit 1970–1988. Total sexual offences and episodes		Radzinowicz (1957) Sex offenders brought to trial	Criminal Statistics (1988) Offenders found guilty or cautioned for indictable sex offences
Indecent exposure	47 (24.6%)		90 (24.7%)	—
Heterosexual				
Rape and attempted rape	1 (0.5%)	[1%]	22 (1.1%)	540 (5%)
ABH	3 (1.5%)	[3%]	—	—
Unlawful SI (under 13 yrs)	1 (0.5%)	[1%]	11 (0.5%)	214 (1.99%)
Unlawful SI (13–16 yrs)	3 (1.5%)	[3%]	45 (2.3%)	1555 (14.5%)
Exploiting SMH	5 (2.6%)	[5%]	5 (0.2%)	—
Indecent assault: serious	14 (7.3%)	[14%]	⎧ 396 (20%)	3961 (36.9%)
minor	48 (25%)	[48%]	⎩	—
Incest	—		30 (1.5%)	245 (2.2%)
Associating with underage girl	1 (0.5%)		—	—
Loitering with intent	1 (0.5%)		—	—
Inappropriate advances/ suggestions	23 (12%)		—	—
Following	3 (1.5%)		—	—
Peeping	2 (1%)		—	—
Obscene phone call	1 (0.5%)		—	—

Homosexual

Buggery	2 (1%) [2%]	32 (1.6%)	412 (3.8%)
Gross indecency	2 (1%) [2%]	59 (3.0%)	1496 (13.9%)
Indecency under the byelaws	–	451 (22.7%)	–
Indecency with male under 16 yrs	2 (1%) [2%]	–	334 (3%)
Indecent assault on a male	12 (6.3%) [12%]	167 (8.4%)	736 (6.55%)
Indecent advances/ suggestions	6 (3.1%) [6%]	–	–
Soliciting/importuning	-	278 (14.0%)	699 (6.5%)

Other

Breach of peace (cross-dressing)	8 (4.2%)	–	–
Stealing female underwear	6 (3.1%)	–	–

( ) = % of total
[ ] = % of indictable offences

sexual feelings rather than a specific sexual deviation. There appears, however, to be little difference between mentally handicapped and non-handicapped homosexual offenders. In both groups a high percentage of victims are well known to the offender and there is evidence of victim compliance and a lengthy association in many (Day, in press; Gebhard et al., 1965).

Mentally handicapped sex offenders show the same range of adverse psycho-social factors in their backgrounds as non-handicapped sex offenders (Gebhard et al., 1965; Radzinowicz, 1957). In a substantial proportion of cases the home is characterised by multiple family pathology with gross marital disharmony, parental separation, violence, neglect and poor control (Day, in press; Gilby, Woolf, and Goldberg, 1989). In one study (Gilby, Woolf, and Goldberg, 1989) 20% of patients had suffered sexual abuse as children. Similarly many have a history of school adjustment and relationship problems, behaviour problems, psychiatric illness and other delinquent behaviour (Day, in press; Gilby, Woolf, and Goldberg, 1989). Sexual naivety, inability to understand normal sexual relationships, lack of relationship skills, difficulties in mixing with the opposite sex, poor impulse control and susceptibility to the influence of others have been repeatedly reported as prominent features (Day, in press; Gebhard et al., 1965; Gilby, Woolf, and Goldberg, 1989; Hingsburger, 1987; Radzinowicz, 1957). Nearly two-thirds of the mentally handicapped sex offenders studied by Day, for example, had had no sexual experience involving another individual prior to their first sexual incident, and only 10% had ever been married or cohabiting. In the large-scale study by Gebhard et al. (1965), 90% of sex offenders had experienced heavy petting, and the incidence of pre-marital coitus ranged from 67% and 90% and of marriage from 40% and 85% in the various offence categories.

Day differentiated two groups of mentally handicapped sex offenders in his study: those who commit sex offences only, and a smaller group whose sex offending is part of a wider tapestry of offending behaviour and social problems. A similar dichotomy has been described in non-handicapped sex offenders (Gebhard et al., 1965; Radzinowicz, 1957). The sex-offences-only group displayed less psychosocial pathology, tended to function at the lower end of the mildly mentally handicapped range, showed little specificity for type of offence and type of victim and had a better prognosis. Their sex offending would seem to be explainable in terms of a normal sex drive coupled with lack of normal outlets compounded by sexual naivety, poor impulse control, social ineptness, and a lack of social awareness. More enlightened approaches to the sexuality of mentally handicapped people should significantly reduce the incidence of this type of offending in the future. Treatment measures should be directed at sex education and counselling, relationship skills and improving self-image and self-confidence (Craft and Craft, 1983). The group who committed both sex and other offences were more damaged individuals who showed marked adverse psychosocial factors in their backgrounds and tended to be sociopathic personalities. They were likely to become persistent offenders and commit serious offences. Highly specialised assessment and treatment services are required for this group.

ARSON

Despite the reported association between arson and mental handicap the topic has received little attention. McKerracher and Dacre (1966) examined 20 male 'subnormal' arsonists admitted to Rampton Hospital and found that they had a higher incidence of aggression to property (other than arson), attempted suicide, self-wounding and psychotic overlay, and a lower incidence of aggression to others and sex offences than a comparative group of non-arsonist subnormal male offenders admitted during the same period. Sex offences committed by the arsonists were largely heterosexual in nature and rarely involved aggression. Similar findings emerged from a study of 57 female arsonists with a mean IQ of 77.5, one-third of whom were classified as subnormal or severely subnormal, admitted to three Special Hospitals (Tennent, McQuaid, and Lougnane, 1971). In comparison to a control group matched for age, length of stay and IQ distribution the arsonists had a lower history of aggression to others preceding admission and a greater history of damage to property. There were no differences in psychiatric symptomatology or in the incidence of suicidal attempts or self-mutilation between the two groups but the arsonists had significantly more problems related to sexual development and sexual relationships. In 39% of cases the arson had occurred in a setting of direct conflict with authority and in 69% the fire was in the immediate living area of the patient. Yesevage *et al.* (1983) studied two groups of adult male arsonists—27 mentally disordered, of whom 46% were mentally retarded, and 23 who were not mentally disordered. Broken homes and seriously disturbed family relationships were present in a high proportion of both groups. The most commonly cited motives in the mentally disordered group were vengeance and pleasure and over half the fires were started at or around the subject's work place or home. Studies of non-handicapped arsonists on remand or in hospitals or special prisons (Bradford, 1982; Hurley and Monaghan, 1969; O'Sullivan and Kelleher, 1987; Soothill and Pope, 1973) have revealed similar characteristics.

Recidivism appears to be common in mentally disordered arsonists. Of Tennent, McQuaid, and Lougnane's (1971) female arsonists, 61% had set two fires, 18% three or more and only 20% one fire. Yesevage *et al.*'s (1983) mentally disordered group set an average of 2.8 fires per individual. Recidivism rates of 30% over a 15 year period were reported by Lewis and Yarnell (1951), and of 35% over a 10-year period by O'Sullivan and Kelleher (1987); but in Soothill and Pope's (1973) 20-year follow-up of 82 individuals charged with arson the recidivism rate was only 3%. Clinical experience and anecdotal evidence indicate similar high recidivism rates in mentally handicapped arsonists but there are no specific follow-up studies.

Borrowing the suggestion of Geller and Bertsch (1985) that fire setting might be used as a communicative vehicle by those with poor verbalising skills, O'Sullivan and Kelleher (1987) have hypothesised that this may be the explanation in many cases of arson committed by mentally handicapped individuals. McKerracher and Dacre (1966) also suggested that arson is a form of displaced aggression in passive inadequate individuals who are incapable of interacting at an emotional level with others. Conflict or other stress is certainly frequently associated with episodes of arson committed by the mentally handicapped but in others it is difficult to identify a motive, although sometimes feelings of power and excitement generated by fire setting and its consequences appear to be the explanation (Yesevage *et al.*, 1983). Jackson, Glass, and Hope (1987) have advanced a theoretical paradigm to explain recidivistic arson as a basis for management. They hypothesise that personal and environmental disadvantage, dissatisfaction with self and/or life and actual or perceived ineffective social interaction are key contextual elements; that special factors direct the arsonist towards fire, and that fire-setting episodes are triggered by the absence of a 'person target' in situations which the individual feels powerless to change. They advise that management strategies should therefore focus upon helping the arsonist to develop alternative and successful methods for effecting social influence through the development of interaction skills and training in appropriate assertiveness. Clare, Murphy, Cox and Chaplin (1992) have reported the successful treatment, using this approach, of a mildly mentally handicapped male arsonist.

FEMALE OFFENDERS

In studies of hospital order patients males outnumber females in ratios of 4 : 1 (Walker and McCabe, 1973) and 7 : 1 (Gibbens and Robertson, 1983a, b). The majority of mentally handicapped females who come before the courts do so because of behavioural problems and sexual misdemeanours and are usually committed to care or hospital because of concern for their welfare. Morris (1948), in a study of mentally handicapped patients in Norfolk County Council's institutions, identified 49 female offenders with an average IQ of 59 and an average age of 19.9 years. The vast majority had been committed for sex-related offences— 43% were found to be in moral danger, 33% had been convicted for prostitution, and 4% had been involved in incest; larceny was the index offence in only 12% of cases. An analysis of 80 female patients with an average mental age of 9.42 years admitted to Rampton Hospital (Milner, 1949) revealed that sexual delinquency was a pre-admission problem in 52%, violence in 33% and acquisitive offences in 37%. Wildenskov (1962) reported on 50 institutionalised mentally handicapped women offenders in Denmark; 70% had been committed for leading an 'immoral life ranging from prostitution to moral laxity' (p. 219), and only 16% for theft or other crimes against property. Kugel, Trembath, and Sagar (1986) examined 52 female patients committed to the state institution of Rhode Island: the mean IQ of the group was 58 and the vast majority were under the age of 30 years. The principal reasons for committal were promiscuity 28%, behaviour problems 32% and being neglected 17%; conventional offences were uncommon (acquisitive 7%, arson 3%, and violence 2%).

McKerracher, Street, and Segal (1966), in a study of 23 female patients with an average IQ of 70 admitted to Rampton Hospital, found that the main reasons for admission were self-wounding and mutilation, attempted suicide and indiscriminate aggressive acts to property and persons. Compared to a group of male patients matched for age, IQ and length of stay the females showed persistent grossly disturbed behaviour and emotional lability following admission. The greater propensity of females to commit damage to property was also reported by Parker (1974) in a study of mentally handicapped patients at Rampton and Moss Side Special Hospitals. In Walker and McCabe's (1973) hospital order cohort 9% of the 86 subnormal female patients had been convicted for a sex offence (mainly soliciting), and a further 24% for vagrancy including sexual misconduct; 53% had been convicted for property offences (mainly shoplifting and minor larceny), 5% for violence against the person, and 3.4% for arson. In a 15-year follow-up of an expanded cohort, 33% of the female 'subnormal' patients had been reconvicted—69% for acquisitive offences, 9% for soliciting, 7% for assault, and 1% for arson (Robertson, 1981).

The rare and unusual crime of baby stealing is occasionally committed by mentally handicapped women. According to d'Orban (1976) such offences may be comforting, manipulative or psychotic in origin. Comforting offences are a consequence of the woman's feelings of deprivation and loneliness and a desire to comfort herself by playing with or mothering a young child—usually that of a relative or friend. In the manipulative group the baby is stolen in an attempt to control a crisis in interpersonal relationships or to manipulate a partner and tends to involve a stranger's child. In the third group the offence is usually committed in an acute psychotic state, sometimes as a consequence of delusional ideas. There is a risk of repeat offending, particularly in the 'comforting offences' (d'Orban, 1990). A quarter of 24 cases reported by d'Orban (1976) were mentally handicapped; in four the offence was classified as comforting and in two it was associated with superadded transient psychotic illness.

Female mentally handicapped offenders usually have grossly disturbed family backgrounds. The only detailed study is that by Morris (1948), which although more than 40 years old, matches well with clinical experience today. Of the 49 female patients he studied only 16% came from what were described as good or superior homes, 45% were from poor homes, and 32% from bad homes. Evidence of 'defective family relationships' was shown by 22%, 29% came from households where discipline was considered to be defective, and in 37% the home environment was described as 'vicious'. In over 50% one or both parents were of dull intelligence and in 18% either mentally defective or psychotic. Promiscuity, illegitimacy, incest and criminal behaviour were all prominent in the family histories.

MANAGEMENT AND TREATMENT

Offending in the mentally handicapped is usually the consequence of under-socialisation, poor internal controls and faulty social learning: educational under-achievement, lack of social and occupational skills and poor self-image are frequently additional factors. The aims of treatment, therefore, are to assist maturation, facilitate the development of adequate levels of self-control, instil a sense of personal worth and personal responsibility, establish acceptable social mores and improve social, occupational and educational skills. A properly formulated treatment programme with explicitly stated goals is essential. All personnel involved in care should work together to an agreed strategy and meet regularly to monitor progress and review plans. The principal elements of the treatment package are socialisation programmes, practical skills training, further education, counselling/supportive psychotherapy and in some cases specific behavioural programmes and sex suppressant or anti-aggressive medication (Day, 1990a, b).

The majority of mentally handicapped offenders can be managed in the community, supported by the mental handicap services and where appropriate the probation service. Hospitalisation is indicated when the offence committed is a serious one, when the patient is considered to be dangerous, or where the general needs of an individual for training, control and care cannot be met in a community setting (Day, 1990a).

A number of institutional programmes based on token economy regimes have been developed for mentally handicapped offenders (Burchard, 1967; Day, 1988; Denkowski and Denkowski, 1984; Denkowski, Denkowski, and Mabli, 1984; Fidura, Lindsey, and Walker, 1987; Sandford, Elzinga, and Grainger, 1987; Santamour and Watson, 1982). They aim to link personal behaviour with its consequences through the systematic issuing of tokens or points which can be exchanged for a range of back-up reinforcers contingent upon appropriate behaviour. They are applied on a group basis and involve a staged progression from secure to open care. Proper application requires a controlled environment, high staff to patient ratios, well-trained and experienced personnel and intensive support from a multidisciplinary team, and they are only suitable for use in specialised units. Good results have been reported (Day, 1988; Sandford, Elzinga, and Grainger, 1987). Holland and Murphy (1990) have criticised such a 'blanket', 'whole environment approach' on the grounds that it ignores individual needs and is difficult to transfer to the natural environment and advocate individually tailored treatment. The two are, however, by no means incompatible and individualised packages of social and personal skills training, further education and counselling are an essential feature of most schemes.

Psychological treatments which have been successful with non-handicapped offenders are only just beginning to be used for mentally handicapped offenders. Foxx, Bittle, Bechtel, and Livesay (1986) reviewed the available studies of behavioural treatments for sexually deviant behaviour in mentally handicapped individuals and concluded that while the majority lacked scientific rigour the results were in many cases favourable. Self-management techniques, so far used mainly in the management of disruptive and other inappropriate behaviours in severely mentally handicapped people (Gardner, Cole, Berry, and Nowinski, 1983; Woods and Lowe, 1986), have been used with some success in the mildly mentally handicapped presenting conduct difficulties (Cole, Gardner, and Karan, 1985). Milner (1962) has reported his experiences in the use of psychotherapy in the treatment of mentally handicapped delinquents and advanced the hypothesis that in many cases delinquent behaviour is the externalised expression of repressed guilt feelings about sex and death. Swanson and Garwick (1990) have described a successful group therapy programme for mentally handicapped sex offenders. A number of studies have demonstrated the value of the newer tranquillising drugs particularly in their depot forms, in reducing the level of difficult and disruptive behaviour in mentally handicapped patients (Craft and Schiff, 1980; Lynch, Eliatamby, and Anderson, 1985; Mlele and Wiley, 1986; Yar-Khan, 1981), and Day (1988) has reported their successful use as mood stabilisers in emotionally labile and aggressive offenders.

SERVICE PROVISION

Mentally disordered offenders have been provided for under Mental Health legislation in the UK since the early eighteenth century. Mentally handicapped offenders have largely been cared for in mental handicap institutions where some special units have been developed (Craft, 1984; Day, 1988; Mayor, Bhate, Firth, Graham, Knox, and Tyrer, 1990; Shapiro, 1969). The first Special Hospital for the care and treatment of dangerous mentally handicapped offenders was established in 1920 (Parker, 1985). Two reviews of services for mentally disordered offenders in the early 1970s (Butler, 1974; Glancy, 1974) proposed the establishment of Medium Secure Units to provide a level of security and care between that provided by the Special Hospitals and that provided in local units. The original concept included provision for mentally handicapped offenders alongside the mentally ill but this was never realised in practice and it is now accepted that special Medium Secure Units for mentally handicapped offenders are required (DoH, 1989; RCPsych., 1986), although so far few have been established (Isweran and Bardsley, 1987; Isweran and Brener, 1990; Smith, 1988).

There has been a marked reduction in the use of hospital orders for mentally handicapped offenders under the Mental Health Acts 1959, 1983, since the late 1960s in contrast to mentally ill and psychopathic offenders where the use has remained constant (Figure 5.1). Robertson (1981, 1982) has cited changing hospital admission policies consequent upon new philosophies of care, the introduction of the treatability clause into the 1959 and 1983 Mental Health Acts and the provision of alternative community services as the main reasons. However, while there has been a significant increase in the use of guardianship orders for the mentally ill there has been a steady decline in their use for the mentally handicapped since 1975 (Hughes, 1990). It seems more likely that more mentally handicapped offenders are being imprisoned. In a survey of mentally abnormal men remanded to Winchester Prison over a 5-year period, Coid (1988) found that mentally handicapped offenders, along with those with organic brain damage or chronic psychotic illness, were less likely to be accepted by the NHS and more likely to be imprisoned, confirming the conclusion of an earlier review of psychiatric morbidity amongst sentenced prisoners (Coid, 1984). Of reconvicted mentally handicapped offenders followed up by Gibbens and Robertson (1983a, b), 40% received a prison sentence compared to 20% of the mentally ill, and only 14% received a psychiatric disposal compared to 57% of the mentally ill. The prevalence of mental handicap in prison and other penal cohorts is three to four times that in the general population (Table 5.1). Lund (1990) has similarly

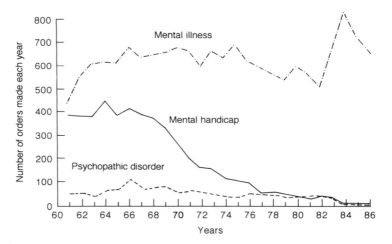

Figure 5.1   Hospital orders since 1961 by year and type of disorder (excluding restriction orders) (NHS figures only from 1983). From Robertson (1982) reproduced by kind permission, updated to 1986

reported a drastic decrease in the numbers of borderline retarded offenders receiving care orders under Danish mental health legislation since 1973. There are, of course, those who argue from principles of normalisation that mentally handicapped people should be treated within the penal system like any other offender. However, as Jackson (1983) aptly points out, this is a fundamental misunderstanding of the principle of normalisation and 'recognition of an individual's human worth does not logically require that society has to accord a retarded citizen identical treatment to that accorded to a non-retarded citizen' (p. 12). Furthermore, studies have demonstrated that mentally handicapped offenders are unable to adjust to prison regimes, are victimised by other prisoners and are much more likely to display aggressive behaviour (Reichard, Spencer, and Spooner, 1982; Smith, Algozzine, Schmid, and Hennly, 1990).

The treatment and care of mentally handicapped offenders has recently been highlighted by the implementation of Care in the Community policies and the planned phasing out of mental handicap hospitals in the UK. Service requirements have been reviewed by a DoH study team (DoH, 1989) and more recently in a major review of health and social services for mentally disordered offenders (DoH and Home Office, 1992). There is general consensus that specialised provision within the mental handicap psychiatry services is required because of the differences between mentally handicapped offenders and other mentally disordered offenders and their specialised treatment, rehabilitation and aftercare needs (Day, 1988, 1990a; DoH, 1989; DoH and Home Office, 1992; RCPsych., 1986). A similar conclusion has been reached in Holland where five specialised regional services for mentally handicapped offenders have been planned, two of which are already operational (Dosen, personal communication) and in the USA

Table 5.6 A comprehensive service model for the treatment and management of mentally handicapped offenders

Level	Facility	Role	No. places
National	Special Hospitals	Maximum security Medium- to long-term care	5/million popn [a]
Regional	Medium Secure Units	Medium security Medium-term care Rehabilitation of Special Hospital patients	10/million popn [b]
Sub-regional	Local Secure Units	Semi-security Medium- to long-term care Rehabilitation of Special Hospital and MSU patients	20/500 000 popn [c] (male) 10/500 000 popn (female)
Local community services	Specialised day and residential care services	Rehabilitation Aftercare Continuing care	
	Multiprofessional support teams	Assessment Treatment Support	

[a] Existing provision
[b] Oxford Regional Health Authority (1976)
[c] Day (1983)

where specialised units and management programmes have been developed in many states (Santamour and Watson, 1982).

The Department of Health and Home Office reviews (DoH, 1989; DoH and Home Office, 1992) concluded that a comprehensive range of specialised facilities is required, from community services for the majority to high-security provision for the most dangerous offenders, together with specialised rehabilitation and aftercare services for hospitalised offenders and some long-term facilities for those requiring continuing care with minimal security. The principal components of this service, together with estimates of bed requirements, are listed in Table 5.6. The local hospital unit is the mainstay of the service, providing the main treatment facility and acting as a base for professional staff and community services. Invariably, because of the small numbers involved and the need for economic and therapeutic viability, such units need to be provided on a regional or sub-regional basis. Day (1988) has described such a unit based in a mental handicap hospital and Murphy and her colleagues (Murphy, Holland, Fowler, and Reap, 1991; Murphy and Clare, 1991) have described a similar but smaller unit established within a general psychiatric hospital. There is debate as to the extent to which containment and locked facilities are required; it is suggested that this can be avoided with high staffing levels (Murphy *et al.*, 1991). A comprehensive package of aftercare, including domiciliary support, occupational placement, residential placement where required and leisure activities, is essential if social breakdown and drift back into offending are to be avoided (Craft, 1984; Day, 1988; Hunter, 1979; Walker and McCabe, 1973). Experience indicates that mentally handicapped offenders can rarely be satisfactorily managed in regular occupational and residential services for mentally handicapped people which are not geared to catering for their continuing need for structure and supervision (Day, 1988; Murphy and Clare, 1991). Specialised provision is required in the early stages of rehabilitation for the majority and on a continuing care basis in some cases.

REFERENCES

Aitken, J., Brunton, M., Jacobs, P. A., Price, W. H., and MacColl, K. (1971). Chromosome studies on male patients at a mental subnormality hospital. *Clinical Genetics*, **2**, 338–54.

Akesson, H. O., Forssman, H., Wahlstrom, J., and Wallin, L. (1974). Sex chromosome aneuploidy among men in three Swedish hospitals for the mentally retarded and maladjusted. *British Journal of Psychiatry*, **125**, 386–9.

Bearcroft, J. S., and Donovan, M. D. (1965). Psychiatric referrals from courts and prisons. *British Medical Journal*, **2**, 1519–23.

Bluglass, R. (1966). A psychiatric study of Scottish convicted prisoners. MD Thesis, University of St Andrews, Scotland.

Bluglass, R. (1980). Indecent exposure in the West Midlands. In D. J. West (ed.), *Sex Offenders in the Criminal Justice System*, Cropwood Conference Series No. 12. Cambridge: University of Cambridge Institute of Criminology, pp. 171–80.

Bowden, P. (1978). Men remanded into custody for medical reports. The selection for treatment. *British Journal of Psychiatry*, **132**, 320–31.

Bradford, J. M. W. (1982). Arson: a clinical study. *Canadian Journal of Psychiatry*, **27**, 188–93.

Bromberg, W., and Thompson, C. B. (1937). The relation of psychosis, mental defect and personality type to crime. *Journal of Criminal Law and Criminology*, **28**, 70–89.

Brown, B. S., and Courtless, T. F. (1968) The mentally retarded offender. In R. G. Allan, E. Z. Ferster, and J. G. Rubin, (eds), *Readings in Law and Psychiatry*. Baltimore, MA: Johns Hopkins Press, pp. 361–78.

Burchard, J. D. (1967). Systematic socialisation: A programmed environment for the rehabilitation of antisocial retardates. *Psychosocial Record*, **17**, 461–76.

Butler Committee (1974). Interim Report of the Committee on Mentally Abnormal Offenders, Cmnd. 5698. London: HMSO.

Casey, M. D. (1970). Criminological implications of chromosome abnormalities. In D. J. West, (ed.), *Proceedings of the Crockford Round Table Conference 1969*. Cambridge: Institute of Criminology, pp. 49–60.

Casey, M. D., Blank, C. E., Mobley, T., Kohn, P., Street, D. R. K., McDougall, J. G., Gooder, J., and Platts, J. (1971). *Special Hospitals Report No. 2*. HMSO: London.

Casey, M. D., Segal, L. J., Street, D. R. K. and Blank, C. E. (1966). Sex chromosome abnormalities in two state hospitals for patients requiring special security. *Nature*, **209**, 641–2.

Clare, I. C. H., Murphy, G. H., Cox, D., and Chaplin, E. H. (1992). Assessment and treatment of fire-setting: A single case assessment. *Criminal Behaviour and Mental Health*, **2**, 253–68.

Coid, J. (1984). How many psychiatric patients in prison? *British Journal of Psychiatry*, **145**, 78–86.

Coid, J. W. (1988). Mentally abnormal offenders on remand: 1.—Rejected or accepted by the NHS? *British Medical Journal*, **296**, 1779–82.

Cole, C. L., Gardner, W. I., and Karan, O. C. (1985). Self management training of mentally retarded adults presenting severe conduct difficulties. *Applied Research in Mental Retardation*, **6**, 337–47.

Court-Brown, W. M., (1968). Males with an XYY sex chromosome complement. *Journal of Medical Genetics*, **5**, 341–59.

Craft, M. (1969). The moral responsibility for Welsh psychopaths. In A. V. S. de Reuck and R. Porter, (eds), *The Mentally Abnormal Offender*. London: Churchill, pp. 91–4.

Craft, M. (1984). Should one treat or gaol psychopaths. In M. and A. Craft (eds), *Mentally Abnormal Offenders*. London: Ballière Tindall, pp. 384–96.

Craft, A., and Craft, M. (1983). *Sex Education and Counselling for Mentally Handicapped People*. Tunbridge Wells: Costello Press.

Craft, M., and Schiff, A. A. (1980). Psychiatric disturbance in mentally handicapped patients. *British Journal of Psychiatry*, **137**, 250–5.

Daly, R. F. (1969). Mental illness and patterns of behaviour in 10 XYY males. *Journal of Nervous and Mental Disease*, **149**, 318–27.

Day, K. (1983). A hospital based psychiatric unit for mentally handicapped adults. *Mental Handicap*, **11**, 137–40.

Day, K. (1988). A hospital based treatment programme for male mentally handicapped offenders. *British Journal of Psychiatry*, **153**, 635–44.

Day, K. (1990a). Mental retardation: Clinical aspects and management. In R. Bluglass and P. Bowden (eds), *Principles and Practice of Forensic Psychiatry*. Edinburgh: Churchill Livingstone, pp. 399–418.

Day, K. (1990b). Treatment of antisocial behaviour. In A. Dosen, A. Van Gennep, and G. J. Zwanikken (eds), *Treatment of Mental Illness and Behavioural Disorder in the Mentally Retarded*, Proceedings of the International Congress, 3 and 4 May 1990, Amsterdam. Leiden, Netherlands: Logon Publications, pp. 103–22.

Day, K. (in press). Mentally handicapped sex offenders: A clinical study. The 22nd Blake Marsh Lecture, Royal College of Psychiatrists, January 1989.

Denkowski, G. C., and Denkowski, K. M. (1984). Community based residential treatment model for mentally retarded adolescent offenders. In J. M. Berg, (ed.), *Perspectives and Progress in Mental Retardation*, vol. 1. *Social, Psychological and Educational Aspects*. Baltimore: University Park Press, pp. 303–311.

Denkowski, G. C., Denkowski, K. M. and Mabli, J. (1984). A residential treatment model for MR adolescent offenders. *Hospital and Community Psychiatry*, **35**, 279–81.

Department of Health (1989). Needs and Responses: Services for adults with mental handicap who are mentally ill, who have behaviour problems or who offend. London: Department of Health Leaflets Unit.

Department of Health and Home Office (1992). Review of health and social services for mentally disordered offenders and others requiring similar services. Final summary report. CM 2088. London: HMSO.

d'Orban, P. T. (1976). Child stealing: A typology of female offenders. *British Journal of Criminology*, **16**, 275–81.

d'Orban, P. T. (1990). Kidnapping, abduction and child stealing. In R. Bluglass and P. Bowden (eds), *Principles and Practice of Forensic Psychiatry*. Edinburgh: Churchill Livingstone, pp. 797–804.

Dyggve, H., and Kodahl, T. (1979). Disease pattern among 942 mentally retarded persons in a Danish county. *Acta Psychiatrica Scandinavica*, **59**, 381–94.

East, W. N., Stocks, P., and Young, H. T. P. (1942). The adolescent criminal: A medico-sociological study of 4000 male adolescents. London: J. and A. Churchill.

Eysenck, H. J. (1977). *Crime and Personality*. Third edition. London: Routledge and Kegan Paul.

Eysenck, H. J., and Gudjonsson, G. H. (1989). *The Causes and Cures of Criminality*. New York: Plenum Press.

Farrington, D. P., Biron, L., and Le Blanc, M. (1982). Personality and delinquency in London and Montreal. In J. Gunn and D. P. Farrington (eds), *Abnormal Offenders, Delinquency and the Criminal Justice System*. Chichester: Wiley, pp. 153–201.

Faulk, M. (1976). A psychiatric study of men serving a sentence in Winchester Prison. *Medicine, Science and the Law*, **16**, 244–51.

Fidura, J. G., Lindsey, E. R., and Walker, G. R. (1987). A special behaviour unit for treatment of behaviour problems of persons who are mentally retarded. *Mental Retardation*, **25**, 107–11.

Foxx, R. M., Bittle, R. G., Bechtel, D. R., and Livesay, J. R. (1986). Behavioural treatment of the sexually deviant behaviour of mentally retarded individuals. *International Review of Research in Mental Retardation*, **14**, 291–317.

Gardner, W. I., Cole, C. L., Berry, D. L., and Nowinski, J. M. (1983). Reduction of disruptive behaviours in mentally retarded adults: A self management programme. *Behaviour Modification*, **7**, 76–96.

Gebhard, P. H., Gagnon, J. H., Pomeroy, W. B., and Christenson, C. V. (1965). *Sex Offenders: An Analysis of Types*. London: Heinemann.

Geller, J. L., and Bertsch, G. (1985). Fire setting behaviour in the histories of a state hospital population. *American Journal of Psychiatry*, **142**, 464–8.

Gibbens, T. C. N. (1963). *Psychiatric Studies of Borstal Lads*. Maudsley Monographs No. 11. Oxford: Oxford University Press.

Gibbens, T. C. N. (1966). Aspects of Aftercare. Annual Report. London: Royal London Prisoners Aid Society Ltd, pp. 8–11 (quoted by Faulk, 1976).

Gibbens, T. C. N., and Robertson, G. (1983a). A survey of the criminal careers of hospital order patients. *British Journal of Psychiatry*, **143**, 362–9.

Gibbens, T. C. N., and Robertson, G. (1983b). A survey of the criminal careers of restriction order patients. *British Journal of Psychiatry*, **143**, 370–5.

Gibbens, T. C. N., Soothill, K. L., and Way, C. K. (1981). Sex offences against young girls: A long term record study. *Psychological Medicine*, **11**, 351–7.

Gilby, R., Woolf, L., and Goldberg, B. (1989). Mentally retarded adolescent sex offenders. A survey and pilot study. *Canadian Journal of Psychiatry*, **34**, 542–8.

Glancy, J. (1974). Revised Report of the Working Party on Security in NHS Psychiatric Hospitals. London: DHSS.

Glueck, B. (1918). A study of 608 admissions to Sing Sing Prison. *Mental Hygiene*, **2**, 85–151.

Goddard, H. H. (1920). *Human Efficiency and Levels of Intelligence*. Princetown: Princetown University Press.

Goring, C. (1913). *The English Convict*. London: HMSO.

Gostason, R. (1985). Psychiatric illness among the mentally retarded: A Swedish population study. Supplement No. 318, *Acta Psychiatrica Scandinavica*, **71**.

Gunn, J., and Fenton, G. (1969). Epilepsy in prisons: A diagnostic survey. *British Medical Journal*, **4**, 326–8.

Gunn, J., Maden, A., and Swinton, M. (1991). Mentally disordered prisoners. Home Office Report. London: HMSO.

Guze, S. B. (1976). *Criminality and Psychiatric Disorders*. Oxford: Oxford University Press.

Haskins, J., and Friel, C. (1973). *Project CAMIO: A national survey of the diagnosis and treatment of mentally retarded offenders in correctional institutions*, vol. 8. Huntsville Tax: Sam Houston State University (quoted by MacEachron, 1979).

Hingsburger, D. (1987). Sex counselling with the developmentally handicapped. The assessment and management of seven critical problems. *Psychiatric Aspects of Mental Retardation Review*, **6**, 41–6.

Hirschi, T., and Hindelgang, M. J. (1977). Intelligence and delinquency: A revisionist review. *American Sociological Review*, **42**, 571–87.

Holland, T., and Murphy, G. (1990). Behavioural and psychiatric disorder in adults with mild learning difficulties. *International Review of Psychiatry*, **2**, 117–35.

Home Office (1990). Statistics of mentally disordered offenders, England and Wales 1988. *Statistical Bulletin*, June 1990. Croydon, Surrey: Statistical Department, Home Office.

Home Office and DHSS (1987). Interdepartmental working group of Home Office and DHSS officials on mentally disturbed offenders in the prison system in England and Wales—Report May 1987.

Hook, E. B. (1973). Behavioural implications of the human XYY genotype. *Science*, **179**, 139–50.

Hughes, G. (1990). Trends in guardianship usage following the Mental Health Act 1983. *Health Trends*, **22**, 145–7.

Hunter, H. (1969). A controlled study of the psychopathology and physical measurements of Klinefelter's syndrome. *British Journal of Psychiatry*, **115**, 443–8.

Hunter, H. (1977). XYY males: Some clinical and psychiatric aspects deriving from a survey of 1811 males in hospitals for the mentally handicapped. *British Journal of Psychiatry*, **131**, 468–70.

Hunter, H. (1979). Forensic psychiatry and mental handicap. In F. E. James and R. P. Snaith (eds), *Psychiatric Illness and Mental Handicap*. London: Gaskell Press, pp. 141–6.

Hurley, W., and Monahan, T. M. (1969). Arson: The criminal and the crime. *British Journal of Criminology*, **9**, 4–21.

Isweran, M. S., and Bardsley, E. M. (1987). Secure facilities for mentally impaired patients. *Bulletin, Royal College of Psychiatrists*, **11**, 52–4.

Isweran, M. S., and Brener, N. (1990). Psychiatric disorders in mentally retarded patients and their treatment in a Medium Secure Unit. In A. Dosen, A. van Gennep and G. J. Zwanikken (eds), *Treatment of Mental Illness and Behavioural Disorder in the Mentally Retarded*. Leiden, Netherlands: Logon Publications.

Jacobs, P. A., Brunton, M., Melville, M. M., Brittain, R. P., and McClemont, W. F. (1965). Aggressive behaviour, mental subnormality and the XYY male. *Nature*, **208**, 1351–2.

Jacobs, P. A., Price, W. H., Brown, W. M. C., Brittain, R. P., and Whatmore, P. B. (1968). Chromosome studies on men in a maximum security hospital. *Annals of Human Genetics*, **31**, 339–58.

Jackson, H. F., Glass, C., and Hope, S. (1987). A functional analysis of recidivistic arson. *British Journal of Clinical Psychology*, **26**, 175–85.

Jackson, R. (1983). Mental retardation and criminal justice: Some issues and problems. *Mental Subnormality*, **29**, 7–12.

Jones, D. A. (1976). The health risk of imprisonment. Lexington, Mass.: Lexington Books.

Koller, H., Richardson, S. A., and Katz, M. (1983). Behaviour disturbance since childhood among a five year birth cohort of all mentally retarded young adults in a city. *American Journal of Mental Deficiency*, **87**, 386–95.

Koller, H., Richardson, S. A., Katz, M., and McLaren, J. (1982). Behaviour disturbance in childhood and early adult years in populations who were and were not mentally handicapped. *Journal of Preventive Psychiatry*, **1**, 453–68.

Koller, H., Richardson, S. A., and Katz, M. (1987). Antecedents of behaviour disturbance in mildly retarded young adults. *Upsala Journal of Medical Science*, Supplement 44, 105–10.

Kugel, R. B., Trembath, J., and Sagar, S. S. (1968). Some characteristics of patients legally committed to a state institutional for the mentally retarded. *Mental Retardation*, **6**, 2–8.

Leonard, M. F., and Sparrow, S. (1986). Prospective study of development of children with sex chromosome anomalies: A New Haven study in adolescence. In S. G. Ratcliffe and N. Paul (eds), *Prospective Studies on Children with Sex and Chromosome Aneuploidy*. New York: Alan R. Liss, pp. 221–49.

Levy, S. (1954). The role of mental deficiency in the causation of criminal behaviour. *American Journal of Mental Deficiency*, **58**, 455–64.

Lewis, N. D. C., and Yarnell, H. (1951). Pathological fire setting. Nervous and mental diseases. Monograph No. 82, New York: Coolidge Foundation.

Lund, J. (1990). Mentally retarded criminal offenders in Denmark. *British Journal of Psychiatry*, **156**, 726–31.

Lynch, D. M., Eliatamby, C. L. S., and Anderson, A. A. (1985). Pipothiazine Palmitate in the management of aggressive mentally handicapped patients. *British Journal of Psychiatry*, **146**, 525–9.

Maberly, A. (1950). Delinquency in handicapped children. *British Journal of Delinquency*, **1**, 125–8.

Mayor, J., Bhate, M., Firth, H., Graham, A., Knox, P., and Tyrer, S. (1990). Facilities for mentally impaired patients: Three years experience of a semi-secure unit. *Psychiatric Bulletin, Royal College of Psychiatrists*, **14**, 333–5.

McClintock, F. H. (1963). *Crimes of Violence*. London: Macmillan.

McCord, J. (1979). Some child rearing antecedents of criminal behaviour in adult men. *Journal of Personality and Social Psychology*, **37**, 1477–86.

MacEachron, A. E. (1979). Mentally retarded offenders: Prevalence and characteristics. *American Journal of Mental Deficiency*, **84**, 165–76.

McGarvey, B., Gabriele, W. F., Bentler, P. M., and Mednick, S. A. (1981). Rearing, social class, education and criminality: A multiple indicator model. *Journal of Abnormal Psychology*, **90**, 354–64.

McGuffin, P. (1984). Intelligence and mental handicap. In P. McGuffin, M. F. Shanks and R. J. Hodson (eds), *The Scientific Principles of Psychopathology*. London: Academic Press, pp. 173–90.

McKerracher, D. W., and Dacre, A. J. I. (1966). A study of arsonists in a special security hospital. *British Journal of Psychiatry*, **112**, 1151–4.

McKerracher, D. W., Street, D. R. K., and Segal, L. J. (1966). A comparison of the behaviour problems presented by male and female subnormal offenders. *British Journal of Psychiatry*, **112**, 891–7.

Mein, R. (1957). A survey of mentally defective sexual offenders in Harperbury Hospital. Unpublished.

Melnyk, J., Derencseny, I. A., Vanasek, F., Rucci, A. J., and Thompson, H. (1969). XYY survey in an institution for sex offenders and the mentally ill. *Nature*, **224**, 369–70.

Messinger, E., and Apfelberg, B. (1961). A quarter century of court psychiatry. *Crime and Delinquency*, **7**, 343–62.

Miller, M. E., and Sulkes, S. (1988). Fire setting behaviour in individuals with Klinefelter syndrome. *Paediatrics*, **82**, 115–17.

Milner, K. O. (1949). Delinquent types of mentally defective persons. *Journal of Mental Science*, **95**, 842–59.

Milner, K. O. (1962). The treatment of delinquent mental defectives by psychotherapy. In B. W. Richards (ed.), *Proceedings of the First Conference on Scientific Study of Mental Deficiency*. Dagenham, England: May & Baker, pp. 258–62.

Mlele, T. J. J., and Wiley, Y. V. (1986). Clopenthixol Decanoate in the management of aggressive mentally handicapped patients. *British Journal of Psychiatry*, **149**, 373–6.

Moffitt, T. E., Gabriele, W. F., Mednick, S. A., and Schulsinger, F. (1981). Socio-economic status, IQ and delinquency. *Journal of Abnormal Psychology*, **90**, 152–6.

Morris, J. V. (1948). Delinquent defectives—a group study. *American Journal of Mental Deficiency*, **52**, 345–69.

Murphy, G., and Clare, I. (1991). MIETS (Mental Impairment, Evaluation and Treatment Service). II. Psychological assessment and treatment, outcome for clients and service effectiveness. *Mental Handicap Research*, **4**, 180–206.

Murphy, G., Holland, A., Fowler, P., and Reap, J. (1991). MIETS: A service option for people with mild mental handicaps and challenging behaviour or psychiatric problems. I. Philosopy, service and service users. *Mental Handicap Research*, **4**, 41–66.

Murphy, W. D., Coleman, E. B., and Haynes, M. R. (1983). Treatment and evaluation issues with the mentally retarded offender. In J. D. Greer and I. R. Stuart (eds), *The Sexual Aggressor. Current Perspectives on Treatment*. New York: Van Nostrand Reinholt.

Murray, G. J., Briggs, D., and Davis, M. S. (1992). Psychopathic disordered, mentally ill and mentally handicapped sex offenders: A comparative study. *Medicine, Science and the Law*, **32**, 331–336.

Netley, C. T. (1986). Summary overview of behavioural development in individuals with neonatally identified X and Y aneuploidy. In S. G. Ratcliffe and N. Paul (eds), *Prospective Studies on Children with Sex and Chromosome Aneuploidy*. New York: Alan R. Liss, pp. 293–306.

Newton, M. S., Jacobs, P. A., Price, W. H., Woodcock, G., and Frazer, I. A. (1972). A chromosome survey of a hospital for the mentally subnormal. *Clinical Genetics*, **3**, 215–55.

Nielsen, J. (1970). Criminality among patients with Klinefelter's syndrome and the XYY syndrome. *British Journal of Psychiatry*, **117**, 365–9.

Nielsen, J., and Henricken, F. (1972). Incidence of chromosome aberrations among males in a Danish Youth Prison. *Acts Psychiatrica Scandinavica*, **48**, 87–102.

O'Sullivan, G. H., and Kelleher, M. J. (1987). A study of fire setters in the south west of Ireland. *British Journal of Psychiatry*, **151**, 818–23.

Oxford Regional Health Authority (1976). A survey of the need for secure psychiatric facilities in the Oxford region. Oxford: Department of Psychiatry, University of Oxford.

Parker, E. (1974). Survey on incapacity associated with mental handicap at Rampton and Moss Side Special Hospitals. Special Hospitals Research Report No. 11. Special Hospitals Research Unit. London: HMSO.

Parker, E. (1985). The development of secure provision. In L. Gostin (ed.), *Secure Provision*, London and New York: Tavistock, pp. 15–65.

Payne, C., McCabe, S., and Walker, N. (1974). Predicting offender—patients recon-
victions. *British Journal of Psychiatry*, **125**, 60–4.

Phillip, J. C., Lundstrom, D. O., and Hirschhorn, K. (1976). The frequency of chromosome aberrations in tall men with special reference to 47XYY and 47XXY. *American
Journal of Human Genetics*, **28**, 404–11.

Pitcher, D. R. (1975). The XYY Syndrome. In T. Silverstone and B. Barraclough (eds),
Contemporary Psychiatry. London: Gaskell Press, pp. 316–25.

Radzinowicz, L. (1957). Sexual offences: A report of the Cambridge Department of
Criminal Science. London: Macmillan.

Ratcliffe, S. G., Murray, L., and Tague, P. (1986). Edinburgh study of growth and
development with sex chromosome abnormalities. 3. In S. G. Ratcliffe and N. Paul
(eds), *Prospective Studies on Children with Sex and Chromosome Aneuploidy*. New
York: Alan R. Liss, pp. 73–118.

Ratcliffe, S. G., and Paul, N. (eds) (1986). *Prospective Studies on Children with Sex
Chromosome Aneuploidy*. New York: Alan R. Liss.

Reichard, C. L., Spencer, J., and Spooner, F. (1982). The mentally retarded defendant
offender. In M. Santamour and P. Watson (eds), *The Retarded Offender*. New York:
Praeger, pp. 121–39.

Reichel, H. (1987). The intelligence—criminality relationship. A critical review. Supplement 66, Department of Psychology, University of Stockholm, pp. 5–47.

Richardson, S. A., Katz, M., Koller, H., McLaren, J., and Rubinstein, B. (1979). Some
characteristics of a population of mentally retarded young adults in a British city. A
basis for estimating some service needs. *Journal of Mental Deficiency Research*, **23**,
275–85.

Richardson, S. A., Koller, H., and Katz, M. (1985). Relationship of upbringing to later
behaviour disturbance of mildly mentally retarded young people. *American Journal of
Mental Deficiency*, **90**, 1–8.

Robertson, G. (1981). The extent and pattern of crime amongst mentally handicapped
offenders. *Journal of the British Institute of Mental Handicap*, **9**, 100–3.

Robertson, G. (1982). The 1959 Mental Health Act of England and Wales: Changes in the
use of its criminal provisions. In J. Gunn and D. P. Farrington (eds), *Abnormal
Offenders, Delinquency and the Criminal Justice System*. Chichester, UK: Wiley,
pp. 245–68.

Robinson, C. B., Patten, J. W., and Kerr, W. S. (1965). A psychiatric assessment of
criminal offenders. *Medicine, Science and the Law*, **5**, 140–6.

Rooth, F. G. (1971). Indecent exposure and exhibitionism. *British Journal of Hospital
Medicine*, **5**, 521–33.

Roper, W. F. (1950). A comparative study of Wakefield Prison populations in 1948. Part
1. *British Journal of Delinquency*, **1**, 15–28.

Roper, W. F. (1951). A comparative study of the Wakefield Prison population in 1948 and
1949. Part 2. *British Journal of Delinquency*, **1**, 243–70.

Royal College of Psychiatrists (1980). *Secure facilities for Psychiatric Patients: A
Comprehensive Policy*. London.

Royal College of Psychiatrists (1986). Psychiatric services for mentally handicapped adults
and young people. *Bulletin, Royal College of Psychiatrists*, **10**, 321–2.

Sandford, D. A., Elzinga, R. H., and Grainger, W. (1987). Evaluation of a residential
behavioural programme for behaviourally disturbed mentally retarded young adults.
American Journal of Mental Deficiency, **91**, 431–4.

Santamour, M. B., and Watson, P. S. (eds) (1982). *The Retarded Offender*. New York:
Praeger.

Schilling, R. F., and Schinke, P. (1988). Mentally retarded sex offenders: Fact, fiction and
treatment. *Journal of Social Work and Human Sexuality*, **7**, 33–48.

Schroder, J., De La Chapelle, A. *et al.* (1981). The frequency of XYY and XXY men
among criminal offenders. *Acta Psychiatrica Scandinavica*, **63**, 272–6.

Shapiro, A. (1969). Delinquent and disturbed behaviour within the field of mental deficiency. In A. V. S. de Reuck and R. Porter (eds), *The Mentally Abnormal Offender*. London: Churchill, pp. 76–90.

Smith, C., Algozzine, B., Schmid, R., and Hennly, T. (1990). Prison adjustment of youthful inmates with mental retardation. *Mental Retardation*, **28**, 177–81.

Smith, J. (1988). An open forensic unit for borderline mentally impaired offenders. *Bulletin, Royal College of Psychiatrists*, **12**, 13–15.

Soothill, K. L., and Gibbens, T. C. N. (1978). Recidivism of sexual offenders: A reappraisal. *British Journal of Criminology*, **18**, 267–76.

Soothill, K. L., and Pope, P. J. (1973). Arson: A 20 year cohort study. *Medicine, Science and the Law*, **13**, 127–38.

Sourial, N., and Fenton, F. (1988). Testosterone treatment of an XYY male presenting with aggression: A case report. *Canadian Journal of Psychiatry*, **33**, 846–50.

Stott, D. H. (1962). Evidence for a congenital factor in maladjustment and delinquency. *American Journal of Psychiatry*, **118**, 781–91.

Sutherland, E. H. (1931). Mental efficiency and crime. In K. Young (ed.), *Social Attitudes*, New York: Holt.

Svendsen, B. B., and Werner, J. (1977). Offenders within ordinary services for the mentally retarded in Denmark. In P. Mittler (ed.), *Research to Practice in Mental Retardation*, Baltimore: University Park Press, pp. 419–24.

Swanson, C. K., and Garwick, G. B. (1990). Treatment for low functioning sex offenders: Group therapy and inter-agency co-ordination. *Mental Retardation*, **28**, 155–61.

Taylor, P. J., and Gunn, G. (1984). Violence and Psychosis. 1. Risk of violence among psychotic men. *British Medical Journal*, **288**, 1945–9.

Tennent, G., McQuaid, A., and Lougnane, T. (1971). Female arsonists. *British Journal of Criminology*, **9**, 4–21.

Thompson, C. B. (1937). A psychiatric study of recidivists. *American Journal of Psychiatry*, **94**, 591–604.

Tong, J. E., and Mackay, G. W. (1969). A statistical follow up of mental defectives of dangerous or violent propensities. *British Journal of Delinquency*, **9**, 276–84.

Tutt, N. S. (1971). The subnormal offender. *British Journal of Subnormality*, **17**, 42–7.

Walker, N., and McCabe, S. (1973). *Crime and Insanity in England*, vol. 2, Edinburgh: Edinburgh University Press.

West, D. J., and Farrington, D. P. (1973). *Who Becomes Delinquent?* London: Heinemann.

West, D. J., and Farrington, D. P. (1977). *The Delinquent way of Life*. London: Heinemann.

Wiener, S., Sutherland, G., Bartholomew, A. A., and Hudson, B. (1968). XYY males in a Melbourne Prison. *Lancet*, **1**, 150 (letter).

Wildenskov, H. O. T. (1962). A long term follow up of subnormals originally exhibiting severe behaviour disorders or criminality. In *Proceedings of the London Conference on the Scientific Study of Mental Deficiency*. Dagenham, London: May and Baker, pp. 217–22.

Witkin, H. A., Mednick, S. A., Schulsinger, F., Bakkestrom, E., Christiansen, K. O., Goodenoff, D. R., Hirschhorn, K., Lundsteen, C., Owen, D. R., Phillip, J., Rubin, D. B., and Stocking, M. (1976). Criminality in XYY and XXY men. *Science*, **193**, 547–55.

Woods, P. A., and Lowe, C. F. (1986). Verbal self-regulation of inappropriate social behaviour with mentally handicapped adults. In J. M. Berg (ed.), *Science and Service in Mental Retardation*. London: Meuthen, pp. 353–62.

Woodward, M. (1954). The role of low intelligence in delinquency. *British Journal of Delinquency*, **5**, 281–303.

Yar-Khan, S. (1981). The psychiatrically violent patient. *British Medical Journal*, **282**, 1400–1.

Yesevage, J. A., Benezech, M., Ceccaldi, S., Bourgeois, M., and Addad, M. (1983). Arson in mentally ill and criminal populations. *Journal of Clinical Psychiatry*, **44**, 128–30.

6

The Treatment of People with Learning Disabilities Who Offend

CHRIS CULLEN
Psychological Laboratory, University of St Andrews, Scotland, UK

THE NATURE OF THE PROBLEM

The extent to which having a learning disability (a preferable term to the more common 'mental handicap') predisposes a person towards offending, and the extent to which learning disabilities are over- or under-represented amongst offenders, are questions which have been of interest for decades. Earlier opinions have been shown to be based on false premises. For example, Goring's (1913) claim that 'the greatest single cause of delinquency and crime is low grade mentality, much of it within the limits of feeblemindedness' can be seen nowadays to be without foundation.

As discussed in Chapter 5, estimates of the proportion of offenders with a learning disability vary considerably from study to study: for example from 2% (Denkowski and Denkowski, 1985) to 10% (Marsh, Friel and Eissler, 1975). The picture is complicated further by differing interpretations of what constitutes a learning disability (e.g. before what point on an intelligence scale should a person be before being classified as having a learning disability rather than, in older terminology, merely being 'slow'). While prevalence figures are relevant for some purposes the issue will be side-stepped in this chapter in favour of considering some of the factors which might be relevant to helping people with a learning disability who offend. Anyway, the general principles which are outlined here are, I believe, of relevance to all people; those with a learning disability are not radically and qualitatively different.

Clinical Approaches to the Mentally Disordered Offender
Edited by K. Howells and C. R. Hollin © 1993 John Wiley & Sons Ltd

Some aspects of the relation between learning disability and criminality have been described concisely by Lund (1990):

(a) there is a slightly increased prevalence of the mildly and borderline retarded among offenders,
(b) there is a slightly increased incidence of crime among the mildly and borderline retarded,
(c) the higher prevalence should be expected because of the higher risk of detection for this population,
(d) there is a clearly decreased incidence of crime among the severely and profoundly retarded,
(e) in relation to other offenders there are more arsonists and sexual offenders among mentally retarded criminals,
(f) borderline retarded offenders exhibit more recidivism. (p. 726)

Kunjukrishnan and Varan (1989) also provide a summary of some of the relevant parameters—although these authors inexplicably use the old-fashioned (and probably offensive) term 'mental subnormality' in their paper:

> The reported incidence of crime among the MS varies, depending on the setting of the study, the population studied and the parameters used in diagnosing mental subnormality. The MS have multiple handicaps—in the intellectual, emotional and socio-economic aspects of their life, and hence they have difficulty in conforming to the societal norms. As a result they come in contact with the criminal justice system—they are tempted to commit crimes as they do not always understand the full consequences of their actions; they are often used by others to commit offences for them; they are more easily caught, as they are not as capable of avoiding detection as others; they are not as able, as others, to defend themselves, even with the help of legal counsel. Hence, they are more often convicted and sentenced than others. (p. 448)

Drawing some common threads from these reviews it is apparent that there is a problem, of significant extent, both for people with learning disabilities who offend *and* for the criminal justice system. This problem is multifaceted, and different specialists will each have their own contribution to make to the field. For my own part there are some skill repertoires which people with learning disabilities lack with which I shall not be concerned in what follows, including the ability to commit offences and escape detection, and to conduct a skilful defence in court. It is not that I do not think these to be important; instead I want to look at how to help people to avoid offending. To anticipate later parts of the chapter, it seems that poor self-control and an absence of more appropriate repertoires, together with behaviour which is under the control of immediate rather than longer term contingencies, are all at the core of the problem for many offenders with learning disabilities. I want to consider some of the practical and conceptual issues which relate to these and which face us when working with this group.

FUNCTIONAL APPROACHES

First I want to establish some ground rules. Because of the obvious complexity of the situation we must avoid simplistic 'solutions' which suggest that offending behaviour simply deserves punishment. I know of no evidence which supports such a view. Although offending is behaviour which is clearly inappropriate, and which in due course has to be eliminated, I am convinced that we have to avoid pathological approaches. These have been defined as:

> Focusing on the elimination of [behaviour] through a variety of means ... Such approaches often consider the problem in terms of a pathology which, regardless of how it was established, or developed, or is maintained, is to be eliminated. (Goldiamond, 1974, p. 14)

There are at least two good reasons for eschewing purely pathological approaches with learning-disabled offenders. Firstly, removing behaviour leaves a vacuum which will then be filled by an alternative repertoire. Unless the alternative repertoire is carefully arranged it could easily turn out to be as problematic as the behaviour it replaces. For example, dealing with aggression towards others, perhaps by some response prevention or punishment procedure, *might* work, but it would not be surprising to find some 'symptom substitution' whereupon the person became self-abusive, tried to run away, counter-attacked, and so on.

A second reason for being wary about pathological approaches is that they are generally not particularly effective, and their supporting literature is often weak. Cullen, Hattersley, and Tennant (1981) reviewed the 1978 volumes of the *Journal of the Experimental Analysis of Behavior* (which publishes basic behavioural research) and the *Journal of Applied Behavior Analysis* (which publishes applied research). Approximately 75% of the papers in *JEAB*, and 80% of the papers in *JABA*, were concerned with *increasing* rather than decreasing behavioural repertoires. A similar review of the 1989 volumes reveals 93% of *JEAB* papers and 91% of *JABA* papers describing procedures for increasing behaviour (Cullen, 1991a). Of course there are occasions when we must deal directly with a repertoire with the intention of eliminating it, but these occasions are fewer than we might imagine.

In place of pathological approaches we should try constructional ones, defined as approaches:

> ... whose solution to problems is the construction of repertoires (or their reinstatement or transfer to new situations) rather than the elimination of repertoires. (Goldiamond, 1974, p. 14)

Being constructional involves a functional approach (cf. Cullen, 1983), that is, knowing something about why a person is behaving in a particular way. Such an analysis tries to identify the contingencies—the setting events and the consequences—which maintain the offending behaviour. Once we know something about these, then it is more likely that adaptive alternative repertoires *which achieve similar consequences and/or which are occasioned by the same setting events* can be established to replace the offending behaviour. As we shall see later in the chapter, contingencies for behaviours which are non-offending are likely to be complex—possibly more complex than those responsible for offending.

Although the constructional approach can be expressed simply enough it is therapeutically sophisticated. However, it is not an impossible prescription for action, and even an incomplete analysis is likely to lead to more effective treatment of offending behaviour than approaches aimed only at dealing with the offending behaviour and which ignore the contingencies of which it is a function.

It is important to emphasise that the constructional approach does not simply lead to ignoring maladaptive behaviour. There will be occasions when the offending behaviour cannot be left to one side while alternatives are established (cf. Cullen and Tennant, 1991). Donnellan and her colleagues have developed an organisational model for planning interventions which takes into account the need to be reactive to maladaptive behaviour while at the same time dealing with the problem by establishing repertoires (cf. Donnellan, LaVigna, Negri-Shoultz, and Fassbender, 1988; LaVigna, Willis, and Donnellan, 1989). In considering treatment issues I shall touch upon the different elements to this model. There are four, each of which has an important role in dealing with offending behaviour. They are:

(1) Reactive strategies are those which deal immediately with the behaviour and its effects.
(2) Proactive strategies are those whose function is to change the frequency of the problem behaviour over time, and for establishing acceptable alternative repertoires.

Proactive strategies may be of three kinds:

(2a) Ecological changes—in which some of the setting events are manipulated to affect the problem behaviour and to set the occasion for acceptable behaviour.
(2b) Positive programming—to establish new behaviour which might ultimately displace or replace offending behaviour.
(2c) Direct treatment—to achieve more immediate change than is usually possible by ecological manipulations and positive programming.

Most comprehensive 'treatment programmes' for offending behaviour will have aspects coming under each of these headings, and I cannot imagine an effective programme which would not have each element. Consider, for example, the hospital-based treatment programme for offenders with learning disabilities described in Day (1988). There is a *skills training* component, to establish personal, domestic, leisure and occupational skills, which is essentially *positive programming* aimed towards establishing more useful repertoires. An *incentive scheme*, which is based on the token economy system, is partly an *ecological manipulation* to establish an environment in which adaptive behaviour is more likely to occur and be maintained. *Counselling and supportive psychotherapy* probably involves both positive programming and ecological changes (i.e. arranging an environment wherein complaints and problems can be resolved without recourse to offending), and the *drug therapy* which is offered may be partly a *reactive strategy* aimed at calming a person during a crisis, and partly a *direct treatment strategy*, to achieve a degree of calmness and tranquillity more quickly than would be possible with other aspects of the programme.

When thinking about approaches for helping offenders with learning disabilities, therefore, Donnellan's model acts as a useful prompt for ensuring that the programme is comprehensive. We shall return to this later.

THERAPEUTIC INTERVENTIONS

Successful programmes should contain both reactive and proactive strategies. Unfortunately, though, there are remarkably few programmes which are specifically aimed at learning-disabled offenders. Morris and Braukmann's *Behavioral Approaches to Crime and Delinquency: A Handbook of Application, Research and Concepts* (1987) mentions none. Denkowski and Denkowski (1985) describe a community-based residential treatment programme for learning-disabled adolescent offenders; Swanson and Garwick (1990) describe a group therapy approach for sex offenders who are low-functioning. There are others scattered throughout the literature, but it is not my intention to try to identify them all in this chapter. What I want to do is to look at some of the general principles involved in designing clinical interventions for learning-disabled offenders, and to consider whether there are still further avenues to be explored.

It is important to do this because there is generally recognised to be a problem with all interventions for offending, particularly those that have set out to permanently 'cure' the problem. Wolf, Braukmann, and Ramp (1987) put it thus:

> The consensus seems to be that, to date, there have not been any clear and convincing demonstrations of effective strategies for curing or preventing the problems of serious anti-social children or adults. Almost every review of delinquency treatment and prevention research has been largely pessimistic .... [T]he many behavioural efforts to remediate criminal and delinquent behaviour, though meritorious in many respects, have not, as a rule, demonstrated long-term differential effects. (p. 352)

There is no reason to expect other than that this conclusion holds for programmes with learning-disabled offenders. However, the nature of the learning disability might have an influence on what steps we should be taking to increase the efficacy of our approaches.

Many offenders who have learning disabilities seem to have what might loosely be called a lack of self-control. In fact one author has recently suggested that over-susceptibility to immediate contingencies and a failure to self-regulate behaviour might be particularly characteristic of people with learning disabilities (Whitman, 1990). In the terminology of applied behaviour analysis, behaviour is contingency-shaped rather than rule-governed, a topic returned to later in the chapter. The ability to say 'I should not do this because of …. Instead it would be better to do …' is often missing. Realising this, and seeing that many apparently straightforward environmental measures have failed to control behaviour, has prompted researchers and clinicians in recent years to investigate the possibility of helping people with learning disabilities to acquire self-control repertoires. If we can help someone to regulate or control their own behaviour, perhaps they will be less likely to offend?

I want first to look at this literature in general, and then at a specific sub-category which has been of much interest in recent years—anger control.

Self-control

There is now an abundance of literature which shows that, under some circumstances, some people with learning disabilities can acquire repertoires which may be described as self-control. The qualifiers are important for reasons which will become apparent later. One of the most quoted and well controlled studies will serve to illustrate some of the important aspects of self-control procedures.

Cole, Gardner, and Karan (1985) addressed the issue of severe conduct difficulties in six mentally retarded adults. Their subjects had reputations for 'potentially dangerous behaviour' and several had found themselves in trouble with the law as a result. The behaviour of all six subjects had resulted in dismissal from, or precluded entry into, community vocational schemes. Most of them reacted 'impulsively' to provocation in work settings. A treatment package was designed to provide individualised coping responses which would be managed by the subjects themselves.

The treatment package consisted of establishing the skills of:

(1) Self-monitoring and labelling of behaviours such as shouting, working quietly, hitting and using self-control.
(2) Self-evaluation by means of discriminating appropriate and inappropriate behaviours and displaying the relevant card with the words Good Adult Worker or Not Adult Worker (together with a photograph of the subject smiling while working or frowning while not working).
(3) Self-consequation with coins for Good Adult Worker behaviour.
(4) Self-instruction of appropriate behaviour.

To establish these behaviours a variety of procedures were used, including modelling and role-play using video and audiotape. After intensive training each subject returned to the workplace and at the end of specified intervals *and* upon each occurrence of inappropriate behaviour the subject was prompted by a trainer to self-monitor (describe their behaviour at that time); to self-evaluate (use the Good/Not Adult Worker card); and self-consequate (accept coin and/or say whether he/she was proud of behaving that way). Subjects were also encouraged to self-instruct and to rehearse appropriate strategies.

During the next phase, trainer intervention was provided less often, and after a few days was not needed. The work-interval was increased gradually from 5 minutes to 75 minutes. A further, maintenance, phase resulted in the timer and the display card being removed. Follow-up data were collected for 9 months.

This treatment package resulted in immediate decreases in disruptive behaviour. A 1-day probe when the money containers were removed and subjects told that earnings would be credited to their accounts resulted in a slight increase in verbal and physical disruption, an effect which was reversed by a return to maintenance conditions. Clearly the results are important and show that such procedures can be effective. However, a number of issues arise from this and similar studies (cf. Gardner and Cole, 1989; Shapiro, 1986).

Many of the inappropriate behaviours which have been addressed by such studies have been high-frequency conduct disorders and disruption. Much offending (e.g. sex offences and arson) is relatively low rate, and would not, therefore, lend itself to interventions which require direct alternative or incompatible behaviours. Also, although studies are often presented as dealing with seriously challenging behaviour they rarely do so. Gardner and Cole's (1989) chapter is in a volume on 'The treatment of severe behaviour disorders' but they acknowledge that 'relatively minimal attention has been devoted to investigating the effects of self-management approaches on clinically significant aberrant behaviour' (p. 21).

While there is some evidence to persuade us that treatment packages can have an effect, it has not yet been possible to identify how much each of the components of a package contributes to the effect. Although this may be less important from a pragmatic point of view than it is from a scientific one, it does mean that clinicians still lack clear guidance on what procedures and in which combinations to try for particular clients. This is important because research so far tells us that not all subjects acquire the self-management strategies. It would be useful to know whether this is entirely a function of the person's lack of cognitive and other abilities or whether it is partly a function of the procedures. It is this latter possibility which I shall investigate later in the chapter.

What seems clear from all the descriptions of self-management programmes is that they generally involve a good deal of external control by the person's environment. Shapiro (1986) describes this as self-control through contingency management, which nicely side-steps the argument about whether self-control is 'really' behavioural control from within the person. Catania (1975, 1976) for example talks of the 'myth of self-reinforcement' because the environmental contingencies which are responsible for arranging consequences for one's own behaviour are overlooked when the prefix 'self' is attached to a word. However, there is another, a more 'cognitive', variety of self-control which Shapiro (1986) calls self-control by cognitive change, and it is to this I now turn.

Anger Control

It is a debatable point to what extent behaviour is *caused* by internal events. Most psychologists adopt the view that internal—or private (cf. Skinner, 1945)—

events, often labelled as thoughts, cognitions, feelings, impulses and so on, are so closely implicated in the control of behaviour, including offending behaviour, that people must be taught how to manipulate them. Even for behaviour analysts private events are relevant, at least as setting events for behaviour (cf. Cullen, 1991b). It makes sense, therefore, if it is at all feasible, to teach people how to control their private events.

With respect to offending behaviour, *anger* is an emotion which seems *prima facie* to be involved. Temper control is often seen to be a major difficulty for many clients and there have been many therapeutic packages designed to deal with the problem. The most popular has been that devised by the American psychologist Raymond Novaco (Novaco, 1975, 1985). This programme has a number of elements, not all of which are suitable for people with learning disabilities (e.g. keeping a diary), and clinicians who have adopted Novaco's approach have had to make some adaptations.

Benson, Rice, and Miranti (1986) devised an anger management programme for a group of 54 mildly or moderately disabled volunteers, building on a programme which Benson and other colleagues had adapted for institutionalised children. Treatment groups of 5–9 people met in 12 weekly, 90-minute sessions. Anger management training involved relaxation (using the Jacobson tension-release method); self-instruction (discriminating between 'coping' statements and 'trouble' statements and then practising making coping statements at first aloud and then silently); and problem-solving (involving a four-step plan to solve the problems arising during an anger-arousing situation). Three comparison groups receiving only one each of these elements were also involved in this study.

Unfortunately, outcome data are presented as statistical probability levels and it is impossible to assess the clinical significance of any effects. Benson, Rice, and Miranti (1986) report that 'a cognitive-behavioural approach to [anger management] may be effective with mentally retarded adults .... The general lack of between-group differences, coupled with the absence of a no-treatment group, makes it difficult to interpret treatment effects. Each component of training ... may all have influenced improved responding' (p. 729).

Influenced partly by this, and by the apparent successes of Navaco's approach, I and a group of colleagues (Black, Cullen, Dickens, and Turnbull, 1988) carried out a pilot study to investigate the therapeutic effectiveness of an anger control procedure for learning-disabled clients with temper control problems. Our 12 participants had histories of aggressive outbursts, damage to persons (including themselves) and to property. Two lived at home with their parents, although they were in imminent danger of being taken into special residential facilities. The other ten were all resident in locked hospital wards or on a special Behaviour Disorder Unit. None of the participants had psychotic symptoms and all were in the mild or moderate range of learning disability. Their mean age was 35.6 years, with a range of 21–53 years. The project proceeded through the following stages.

Baseline was a period during which no specific interventions were introduced, but participants learned to use tape-recorders to record 'angry' incidents at the end of each day; what had led up to them; how they had behaved; and what had been the consequences of their actions. This information was used to focus discussion during the therapeutic stages of the project.

Stage 1 was an *education phase* and it involved discussions about the nature of anger. Using actual incidents in which people had been involved (gleaned from listening to the tape diaries) and video tapes (e.g. from popular television programmes) participants learned to describe the events leading up to feelings, and expressions, of anger; the consequences of temper outbursts; the ways in which feelings of anger could be useful in identifying the need to think of different courses of action; what those courses of action might be; and the different consequences of alternative ways of expressing anger. This was carried out in groups of 2 or 3 individuals for most people involved, although some participants were unwilling to work with others and were seen alone. In order to ensure that each participant had an equivalent intervention a standard protocol was used which outlined the topics to be covered and the manner in which they were to be discussed in the therapy sessions. Sessions were twice weekly for each participant (once weekly for the 2 subjects who were living at home), lasting one hour and were conducted by a clinical psychologist or a research nurse. An unexpected finding during this phase of the project was that few people initially were able to describe their own anger and had to be taught self-disclosure. Phase 1 lasted some five months for most subjects— a period far in excess of that reported by workers such as Benson and Novaco.

Stage 2 was a *skill acquisition phase* concerned with acquiring new ways of dealing with anger. This involved role-plays with video feedback of different approaches to dealing with provoking situations and specific training in problem-solving procedures. For example, using a scenario from their own experience, or a scene from a television programme, participants would be taught to say how the problem could be dealt with differently and what would be the different outcome. Each participant was taught to use relaxation procedures as a helpful way of dealing with the tension which is often concurrent with anger. They were taught that their own arousal would be the signal to engage in relaxation procedures. 'Homework' assignments were set in which participants practised their new skills outwith therapeutic sessions. Again a protocol was used to ensure that comparative interventions were received by each participant. This stage lasted up to 30 weeks for each subject.

The final stage of the project was a *follow-up phase* during which therapy was discontinued but outcome measures were collected. Because it was not obvious at the outset which data would be helpful in assessing whether or not the package would be effective, we collected a number of different kinds of information. Some purpose-made rating scales of social behaviour showed no differences before and after therapy, although other measures indicated great variability amongst subjects and between stages. One of our main dependent variables was a measure of the frequency of anger outbursts and a standard data collection form was devised for this purpose. Participants were very different on this measure. All of those who had a significant number of outbursts during baseline showed a decrease to near zero at follow-up, but this improvement could not be tied to a particular stage of the project. Each participant showed marked weekly variations in frequency of anger outbursts.

Other measures, such as changes in different aspects of adaptive behaviour, also showed changes between participants, with some people improving as the project went on while others showed no change. A measure of how easily people could be provoked (adapted from Novaco's Provocation Inventory) seemed to indicate that some people were less easily provoked at the end of the project while others were more easily provoked!

What can we say, therefore, about self-control procedures for people with learning disabilities and seriously antisocial behaviour? We are not in a position to claim that anger management and similar programmes are or are not effective, nor are we in any strong position when it comes to designing a package of therapeutic procedures which might be tried. However, it does seem that our work, taken together with that of others who have investigated self-control procedures, indicates that it is not impossible for people with learning disabilities to acquire self-control procedures, but that there is no clear way of establishing such skills. Perhaps we ought to step back from the hurly-burly of therapy to more manageable experimental situations to see whether we have a clear enough understanding of some of the basic processes which are involved in self-control.

SELF-REGULATION, CORRESPONDENCE AND RULE-GOVERNED BEHAVIOUR

To summarise the case so far, it has been suggested that: (i) offending behaviour probably involves a lack of self-control for many offenders who have learning disabilities; (ii) partly because of the absence of effective programmes of direct contingency management, and partly because it is widely assumed that self-control is somehow 'better' than externally imposed control, researchers have investigated the efficacy of self-control procedures, but unfortunately; (iii) self-control studies have not so far been generally helpful because either they deal with behaviours which are not of clinical interest (so far as this chapter is concerned) such as work productivity or, if they deal with clinically important behaviour, as in our own anger-management project described above, the results are inconclusive.

There are different interpretations of this situation. One is that learning-disabled clients cannot reliably achieve self-control, especially for serious anti-social behaviour. This seems unduly pessimistic, especially as an across-the-board generalisation. Another possibility is that we have an incomplete and inadequate analysis of the concept of self-control, and it is this which leads to the failures in much of the research. Let us pursue this a little further.

What are the essential characteristics of the behaviour we refer to as self-control? One is that behaviour comes under the control of distant or indirect consequences; a corollary of this is that immediate consequences (such as the gratification which might immediately follow a sexual assault) are eschewed in favour of more distant or indirect consequences. Malott (1989) provides a comprehensive analysis of the distinction between contingencies that are direct-acting and those that are not. This analysis might be helpful to us in understanding the concept of self-control.

Contingencies that are direct-acting are those in which behaviour produces outcomes which function as reinforcers or punishers for that behaviour. Assaulting a person, for example, might result in violent retribution, which could act as a punisher for that behaviour. Alternatively aggression, under some circumstances, could be reinforced if it did not lead to a counter-attack but resulted in some gain, such as being able then to take the victim's money. Direct-acting contingencies involve immediate, probable and/or sizeable outcomes and are generally very effective. They have been studied extensively in the laboratory and in natural settings for many years and we know a good deal about them. It is clear that for many people with learning disabilities such contingencies occupy the greater part of their behavioural ecology.

Contingencies which are not direct-acting involve outcomes which are not effective consequences (i.e. reinforcers or punishers) for the behaviour which they follow because these consequences are improbable, delayed and/or small. These contingencies may be described by statements such as 'behave this way and in the future you will get ...' or 'if you do this you may get ... but the likelihood is slight'. Malott (1989) uses examples such as the relation between dental flossing and long-term healthy outcomes, but offending/not offending clearly fits the same scenario, and demonstrates the conflict between direct- and indirect-acting contingencies. If you attack this person and steal his money, you get an immediate and powerful consequence. There may or may not be a longer-term consequence, *if* you are caught, but it will be considerably delayed. If you do not attack and steal, but do something else, the immediate consequence, if there is any, will almost certainly be less powerful than having the person's money.

Malott's analysis of the experimental behavioural literature and of everyday logic leads him to the conclusion that *only* outcomes which are immediate, probable and sizeable can be effective. Since it is undeniable that contingencies which are not direct-acting do control the behaviour of many people, our task is to discover what it is that is mediating between behaviour and the distant outcomes. That is, how might indirect contingencies be mediated in those many instances when behaviour produces improbable, delayed and/or small consequences? One obvious candidate is self-regulation or self-instruction, which is a component of most of the self-control procedures. A clinical anecdote will illustrate.

A 21-year-old man with mild learning disabilities lived in a hostel which was situated on an inner city housing estate. Often he was teased and taunted by children when he left the hostel, and his way of dealing with this was to chase the children and hit them. Not surprisingly this was frowned upon, especially by the children's parents. I suggested a simple self-regulation procedure which involved the following steps. Each morning he was asked to appear in the hostel manager's office and recite, out loud: 'When anyone shouts at me, or teases me, I must not throw things or chase them. Instead I must turn around and walk away.' Next, he had to whisper the words, and then finally stand in silence and say them to himself. Immediately on completion of this third step a tick would be placed in the appropriate part of a chart which he took back to his room. At the end of each week, 5 ticks could be exchanged for a visit, with me, to a local gym.

This was an uncomplicated clinical intervention, with no experimental design, but the result was a decrease to zero of assaults on children. The young man was asked to report all incidents of teasing (which decreased once he stopped chasing the children) and it seemed that there might have been some sort of relationship between the self-talk and the successful self-control.

What is of interest is *how* such a procedure might be having an effect. Was it anything to do with the self-talk, or was it only that he knew he got to come to the gym with me if he behaved himself? During the past decade there has been an increasing literature on say-do correspondence which has tried to address the issue. The relation between verbal and non-verbal behaviour has long been acknowledged as central to development processes (cf. Luria, 1961) and to some aspects of clinical work (especially in psychotherapy), and behaviour analysts began to take a keen interest in the topic when Israel (1978) identified some of the conceptual and methodological issues which are raised by investigations of the correspondence (or lack of it) between saying and doing.

Karlan and Rusch (1982) have identified a number of possible relations such as *positive correspondence* (saying then doing); *negative correspondence* (not saying then not doing); and *non-correspondence* (saying then not doing OR not saying then doing). These are relations concerned with the production of behaviour, but, especially relevant for offenders, we should also be aware of relations which are concerned with inhibiting behaviour. These would be *positive correspondence* (saying not then not doing); *negative correspondence* (not saying not then doing); and *non-correspondence* (saying not then doing OR not saying not then not doing).

I cannot consider here the research related to each of these; suffice it to say that the concept of say-do correspondence gives us a way of thinking about verbal self-regulation. What we now need to address is the question of relevant parameters. Let us consider first the typical paradigm in teaching say-do correspondence. A response (X) is chosen which is at low frequency in the person's repertoire. A verbal response such as 'I will do X' is taught to the person and they are then rewarded for doing X after having said 'I will do X', that is, the chain of behaviour rather than either of its components is reinforced. A number of questions now become important:

(1) Can maintenance be demonstrated, i.e. will subjects continue to do what they say they will do even when reinforcement is discontinued?
(2) Can generalisation be demonstrated, i.e. will subjects perform a behaviour which has not been directly reinforced?
(3) What are the necessary and/or sufficient relations between the statement and the behaviour?

All of these have been investigated during the past few years, usually with children, and across a wide variety of behaviours (although, unfortunately, not yet offending or seriously antisocial behaviour). We now know that say-do correspondence can be taught; it may be maintained in the absence of external reinforcement; and it sometimes generalises to untaught behaviour.

Deacon and Konarski (1987) have explored what might be involved in say-do correspondence, and this analysis may have some practical relevance to those who are interested in how this paradigm might apply to offenders. They investigated whether verbalisations are an important aspect of say-do correspondence by comparing a reinforcement (do only) procedure with a correspondence (say-do) training. Their subjects were 12 people with learning disabilities who had to perform a variety of table-top tasks (such as pressing one of a number of different buttons) each of which had a specific computer-produced consequence (such as an electronic beeper or flashing green light). Social and monetary reinforcement were used.

After a *baseline* phase, during which the least frequent naturally occurring responses were identified for each subject, there was a *verbal control* phase, during which subjects were taught appropriate verbal responses such as 'I am only going to press (target behaviour)'. These were reinforced with monetary and social rewards (e.g. '[Name], that's good! You said you are going to only [target behaviour]. Because of this you can have this extra money. This extra money is for saying, I will only [target behaviour]'). Which button was pressed was recorded, but pressing was not reinforced.

During the *treatment* phase half the group were given correspondence training while the other half received reinforcement only for pressing. The particular target button was selected at random for each subject. The correspondence training was similar to the verbal control training, but now reinforcement only followed demonstration of correspondence between saying and doing. Verbalisations were followed only by praise. The subjects in the reinforcement group were told that they would have the chance to earn more money—but were not told specifically what they would have to do. The correct response was not even prompted, but it was reinforced if and when it appeared.

After this phase there was a return to the verbal control phase and then a 2-month follow-up. There was a near-zero rate of target behaviour for all subjects at baseline and this was hardly affected by the verbal control stage. There was a total lack of correspondence between saying and doing for all subjects.

The correspondence training and reinforcement treatments produced very similar results with 5 of the 6 subjects in the correspondence group reaching criterion and 3 of the 6 reinforcement subjects reaching criterion, with a further 2 showing large improvement. One person in each group showed no training effect. Reverting to the verbal control condition and at follow-up 4 subjects in each group maintained the trained target response at levels comparable to training and displayed strong evidence of generalisation to untrained responses.

This study demonstrates that it is feasible to establish say-do correspondence, but the process is obviously more complex than simply reinforcing a verbal/nonverbal behavioural sequence. Furthermore, it raises the issue of what is being learned. It might be verbal self-regulation, or it could be another behavioural process. What Deacon and Konarski (1987) suggest is that their procedures of correspondence training and their outcomes may be examples of rule-governed behaviour rather than verbal self-regulation. (See also Baer, Detrich, and Weninger, 1988, who provide some support for this idea, and Ward and Ward, 1990, who suggest that verbal self-regulation may be a necessary condition unless rule-governed behaviour occurs.)

The concept of rule-governed behaviour is one which may have relevance to how to understand how some people are able to behave for deferred, improbable or small consequences, and how they avoid engaging in behaviour (such as offending) which would result in probable, immediate and sizeable outcomes, while other people find these difficult. Rule-governed behaviour has long interested behaviour analysts (cf. Skinner, 1966) and has been the subject of a good many conceptual and experimental analyses in recent years (cf. Hayes, 1989).

Rules are verbal statements which specify contingencies. If Malott (1989) is right and the only effective outcomes are those which are immediate, sizeable and/or probable, what might mediate at least some delayed outcomes are *rules*. The verbal statements in say-do correspondence may be rules for behaving (cf. Zettle, 1990). Self-instructions may be rules which specify contingencies and the self-awareness engendered by some insight therapies might also involves rules. Rules and rule-governed behaviour are ubiquitous and may be at the basis of much 'self-control'.

How do rules control behaviour? Malott (1989) examines various possibilities and suggests that rules often act as motivating operations which increase the effectiveness of behavioural consequences which are contingent on following (or not following) the rules. There are likely to be other behavioural functions which are served by rules, such as acting as a cue or a discriminative stimulus, or providing 'automatic' behavioural consequences such as feelings of guilt (e.g. following the rule statement 'I must work 3 hours on this paper today'), or even providing the opportunity for 'self-reinforcement' or 'self-punishment' (cf. Malott, 1989, for a discussion of each of these). From our point of view, however, what is interesting is whether or not people with learning disabilities can acquire the relevant verbal behaviour. Malott (1989) suggests that there may be problems:

> [A]ll of this rule-control seems to require a highly developed repertoire on the part of the person whose behaviour is being controlled. (p. 302)

which might tell us something about why many people with learning disabilities seem unable to behave with respect to delayed contingencies. However Malott (1989) goes on to suggest five prerequisites for effective control by rules.

(1) Specific rules must be able to control behaviour. That is, the person must be able to respond to verbal behaviour, such as 'do this' and 'don't do that'.

(2) Novel rules must be able to control behaviour. There has to be the possibility of generalised rule control, so that we do not have to train every specific act. The control by specific rules is a necessary precursor of control by novel rules.

(3) Performance must evoke accurate self-evaluation. People have to be able to evaluate their own behaviour to determine whether or not it matches the rule. Inability to do this would mean that self-reinforcement or self-punishment could not occur.

(4) Self-evaluation must evoke the (self-) delivery of behavioural consequences. Once the person has ascertained that there was a match between the rule and their behaviour there has to be some delivery of effective consequences.

(5) Effective behavioural consequences must be available. This means that we would have to have available consequences which were meaningful to the person.

Malott goes on to point out that the necessary existence of such prerequisites might be taken to imply that behaving for delayed outcomes is 'precarious and fragile'—and so it is! For people who do not have learning disabilities as much as those who do.

THE POSSIBILITY OF A CLINICAL PROGRAMME?

What, then, about people with learning disabilities who offend? In this chapter it has been suggested that this is a problem, both for the people themselves and for the community in general, and that there is, as yet, no ready-made 'package' of procedures to use. Certainly simple eliminative/punitive approaches will rarely be the answer, because much offending behaviour is low frequency and any punishing stimuli would be so delayed and/or infrequent as to be largely ineffective.

More promising will be to adopt a constructional approach, establishing behaviour to displace offending. In other words, the person has to be given repertoires which are more worthwhile than the offending, and to do this is a great challenge to the service. The approach will almost certainly have to be multidimensional, and will probably have to have both reactive (to deal directly with the offending behaviour) and proactive elements. Of the proactive elements I have concentrated on positive programming, that is establishing new behaviours to displace offending. Ecological manipulations to make the person's environment more conducive to non-offending, and even direct treatment if offending is persistent, may be necessary, but there is not the space here to cover these—nor is there yet much empirical work available.

Self-control repertoires seem to be essential, but there is a lack of conceptual as well as empirical clarity in this area. Certainly it is possible to use packages of procedures to achieve some self-control, although I have doubts that these would be effective with serious antisocial behaviour. There is no evidence yet available to gainsay this opinion. But I do not think that this is because the whole concept of self-control is inappropriate. We do not yet have a research base for such a pessimistic conclusion. Rather I suspect that we have given insufficient attention to what might be going on when we exhibit self-control.

From a behaviour analytic perspective much behaviour which is described as self-control seems to involve some degree of verbal self-regulation, and some correspondence between *saying* (to others or to oneself) and *doing* (or not doing). I have mentioned some of the research during the past decade into this topic (although it is not concerned with seriously antisocial behaviour). Nevertheless, 'common sense' observation of the behaviour of non-offenders suggests that it is an area which is worthy of more serious consideration by clinicians.

When faced with an offender who clearly has a significant learning disability, what should one do? There are few (if any) 'tried-and-tested' packages of procedures which would contain all the necessary elements, nor even much in the way of reactive procedures, other than restraint (which will work only for as long as the restraint is present). Nor are there direct treatment programmes other than punishment or threats of punishment, in whatever guise, which we know to be largely ineffective and which certainly do not establish more useful, competing, repertoires.

If Malott (1989) is correct in his analysis of the prerequisite behaviours for rule-governed behaviour, it makes sense to assess the extent to which each is present as a strong repertoire for the person, and, for those which are absent, to set up specific teaching programmes to establish them.

Can the person follow instructions, and to what degree of complexity? Can the person make relatively fine discriminations between events in her/his environment, and can she/he make *conditional discriminations*, that is 'do this rather than that under these conditions, but that rather than this under those conditions'? It would not be surprising to find that many people with learning disabilities would need some help to follow rules, especially those involving more complex discriminations.

Next, can the person follow new rules with which they have not previously been in contact? To be a successful part of a self-regulation repertoire, it would be important that such rules were sufficiently dissimilar to the specific rules with which the person had been taught to allow us to have confidence that there was *clinically significant* generalised rule control. The limit to the degree to which rules could be generalised would lie in the hands of the clinician/trainer. How ingenious could one be in devising test situations which were sufficiently far from, yet related to, the specific situations which one had first taught?

Self-evaluation is a quite separate skill, one which needs to be carefully operationalised. Basic distinctions between 'good behaviour' and 'bad behaviour' (cf. Cole, Gardner, and Karan, 1985, described above) are crucial, but on their own would be insufficient. Behaviour is rarely evaluated as simply either positive or negative; it generally falls somewhere along a continuum, and its place on the continuum may depend on circumstances. People should be taught to make conditional evaluations of other's behaviour, as well as their own, ranking behaviours according to the environmental contingencies. For example, as I write there is a war going on in Iraq. We are told that behaviour which under most circumstances would be considered 'bad' (i.e. bombing cities) is actually, under current circumstances, 'good'—or at least 'less bad'. It is not too fanciful to accept that individual behaviours should also be conditionally evaluated. The behaviour of pushing a person to the ground is 'bad' if the intent is to steal their money, but (arguably) much 'less bad' if the intent is to protect a third person from being attacked. It is probably important to teach the person with learning disabilities to evaluate the behaviour of others before evaluating their own behaviour since it seems likely that we learn to label our own behaviour after labelling the behaviour of others (cf. Skinner, 1945).

Donnellan *et al.* (1988) have pointed out the importance of what they call 'ecological manipulation'. Put more simply, a person's environment has to support and maintain new repertoires. Following specific and novel rules, and self-evaluation, all must have some meaning, some worth, for the individual. This means that they must evoke consequences. Something has to change as a result of these new repertoires, and that something has to matter to the person. From a functional point of view (described earlier in the chapter) it would make sense to see whether the consequences which maintain offending can be used to maintain new, adaptive repertoires. Of Malott's five points these last two— self-delivery of consequences and ensuring that meaningful consequences are available on an immediate and powerful basis—are likely to be the most difficult to arrange. Most people with learning disabilities have lives which are characterised by poverty and relative friendlessness. It is not going to be easy to ensure that more adaptive repertoires can be maintained in impoverished circumstances, but this is the challenge of helping people with learning disabilities who offend.

REFERENCES

Baer, R. A., Detrich, R., and Weninger, J. M. (1988). On the functional role of the verbalisation in correspondence training procedures. *Journal of Applied Behavior Analysis*, **21**, 345–58.

Benson, B. A., Rice, C. J., and Miranti, S. V. (1986). Effects of anger management training with mentally retarded adults in group treatment. *Journal of Consulting and Clinical Psychology*, **54**, 728–9.

Black, L., Cullen, C., Dickens, P., and Turnbull, J. (1988) Anger control. *British Journal of Hospital Medicine*, **20**, 325–9.

Catania, A. C. (1975). The myth of self reinforcement. *Behaviorism*, **3**, 192–9.

Catania, A. C. (1976). Self-reinforcement revisited. *Behaviorism*, **4**, 157–62.

Cole, C. L., Gardner, W. I., and Karan, O. C. (1985). Self management training of mentally retarded adults presenting severe conduct difficulties. *Applied Research in Mental Retardation*, **6**, 337–47.

Cullen, C. (1983). Implications of functional analysis. *British Journal of Clinical Psychology*, **22**, 137–8.

Cullen, C. (1991a). Positive teaching and the aversive debate. *Positive Teaching*, **2**, 1–6.

Cullen, C. (1991b). Radical behaviourism and its influence on clinical therapies. *Behavioural Psychotherapy*, **19**, 47–58.

Cullen, C., Hattersley, J., and Tennant, L. (1981). Establishing behaviour: The constructional approach. In G. Davey (ed), *Applications of Conditioning Theory*. London: Methuen.

Cullen, C., and Tennant, L. (1991). Working with people who have severe learning disabilities. In J. S. Marzillier and J. Hall (eds), *What is Clinical Psychology?* (2nd ed.). Oxford: Oxford University Press.

Day, K. (1988). A hospital based treatment programme for male mentally handicapped offenders. *British Journal of Psychiatry*, **153**, 635–44.

Deacon, J. R., and Konarski, E. A. (1987). Correspondence training: An example of rule governed behaviour? *Journal of Applied Behavior Analysis*. **20**, 391–400.

Denkowski, G. C., and Denkowski, K. M. (1985). Community based residential treatment of the mentally retarded adolescent offender: Phase I, reduction of aggressive behaviour. *Journal of Community Psychology*, **13**, 299–305.

Donnellan, A. M., LaVigna, G. W., Negri-Shoultz, N., and Fassbender, L. L. (1988). *Progress Without Punishment: Effective Approaches for Learners with Behavior Problems*. New York: Teachers College Press.

Gardner, W. I., and Cole, C. L. (1989). Self-management approaches. In E. Cipani (ed.), *The Treatment of Severe Behavior Disorders: Behavior Analysis Approaches*. Washington: AAMR.

Goldiamond, I. (1974). Toward a constructional approach to social problems. Ethical and constitutional issues raised by applied behaviour analysis. *Behaviorism*, **2**, 1–84.

Goring, C. (1913). *The English Convict*. London: HMSO.

Hayes, S. C. (ed.) (1989). *Rule Governed Behavior: Cognition, Contingencies, and Instructional Control*. London: Plenum Press.

Israel, A. C. (1978). Some thoughts on correspondence between saying and doing. *Journal of Applied Behavior Analysis*, **11**, 271–6.

Karlan, G. R., and Rusch, F. R. (1982). Correspondence between saying and doing: Some thoughts on defining correspondence and future directions for application. *Journal of Applied Behavior Analysis*, **15**, 151–62.

Kunjukrishnan, P., and Varan, L. R. (1989). Interface between mental subnormality and law: A review. *Psychiatric Journal of the University of Ottawa*, **14**, 439–52.

LaVigna, G. W., Willis, T. J., and Donnellan, A. M. (1989). The role of positive programming in behavioural treatment. In E. Cipani (ed.), *The Treatment of Severe Behavior Disorders: Behavior Analysis Approaches*. Washington: AAMR.

Lund, J. (1990). Mentally retarded criminal offenders in Denmark. *British Journal of Psychiatry*, **156**, 726–31.

Luria, A. R. (1961). *The Role of Speech in the Regulation of Normal and Abnormal Behavior*. New York: Pergamon Press.

Malott, R. W. (1989). The achievement of evasive goals: Control by rules describing contingencies that are not direct acting. In S. C. Hayes (ed.), *Rule Governed Behavior: Cognition, Contingencies and Instructional Control*. London: Plenum Press.

Marsh, R. L., Friel, C. M., and Eissler, V. (1975). The adult MR in the criminal justice system. *Mental Retardation*, **13**, 21–5.

Morris, E. K., and Braukmann, C. J. (eds) (1987). *Behavioral Approaches to Crime and Delinquency: A Handbook of Application, Research and Concepts*. New York: Plenum Press.

Novaco, R. W. (1975). *Anger Control: The Development and Evaluation of an Experimental Treatment*. Lexington, MA: Lexington Books.

Novaco, R. W. (1985). Anger and its therapeutic regulation. In M. A. Chesney and R. H. Rosenman (eds), *Anger and Hostility in Cardiovascular and Behavioral Disorders*. New York: Hemisphere Publishing.

Shapiro, E. S. (1986). Behaviour modification: Self-control and cognitive procedures. In R. P. Barrett (ed.), *Severe Behaviour Disorders in the Mentally Retarded: Nondrug Approaches to Treatment*. London: Plenum Press.

Skinner, B. F. (1945) The operational analysis of psychological terms. *Psychological Review*, **42**, 270–7, 291–4.

Skinner, B. F. (1966). An operant analysis of problem solving. In B. Kleinmuntz (ed.), *Problem Solving: Research, Method and Theory*. New York: Wiley.

Swanson, C. K., and Garwick, G. B. (1990). Treatment for low functioning sex offenders: Group therapy and inter-agency coordination. *Mental Retardation*, **28**, 155–61.

Ward, W. D., and Ward, S. W. (1990). The role of subject verbalisation in generalised correspondence. *Journal of Applied Behavior Analysis*, **23**, 129–36.

Whitman, T. L. (1990). Self-regulation and mental retardation. *American Journal on Mental Retardation*, **94**, 347–62.

Wolf, M. M., Braukmann, C. J., and Ramp, K. A. (1987). Serious delinquent behaviour as part of a significantly handicapping condition: Cures and supportive environments. *Journal of Applied Behavior Analysis*, **20**, 347–59.

Zettle, R. D. (1990). Rule governed behaviour: A radical behavioural answer to the cognitive challenge. *Psychological Record*, **40**, 41–9.

7

Psychopathy and Crime: A Review

ROBERT D. HARE
CATHERINE E. STRACHAN
University of British Columbia, Vancouver, Canada
and
ADELLE E. FORTH
Carleton University, Ottawa, Canada

INTRODUCTION

Given the cluster of traits that define the disorder—impulsivity, callousness, egocentricity, selfishness, lack of guilt, empathy, and remorse, and so forth—it should come as no surprise that psychopathy is implicated in a disproportionate amount of the serious repetitive crime and violence in our society. In this chapter we provide an overview of recent research on psychopathy and crime, with some emphasis on violence. Before doing so, however, it is necessary to clarify what we mean by the term psychopathy. This is a crucial starting point because of the terminological and conceptual confusion that has characterized the clinical and research literature for over 100 years.

THE DEFINITION AND ASSESSMENT OF PSYCHOPATHY

Psychopathy is a personality disorder that is associated with a constellation of affective, interpersonal, and behavioural characteristics (see Cleckley, 1976; Hare and Cox, 1978; McCord and McCord, 1964; Weiss, 1987). Psychopaths display shallow and short-lived emotions, are lacking in empathy, guilt, and remorse, are unable to form lasting bonds with others, and have a general disregard for the consequences of their actions on others. They are glib, egocentric, selfish, deceitful, manipulative, impulsive, sensation-seeking, and irresponsible. Not

Clinical Approaches to the Mentally Disordered Offender
Edited by K. Howells and C. R. Hollin © 1993 John Wiley & Sons Ltd

surprisingly, many psychopaths routinely fail to fulfil social obligations and come into frequent contact with the criminal justice system.

There are many other psychopaths who manage to function more or less within the bounds of the law. Little scientific information is available on these individuals—variously referred to as adaptive, successful, or non-criminal psychopaths—largely because of the difficulties in obtaining enough hard data to make adequate assessments, but also because of the problems involved in getting them to participate in research. As a result, most of the empirical research on psychopathy has been conducted with prison inmates.

Terms such as psychopath, sociopath, and antisocial personality disorder (APD) have all been used to refer to what is often assumed to be the same construct. However, these diagnostic labels differ in terms of the criteria sets used to define them, with the result that there is no assurance that each refers to the same underlying construct. For example, APD, as described by the revised third edition of the *Diagnostic and Statistical Manual of Mental Disorders* (DSM-III-R; American Psychiatric Association, 1987) focuses almost exclusively on easily measured antisocial and criminal behaviours. The result is a diagnostic category that has good reliability but questionable validity (Frances and Widiger, 1986; Hare, Hart, and Harpur, 1991; Widiger, Frances, Pincus, Davis, and First, 1991). The problem is that the criteria for APD fail to capture the affective and interpersonal characteristics of psychopathy long considered fundamental to the disorder. As a consequence of its focus on antisocial behaviours APD is more closely allied with persistent criminality and social deviance than with psychopathy. Indeed, as many as 80% of incarcerated male offenders meet the criteria for APD (Correctional Service of Canada, 1990).

In contrast to the behavioural criteria used for a diagnosis of APD, the *International Classification of Diseases* (ICD-10; Sartorius, Jablensky, Cooper, and Burke, 1988) category F60.2, 'dyssocial personality disorder,' includes both behaviours and personality traits in its list of criteria. This category makes explicit reference to such characteristics as egocentricity, callousness, lack of guilt, and poor interpersonal relationships, traits all considered central to psychopathy.

In England and Wales the term psychopathic disorder is a legal category under the Mental Health Act (MHA) of 1959 and its 1983 amendments. The MHA defines psychopathic disorder as 'a persistent disorder or disability of mind ... which results in abnormally aggressive or seriously irresponsible conduct.' Blackburn (1990) has commented that this definition equates psychopathic disorder with social deviance. In this respect, the MHA definition is not unlike the DSM-III-R specifications for APD. Both differ from conceptualizations that make explicit use of inferences about personality traits (e.g. see Hare, 1991).[1]

---

[1] The American Psychiatric Association's Task Force for the forthcoming DSM-IV is aware of the problems with APD, and is currently conducting field trials that may result in substantial changes in the diagnostic criteria for the disorder (see Widiger *et al.*, 1991). Four sets of items are being evaluated in the APD Field Trials: (i) the current criteria for APD; (ii) a shortened set of the current criteria; (iii) the ICD-10 criteria for dyssocial personality disorder; and (iv) a 10-item set derived from the Hare Psychopathy Checklist-Revised (PCL-R; Hare, 1991).

Self-report inventories are often used in research as the primary method to diagnose psychopathy. However, their use for research purposes is problematic. Many of these inventories lack demonstrated reliability and validity. In addition, self-report scales are susceptible to malingering and impression management, a particular concern with individuals who may be skilled at deception and manipulation (Hare, Forth, and Hart, 1989). Moreover, self-report scales designed to measure psychopathy, such as the Psychopathic Deviate (*Pd*) from the Minnesota Multiphasic Personality Inventory (MMPI), the Socialization (*So*) scale from the the California Psychological Inventory (CPI), or the antisocial scale from the Millon Clinical Multiaxial Inventory (MCMI-II), seem to measure only the social deviance components of psychopathy (Hare, 1985, 1991; Harpur, Hare, Hakstian, 1989; Hart, Forth, and Hare, 1991). Like the DSM-III-R category of APD, these scales do not do a very good job of measuring the affective and interpersonal features of psychopathy.

THE REVISED PSYCHOPATHY CHECKLIST (PCL-R)

A measure of psychopathy that is closely tied to traditional clinical conceptions of the disorder is the 22-item Psychopathy Checklist (PCL; Hare, 1980) and its 20-item revision (PCL-R; Hare, 1991). The PCL and PCL-R are highly correlated and measure the same construct (Hare, Harpur, Hakstian, Forth, Hart, and Newman, 1990). Each version consists of a set of clinical rating scales designed to assess behaviours and personality traits considered fundamental to psychopathy (for an overview of the psychometric properties and correlates of the PCL-R see Hart, Hare, and Harpur, 1991). In fact, the strength of the PCL and PCL-R lies in the inclusion of these essential personality traits.

In contrast to the large percentage of offenders receiving a diagnosis of APD, only about 15% to 25% of offenders meet the PCL-R criteria for psychopathy. An asymmetric association between the two procedures exists: the majority of psychopaths defined by the PCL-R meet the APD criteria, but most offenders with an APD diagnosis do not meet the PCL-R criteria for psychopathy.

The items in the PCL-R are presented in Table 7.1. Each item is scored on a 3-point scale on the basis of extensive institutional files and a semi-structured interview. PCL-R scores range from 0 to 40, and represent the degree to which an individual resembles the prototypical psychopath. For research purposes a cutoff score of 30 (34 for the PCL) has proven useful for the diagnosis of psychopathy. There is a substantial body of evidence attesting to the reliability and validity of the PCL-R (Hare, 1991; Hare *et al.*, 1990; Harpur, Hare, and Hakstian, 1989; Hart, Hare, and Harpur, 1991). With respect to the former, Hart, Hare, and Harpur (1991) reported that the alpha coefficient for the PCL-R, aggregated over seven samples of male prison inmates from Canada, the United States, and England ($N = 1192$), was 0.87; the intraclass correlation was 0.83 for a single rating and 0.91 for the mean of two ratings.

Although they meet statistical criteria for a homogeneous measure of a unidimensional construct, both the PCL and the PCL-R consist of the same two

Table 7.1   Items in the Hare Psychopathy
Checklist-Revised (PCL-R)

Item

---

   (1)   Glibness/superficial charm[a]
   (2)   Grandiose sense of self-worth[a]
   (3)   Need for stimulation/proneness to boredom[b]
   (4)   Pathological lying[a]
   (5)   Conning/manipulative[a]
   (6)   Lack of remorse or guilt[a]
   (7)   Shallow affect[a]
   (8)   Callous/lack of empathy[a]
   (9)   Parasitic lifestyle[b]
  (10)   Poor behavioural controls[b]
  (11)   Promiscuous sexual behaviour
  (12)   Early behaviour problems[b]
  (13)   Lack of realistic, long-term goals[b]
  (14)   Impulsivity[b]
  (15)   Irresponsibility[b]
  (16)   Failure to accept responsibility for actions[a]
  (17)   Many short-term marital relationships
  (18)   Juvenile delinquency[b]
  (19)   Revocation of conditional release[b]
  (20)   Criminal versatility

Source from Hare (1991).
[a] Loads on Factor 1.
[b] Loads on Factor 2.

stable factors (Hare *et al.*, 1990; Harper, Hakstian, and Hare, 1988; see Table 7.1 for the items that define these factors in the PCL-R). Although correlated about 0.5 on average, the factors have differential patterns of intercorrelations with external variables. Factor 1 reflects interpersonal and affective characteristics, such as egocentricity, manipulativeness, callousness, and lack of remorse, considered the essence of the clinical concept of psychopathy. This Factor is correlated with classic clinical descriptions of psychopathy, prototypicality ratings of narcissistic personality disorder, and self-report measures of narcissism, but negatively correlated with self-report measures of empathy and anxiety. It projects onto the Arrogant/Calculating octant of the interpersonal circumplex, an octant that has also been labelled Narcissistic/Exploitative (Wiggins, 1982; Wiggins, Trapnell, and Phillips, 1988). Factor 2 reflects those characteristics of psychopathy associated with an impulsive, antisocial, and unstable lifestyle. This factor is most strongly correlated with diagnoses of APD, criminal behaviours, substance abuse, and self-report measures of psychopathy. It projects onto the Cold-heartedness dimension of the interpersonal circumplex.

Each of the factors can be measured reliably. Thus, in the seven samples of prison inmates described above the alpha coefficient was 0.84 for Factor 1 and 0.77 for Factor 2. The intraclass correlation for a single rating and for the mean of two ratings was, respectively, 0.72 and 0.86 for Factor 1, and 0.83 and 0.91 for Factor 2 (Hart, Hare, and Harpur, 1991).

PSYCHOPATHY AND CRIME

In the review that follows we will focus on research that used the PCL-R, or its predecessor, the PCL, for the assessment of psychopathy. There are two main reasons for doing so. First, there is an extensive literature attesting to their reliability and validity. Second, they provide a common metric for operationalizing the construct of psychopathy, with the result that method variance is considerably reduced.

It is important to note here that several of the PCL and PCL-R items are directly or indirectly related to criminal behaviours. In order to prevent 'bootstrapping' most of the studies of psychopathy and crime described below either took this into account statistically or were careful to delete items that were related to the dependent variables (criminal behaviours) of concern.

As suggested in the Introduction, the personality traits that define psychopathy are compatible with a criminal lifestyle and a lack of concern for societal norms or for the feelings, rights, and welfare of others. Research with adjudicated criminals clearly indicates that psychopaths are indeed more criminally active than are other criminals throughout much of their lifespan.

Hare and Jutai (1983) compared the criminal behaviours of 97 psychopaths and 96 non-psychopaths, defined on the basis of a reliable 7-point rating scale that measured the extent to which an individual matched the prototypical 'Cleckley' psychopath. This scale was a precursor of, and highly correlated with, the PCL (Hare, 1980). The mean number of charges per year free for all offences was 5.06 for the psychopaths and 3.25 for the non-psychopaths. The mean number of charges per year free for violent offences was more than three times higher for the psychopaths (0.91) than for the non-psychopaths (0.27).

Wong (1984) analysed the criminal records of a random sample of 315 male inmates from minimum, medium and maximum security institutions in Canada. Psychopaths were defined by a PCL score of at least 30 and non-psychopaths by a score of 20 or less. Compared with the non-psychopaths, the psychopaths committed more than twice as many offences per year free (mean of 4.4 and 1.9, respectively), almost nine times as many institutional offences (6.3, 0.73), and had their first formal contact with the law at an earlier age (24.1, 17.8).

Hare and McPherson (1984) investigated the association between psychopathy (as measured by the PCL) and violence in a sample of 227 male inmates of a medium-security institution. Because two of the PCL items (poor behavioural controls; many types of offences) reflect violent or criminal behaviours, they were deleted to avoid overlap between the PCL and the dependent variables. The sample was divided into groups with high, medium, and low PCL scores. The percentage of inmates in each group convicted of various types of violent crimes between the ages of 16 and 30 is presented in Table 7.2. It is clear that inmates with high PCL scores (psychopaths) were more likely to have been convicted for

Table 7.2   Percentage of inmates in each PCL group convicted of a violent crime between the ages of 16 and 30

Crime category	PCL group		
	High	Medium	Low
Murder	5.5	5.3	10.1
Possession of weapon	34.2	24.0	13.9
Robbery	49.3	44.0	21.5
Assault	45.2	22.7	19.0
Kidnapping	12.3	4.0	1.3
Rape	9.6	5.3	6.3
Vandalism	16.4	2.7	6.3
Fighting	15.1	8.0	1.3
Any violent crime	84.9	64.0	54.4
N	73	75	79

Source: From Hare and McPherson (1984).
Note: PCL = Psychopathy Checklist (Hare, 1980). The analysis period was age 16 to 30. Group differences were significant at the $p < 0.005$ level for all but murder and rape.

a violent offence than were other inmates. Other analyses indicated that the mean number of convictions per year free for violent offences was considerably greater for inmates with high PCL scores (1.00) than it was for those with medium (0.36) or low (0.27) PCL scores.

In a study of psychopathy and violence, Serin (1991) analysed the criminal histories of 87 male inmates assessed with the PCL-R. He found that psychopaths were more likely to commit a violent offence, to use weapons and to make threats of violence, than were non-psychopaths. The psychopaths also became more angry in response to provocative, hypothetical scenarios than did other inmates.

Kosson, Smith, and Newman (1990) investigated the association between psychopathy and crime in 230 white inmates and 70 black inmates of a state correctional facility. The PCL-R was used for the assessment of psychopathy; item 20 (criminal versatility) was deleted and the scores prorated to a 20-item scale. Psychopaths of both races generally had more extensive criminal histories than did non-psychopaths. Thus, for the white inmates the mean number of charges for violent and nonviolent offences was, respectively, 1.96 and 9.06 for the psychopaths, and 1.23 and 4.08 for the non-psychopaths. For the black inmates the corresponding values were 3.09 and 8.00 for the psychopaths, and 1.80 and 5.40 for the non-psychopaths. In addition, the psychopaths committed a greater variety of different types of offences than did the non-psychopaths. Using raw data provided by the authors we determined that the correlation between PCL-R scores and the total number of charges (violent and non-violent) was 0.40 for whites and 0.30 for blacks. The correlation between PCL-R scores and the number of different types of charges was 0.46 for whites and 0.35 for blacks.

A similar, though weaker, association between psychopathy and crime was found in a sample of 75 young offenders assessed using an 18-item modification of the PCL-R (Forth, Hart, and Hare, 1990). PCL-R scores were significantly correlated ($r = 0.27$) with the number of previous violent offences.

In a sample of 80 consecutive male admissions to a forensic psychiatric hospital (Hart and Hare, 1989) PCL-R scores correlated 0.30 with number of violent offences, 0.35 with number of non-violent offences, 0.37 with number of prison terms served (corrected for age), and 0.33 with months spent in prison (corrected for age).

The psychopathy-crime association found with male offenders may also apply to female offenders. We have found, in an ongoing study, that 31% of a sample of 75 female offenders in a maximum-security institution met the PCL-R research criteria for psychopathy (a score of at least 30); they were responsible for half of the total offences and violent offences committed by the sample.

A theme that runs through most of the recent research on the association between psychopathy and crime is the versatility shown by psychopaths. That is, psychopaths engage in a wider variety of criminal activities (Hare, 1991; Wong, 1984) and use a greater range of drugs (Smith and Newman, 1990) than do other criminals, a reflection, perhaps, of a persistent need for new and exciting experiences (see Kosson, Smith and Newman (1990)). One of the items in the PCL-R measures criminal versatility.

INSTITUTIONAL BEHAVIOUR

There is good evidence that the psychopaths' propensity for violence is not inhibited during incarceration. As part of a study described above, Hare and McPherson (1984) examined the institutional violence and aggression of 227 male inmates. A research assistant used file information to determine whether or not each of eight aggressive behaviours was characteristic of each inmate. Because of the subjective nature of these decisions a second assistant made similar decisions on a subsample of 69 inmates. The percentage of inmates with high, medium, and low scores on the PCL that displayed each form of institutional aggression is presented in Table 7.3; the interrater reliabilities of the aggressive behaviours are also listed. In an additional analysis of the institutional files, a 5-point scale was used to rate the frequency with which each inmate engaged in violent behaviour while in the institution: 0 (never), 1 (rarely), 2 (occasionally), 3 (quite often), 4 (very often). The interrater reliability of these ratings with a subsample of 69 inmates was 0.85. The correlation between the PCL scores and the violence ratings was 0.46.

Similar findings have been reported by other investigators. In the study by Wong (1984), described above, psychopaths committed almost four times as many institutional offences and engaged in significantly more threatening behaviour and acts of violence than did non-psychopaths. Similarly, Serin (1991) found that while in prison psychopaths, defined by the PCL-R, were more aggressive and more likely to admit to the use of instrumental aggression in their dealings

Table 7.3   Percentage of inmates in each PCL group that displayed violent and aggressive behaviour in prison

Behaviour	r^a	Group		
		High	Medium	Low
Attempted suicide	0.85	19.2	10.7	15.4
Self-mutilation	0.80	6.8	4.0	3.8
Verbal abuse	0.62	24.7	9.3	3.8
Verbal threats	0.58	26.0	9.3	9.3
Easily annoyed/irritated	0.71	45.2	28.0	10.3
Belligerent	0.64	46.6	21.3	3.8
Aggressive homosexuality	0.74	6.8	8.0	2.6
Fighting	0.59	50.7	29.3	26.9
Any of above	0.85	86.3	80.0	55.1
N		73	75	79

Source: From Hare and McPherson (1984).
Note: The analysis period was age 16 to 30. H, M, and L refer, respectively, to inmates with high, medium, and low PCL scores. Group differences were significant at the $p < 0.001$ level for all but attempted suicide, self-mutilation, and aggressive homosexuality.
[a] Interrater reliability for a subsample of 69 inmates.

with other inmates. Forth, Hart, and Hare (1990) found that PCL-R scores of male young offenders were significantly correlated with the number of institutional charges for violent or aggressive behaviour ($r = 0.46$).

THE VICTIMS OF PSYCHOPATHS

Some clinicians (e.g. Arieti, 1967; Cleckley, 1976) have suggested that violent and aggressive acts by psychopaths are often motivated by proto-emotions, such as tension or frustration, or by weak emotions breaking through even weaker restraints, rather than by strong emotions such as fear or anger. In many cases, their behaviour may represent little more than a petty reaction to external events, an attempt to show off, or a desire to create and display a macho image of themselves.

Considerations of this sort led Williamson, Hare, and Wong (1987) to hypothesize that although psychopaths commit many offences commonly classified as violent, they are largely offences that have little affective colouring, seldom being described as genuine 'crimes of passion.' Further, because psychopaths have relatively little contact with their families, change their residence often, exhibit little intensity in their interpersonal relationships, and often engage in criminal activities that lack purpose and long-range planning, they also hypothesized that their victims are less often friends, relations, or family members, than is the case with other criminals.

These hypotheses were tested in a study of the offences responsible for the current incarceration of samples of 55 psychopathic and 46 non-psychopathic inmates, defined by the PCL. The official police reports were used to analyse the circumstances surrounding the most serious of the offences committed by each inmate. The results were consistent with the hypotheses. Most of the murders and serious assaults committed by the non-psychopaths occurred during a domestic dispute or during a period of extreme emotional arousal, whereas this was seldom true of the psychopaths. The victims of the non-psychopaths were likely to be female and known to them, but the victims of the psychopaths were likely to be male and unknown to them. The violence of the psychopaths frequently had revenge or retribution as the motive or occurred during a drinking bout. In general, it appeared that most of the psychopaths' violence was callous and cold-blooded or part of an aggressive or macho display, without the affective colouring or understandable motives that accompanied the violence of the non-psychopaths. This study has since been replicated with the same results (Wright and Wong, 1988).

RECIDIVISM AND THE PREDICTION OF VIOLENT BEHAVIOUR

Historically, clinicians and researchers have been rather pessimistic about the value of diagnoses of psychopathy in the prediction of criminal or violent behaviour. However, it is important to note that the research literature on which this pessimism was based has been beset by a number of methodological problems, not the least of which was the use of diagnostic procedures that lacked demonstrated reliability and validity (Hare, 1985). Recent research clearly indicates that a diagnosis of psychopathy can have good predictive validity, providing that careful attention is paid to the psychometric properties of the instrument used to assess the disorder.

Hart, Kropp, and Hare (1988) administered the PCL to 231 male inmates prior to their release from prison on parole or mandatory supervision. In Canada parole is early release granted to selected inmates, typically after they have served at least one-third of their sentence. Mandatory supervision is a form of early release contingent on good behaviour during incarceration, and is granted after two-thirds of a sentence has been served. The PCL assessments and decisions about release were completely independent. Following release, each inmate's progress was followed until: (i) he had his release revoked; (ii) he was convicted of a new offence; (iii) he successfully reached the end of the period of supervised release; or (iv) the end of study period was reached (1 February 1986). An unsuccessful release (failure) was defined as revocation, or conviction for a new offence during the period of supervision. Overall, 107 (46.3%) of the releases ended in failure, 56.4% for mandatory supervision and 25.3% for parole. Outcome (success = 0, failure = 1) was correlated 0.33 with PCL scores. A series of regression analyses demonstrated that the PCL made a significant contribution to the prediction of outcome over and beyond that made by relevant criminal-history and demographic variables.

Several group analyses were also performed. The sample was subdivided into groups with high (H), medium (M), and low (L) PCL scores, using the cutoffs described by Hare (1985). The percentage of criminals in Groups H, M, and L that violated the conditions of release was 65.2, 48.9, and 23.5 respectively. Survival analysis indicated that the probability of remaining out of prison for at least one year was 0.80, 0.54, and 0.38, for Groups L, M, and H respectively. In addition, Group H received more suspensions and presented more supervisory problems during the release period than did those in the other groups. During the release period, inmates in Group H were almost three times more likely to violate the conditions of release, and almost four times more likely to commit a violent crime, than were those in Group L.

Serin, Peters, and Barbaree (1990) administered the PCL to 93 male inmates prior to release from a federal prison on unescorted temporary absence (UTA). Six (37.5%) of the 16 psychopaths in the study, defined by a PCL score greater than 31, violated the conditions of UTA, whereas none of the 16 non-psychopaths, defined by a score less than 17, did so. Subsequently, 77 of the 93 inmates were released on parole; follow-up data were available for 74 of these inmates, including 11 psychopaths and 13 non-psychopaths. The failure (recommittal) rate on parole was 27% for the entire sample, 7% for the non-psychopaths, and 33% for the psychopaths. Moreover, the mean time to failure was significantly shorter for the psychopaths (8.0 months) than it was for the non-psychopaths (14.6 months). The PCL predicted outcome better than did a combination of criminal-history and demographic variables, and several standard actuarial risk instruments, including The Base Expectancy Scale (Gottfredson and Bonds, 1961), The Recidivism Prediction Scale (Nuffield, 1982) and the Salient Factor Score (Hoffman and Beck, 1974).

In a 5-year follow-up of the Serin, Peters, and Barbaree (1990) recidivism study, Serin (in press) reported that the overall failure rate was 67% for the 81 criminals involved in the study, 38% for the nonpsychopaths and 85% for the psychopaths. In Wong's (1984) study of a random sample of 315 male inmates, PCL scores were significantly correlated with the number of revocations of parole ($r = 0.30$) and revocations of mandatory supervision ($r = 0.23$).

Psychopathy appears to be predictive not only of recidivism in general, but also of violent recidivism. In the study by Serin (in press) none of the non-psychopaths, and 25% of the psychopaths, violently recidivated. Standard actuarial instruments were not predictive of violent reoffending.

In a long-term follow-up study of 166 male patients released from a forensic psychiatric unit, Harris, Rice, and Cormier (1991) reported that 77% of 52 psychopaths, defined by a PCL-R score of at least 25, committed a violent crime subsequent to their release from an intensive therapeutic community programme. By way of comparison, the violent recidivism rate for 114 other patients released from the same programme was only 21%. Even with the relatively liberal cutoff for psychopathy (a PCL-R score of 30 is typically used), 78% of the outcomes were correctly predicted, with a relative improvement over chance of 52.6%. In a stringent test of the predictive ability of the PCL-R, the four best criminal history variables (selected from a list of traditionally important predictor variables) were entered into a hierarchical multiple regression analysis. The PCL-R was allowed to enter the analysis only if it produced a significant improvement in the prediction of violent outcome. The addition of the PCL-R increased the multiple correlation with outcome (0 = success, 1 = failure) from 0.31 to 0.45, a significant improvement.

Psychopathy also appears to predict violent recidivism in male young offenders. Forth, Hart, and Hare (1990) found that PCL-R scores in a sample of 75 young offenders were significantly correlated with the number of charges or convictions for violent offences ($r = 0.26$) after release. Though the correlation was small, it is important to note that it was obtained with a relatively homogeneous sample—all but two of the offenders met the DSM-III-R criteria for conduct disorder—that consisted of some of the most seriously criminal and persistent young offenders in the province of British Columbia.

Rice, Harris, and Quinsey (1990) studied 54 rapists released from a maximum security psychiatric hospital. During the follow-up period, which averaged 46 months, 28% of the patients committed a sexual offence and 43% committed a violent offence (all sexual offences were coded as violent). PCL-R scores were predictive of post-release sexual offences ($r = 0.31$) and of violent offences ($r = 0.35$). A combination of PCL-R scores and a phallometric measure of sexual arousal (as measured by penile plethysmography) was as effective at predicting sexual offences as was a battery of demographic, psychological and criminal history variables. These two variables alone correctly predicted the post-release outcome of 76.9% of the rapists, with a relative improvement over chance of 43.8%.

PSYCHOPATHY AND AGE-RELATED CHANGES IN CRIMINAL BEHAVIOUR

Although psychopathy is generally considered to be a disorder that persists across much of the life-span, there is evidence that the antisocial and criminal activities of at least some male psychopaths decrease in frequency and severity with age. Hare, McPherson, and Forth (1988) reported that the criminal activities of male psychopaths were more extensive than were those of other persistent offenders until around age 35 or 40, after which they decreased sharply. These age-related changes were much more dramatic for non-violent crimes than for violent crimes. That is, the violent activities of psychopaths appeared to remain relatively constant even after there had been a sharp drop in non-violent criminal activities. Their capacity for violence apparently did not change with age nearly as much as did their readiness to engage in other forms of illegal and antisocial behaviour. Similar findings have been reported by Harris, Rice, and Cormier (1991).

CONCLUSION

Taken together, these studies provide considerable support for the validity of the psychopathy construct, its strong association with crime and violence, and consequently, its importance to the criminal justice and correctional systems. Clearly, the empirical findings indicate the importance for the criminal justice system to identify psychopathic offenders, and for the correctional system to develop effective ways of treating or managing them.

AUTHOR NOTE

Correspondence concerning this chapter should be addressed to Robert D. Hare, Department of Psychology, University of British Columbia, Vancouver, British Columbia, Canada V6T 1Z4.

REFERENCES

American Psychiatric Association (1987). *Diagnostic and Statistical Manual of Mental Disorders* (3rd edn, revised). Washington, DC: Author.

Arieti, S. (1967). *The Intrapsychic Self*. New York: Basic Books.

Cleckley, H. (1976). *The Mask of Sanity* (5th edn). St Louis, MO: Mosby.

Blackburn, R. (1990). Treatment of the psychopathic offender. In K. Howells and C. R. Hollin (eds), *Clinical Approaches to Working with Mentally Disordered and Sexual Offenders*, Issues in Criminological and Legal Psychology, No. 16. Leicester, England: British Psychological Society, pp. 54–66.

Correctional Service of Canada (1990). *Forum on Corrections Research*, 2, No. 1. Ottawa, Canada: Author.

Forth, A. E., Hart, S. D., and Hare, R. D. (1990). Assessment of psychopathy in male young offenders. *Psychological Assessment: A Journal of Consulting and Clinical Psychology*, 2, 342–4.

Frances, A. J., and Widiger, T. (1986). The classification of personality disorders: An overview of problems and situations. In A. J. Frances and R. E. Hales (eds), *American Psychiatric Association Annual Review* (vol. 5, *Psychiatry Update*). Washington, DC: American Psychiatric Press.

Gottfredson, D. M., and Bonds, J. A. (1961). *A Manual for Intake-base Expectancy Scoring*. San Francisco, CA: California Department of Corrections, Research Division.

Hare, R. D. (1980). A research scale for the assessment of psychopathy in criminal populations. *Personality and Individual Differences*, 1, 111–17.

Hare, R. D. (1985). Comparison of procedures for the assessment of psychopathy. *Journal of Consulting and Clinical Psychology*, 53, 7–16.

Hare, R. D. (1986). Criminal psychopaths. In J. Yuille (ed.), *Police Selection and Training: The Role of Psychology*. Dordrecht, Netherlands: Martinus Nijhoff, pp. 187–206.

Hare, R. D. (1991). *The Hare Psychopathy Checklist-Revised*. Toronto, Ontario: Multi-Health Systems.

Hare, R. D., and Cox, D. N. (1978). Clinical and empirical conceptions of psychopathy, and the selection of subjects for research. In R. D. Hare and D. Schalling (eds), *Psychopathic Behaviour: Approaches to Research*. Chichester, England: Wiley.

Hare, R. D., Forth, A. E., and Hart, S. D. (1989). The psychopath as prototype for pathological lying and deception.. In J. C. Yuille (ed.), *Credibility Assessment*. Dordrecht, Netherlands: Kluwer, pp. 25–49.

Hare, R. D., Harpur, T. J., Hakstian, A. R., Forth, A. E., Hart, S. D., and Newman, J. P. (1990). The revised Psychopathy Checklist: Reliability and factor structure. *Psychological Assessment: A Journal of Consulting and Clinical Psychology*, 2, 338–41.

Hare, R. D., Hart, S. D., and Harpur, T. J. (1991). Psychopathy and the DSM-IV Criteria for Antisocial Personality Disorder. *Journal of Abnormal Psychology*, **100**, 391–8.

Hare, R. D., and Jutai, J. W. (1983). Criminal history of the male psychopath. In K. T. Van Dusen and S. A. Mednick (eds), *Prospective Studies of Crime and Delinquency*. Boston: Kluwer-Nijhoff.

Hare, R. D., and McPherson, L. M. (1984). Violent and aggressive behavior by criminal psychopaths. *International Journal of Law and Psychiatry*, **7**, 35–50.

Hare, R. D., McPherson, L. M., and Forth, A. E. (1988). Male psychopaths and their criminal careers. *Journal of Consulting and Clinical Psychology*, **56**, 710–14.

Harpur, T. J., Hakstian, A. R., and Hare, R. D. (1988). Factor structure of the Psychopathy Checklist. *Journal of Consulting and Clinical Psychology*, **56**, 741–7.

Harpur, T. J., Hare, R. D., and Hakstian, A. R. (1989). Two-factor conceptualization of psychopathy: Construct validation and assessment implications. *Psychological Assessment: A Journal of Consulting and Clinical Psychology*, **1**, 6–17.

Harris, G. T., Rice, M. E., and Cormier, C. A. (1991). Psychopathy and violent recidivism. *Law and Human Behavior*, **15**, 625–37.

Hart, S. D., Forth, A. E., and Hare, R. D. (1991). Assessing psychopathy in male criminals using the MCMI-II. *Journal of Personality Disorders*, **5**, 318–327.

Hart, S. D., and Hare, R. D. (1989). Discriminant validity of the Psychopathy Checklist in a forensic psychiatric population. *Psychological Assessment: A Journal of Consulting and Clinical Psychology*, **1**, 211–18.

Hart, R. D., Hare, S. D., and Harpur, T. J. (1991). The Psychopathy Checklist-Revised (PCL-R): An Overview for Researchers and Clinicians. In J. Rosen and P. McReynolds (eds), *Advances in Psychological Assessment*, vol. 8, New York: Plenum.

Hart, S. D., Kropp, P. R., and Hare, R. D. (1988). Performance of male psychopaths following conditional release from prison. *Journal of Consulting and Clinical Psychology*, **56**, 227–32.

Hoffman, P., and Beck, J. L. (1974). Parole decision-making: A Salient Factor Score. *Journal of Criminal Justice*, **2**, 195–206.

Kosson, D. S., Smith, S. S., and Newman, J. P. (1990). Evaluating the construct validity of psychopathy on Black and White male inmates: Three preliminary studies. *Journal of Abnormal Psychology*, **99**, 250–9.

McCord, W., and McCord, J. (1964). *The Psychopath: An Essay on the Criminal Mind*. Princeton, NJ: Van Nostrand.

Nuffield, J. (1982). *Parole Decision-making in Canada: Research Towards Decision Guidelines*. Ottawa, Ontario: Ministry of Supply and Services.

Rice, M. E., Harris, G. T., and Quinsey, V. L. (1990). A follow-up of rapists assessed in a maximum security psychiatric facility. *Journal of Interpersonal Violence*, **4**, 435–48.

Sartorius, N., Jablensky, A., Cooper, J. E., and Burke, J. D. (eds) (1988). Psychiatric classification in an international perspective. *British Journal of Psychiatry*, Supplement No. 1, 152.

Serin, R. C. (1991). Psychopathy and violence in criminals. *Journal of Interpersonal Violence*, **6**, 423–31.

Serin, R. C. (in press). Violence and recidivism in criminal psychopaths. *Law and Human Behavior*.

Serin, R. C., Peters, R. D., and Barbaree, H. E. (1990). Predictors of psychopathy and release outcome in a criminal population. *Psychological Assessment: A Journal of Consulting and Clinical Psychology*, **2**, 419–22.

Smith, S. S., and Newman, J. P. (1990). Alcohol and drug abuse/dependence disorders in psychopathic and nonpsychopathic criminal offenders. *Journal of Abnormal Psychology*, **99**, 430–9.

Weiss, J. (1987). The nature of psychopathy. *Directions in Psychiatry*. New York: Hatherleight Company.

Widiger, T. A., Frances, A. J., Pincus, H. A., Davis, W. W., and First, M. (1991). Toward an empirical classification for DSM-IV. *Journal of Abnormal Psychology: Special Issue*, **100**, 280–8.

Wiggins, J. S. (1982). Circumplex models of interpersonal behavior in clinical psychology. In P. C. Kendall and J. N. Butcher (eds), *Handbook of Research Methods in Clinical Psychology*. New York: Wiley, pp. 183–221.

Wiggins, J. S., Trapnell, P., and Phillips, N. (1988). Psychometric and geometric characteristics of the revised Interpersonal Adjective Scales (IAS-R). *Multivariate Behavioral Research*, **23**, 517–30.

Williamson, S., Hare, R. D., and Wong, S. (1987). Violence: Criminal psychopaths and their victims. *Canadian Journal of Behavioral Science*, **19**, 454–62.

Wong, S. (1984). Criminal and institutional behaviours of psychopaths. *Programs Branch Users Report*. Ottawa, Ontario, Canada: Ministry of the Solicitor-General of Canada.

Wright, S., and Wong, S. (1988). *Criminal psychopaths and their victims*. Unpublished manuscript, Department of Psychology, University of Saskatchewan, Saskatoon, Saskatchewan.

8

Clinical Programmes with Psychopaths

RONALD BLACKBURN
Ashworth Hospital, Liverpool, UK

INTRODUCTION

The involuntary commitment of 'psychopathic' offenders to special mental health facilities for treatment originates from the early part of this century. In Britain, the nineteenth-century concept of 'moral insanity' was enshrined in the category of *moral imbecile* of the 1913 Mental Deficiency Act. This referred to 'Persons who from an early age display some permanent moral defect coupled with strong vicious or criminal propensities on which punishment has had little or no deterrent effect'. It allowed for the compulsory detention of dangerous mental defectives, but in clinical practice, psychiatrists soon equated moral imbecile with 'psychopathic personality', and it eventually gave way to the category of *psychopathic disorder* in the 1959 Mental Health Act for England and Wales: 'a persistent disorder or disability of mind (whether or not including subnormality of intelligence) which results in abnormally aggressive or seriously irresponsible conduct, and requires or is susceptible to medical treatment'.

Legal recognition of a category of 'psychopath' is by no means universal, and it does not appear in the Mental Health Acts for Scotland and Northern Ireland. Nevertheless, equivalent categories have emerged in other western jurisdictions. Holland, for example, introduced a Psychopaths Act in 1928, and in Denmark, a 'special detention centre' for psychopathic criminals was opened at Herstedvester in 1936 (Higgins, 1984). From 1937 onwards, half of the American States enacted 'sexual psychopath' laws permitting indeterminate detention of dangerous sex offenders in institutions for the criminally insane, and in 1951, Maryland passed a 'defective delinquent' law by which persistent offenders whose 'intellectual deficiency or emotional imbalance, or both' made

Clinical Approaches to the Mentally Disordered Offender
Edited by K. Howells and C. R. Hollin © 1993 John Wiley & Sons Ltd

them 'a danger to society' could be detained indefinitely at Patuxent, a psychiatric treatment prison (Holden, 1978).

Although these statutory measures vary in terminology, they share the common assumption that some violent or chronically antisocial offenders have a psychiatric disorder distinct from traditional mental illness, and that this is amenable to psychiatric treatment. A corollary is that indefinite detention in hospital until cure is achieved will serve the interests of both offender and society more appropriately than determinate legal punishment. However, these assumptions reflect a faith in the powers of psychiatry and behavioural science about which opinion has long been divided. For example, Schneider (1923/1950) cautioned against the optimism of psychotherapists who believed they could change abnormalities of personality, many of which he considered to be constitutionally determined and irreversible. While a few clinicians affirmed their optimism (Jones, 1963; Schmideberg, 1961), criminologists questioned whether indeterminate detention of 'psychopaths' actually protected society. Sutherland (1950), for example, described sexual psychopath laws as 'dangerous and futile', arguing that 'sexual psychopaths' could be neither defined nor identified, and that the laws were influenced more by the professional and economic interests of psychiatrists than by any scientific evidence of treatment efficacy. Civil libertarians also argued that in the absence of such evidence, indeterminate sentencing was unjust. These arguments gained ground as evidence accumulated that clinical predictions of dangerousness were unreliable, and that the effectiveness of efforts to rehabilitate offenders in general had not been demonstrated.

Since the early 1970s, there has been an increasing swing towards pessimism about the treatability of psychopaths. In the United States, most sexual psychopath laws had been repealed by 1980, and Maryland's defective delinquent statute was abolished in 1977. Patuxent remains a treatment prison, but treatability rather than dangerousness is now the primary criterion for admission (Holden, 1978). Similar developments in Denmark resulted in Herstedvester ceasing to be a 'special detention centre'. In Britain, the Butler Committee (Home Office/Department of Health and Social Security, 1975) concluded that there was no evidence that offenders suffering from psychopathic disorder were treatable by medical means, and recommended that psychological treatment should be provided in special units within the prison system. They also suggested changing the Mental Health Act category of psychopathic disorder to 'personality disorder'. Neither recommendation has been taken up, but in the 1983 revision of the Act, the phrase 'which requires or is susceptible to medical treatment' was removed from the definition of psychopathic disorder. At the same time, a treatability criterion was introduced with the requirement that compulsory admission of 'psychopaths' to hospital should be likely to alleviate the disorder or prevent deterioration. Opposition to indeterminate hospital orders appears to have increased among psychiatrists (e.g. Chiswick, 1987; Grounds, 1987), many of whom argue that if hospital treatment is desirable, it can be provided by transfer to hospital during a determinate prison sentence. However, a Home Office attempt to change the law in this direction in 1986 met with considerable opposition from both clinicians and lawyers, and was abandoned (Peay, 1988).

Despite retrenchment in legal provision, offenders deemed psychopathic continue to be admitted to secure facilities for treatment in Britain and elsewhere. A quarter of the 1700 patients detained in the English Special Hospitals fall in the category of psychopathic disorder, and they continue to constitute a similar proportion of new admissions. However, some 'psychopaths' who do not meet the Mental Health Act treatability criteria (or who are not assessed for this purpose) may receive psychological treatment in prison, particularly in special units for violent or 'difficult to manage' prisoners (Cooke, 1989; Walmsley, 1991). This chapter describes the kinds of clinical intervention attempted with this group and examines the evidence for their utility.

LEGAL AND CLINICAL CONCEPTS OF PSYCHOPATHY

While legalistic concern about the treatment of 'psychopaths' has focused on indeterminate detention, the concept of psychopathic personality has long been employed by clinicians working with offenders, whether or not they are legally identified as psychopathic. The relationship between legal and clinical concepts of psychopathy, however, is inevitably tenuous in the light of the controversy surrounding the meaning of the term 'psychopath' (Blackburn, 1988; Bowden, 1992; Millon, 1981; Pichot, 1978). This controversy is reflected in a lack of consensus on two critical issues. The first is the question of *who* is the relevant subject of clinical intervention. The second is the question of *what* are the appropriate goals and targets of intervention.

The legal category of psychopathic disorder is not a clinical diagnosis, and is unhelpful in answering either of these questions. It singles out those whose 'abnormally aggressive or seriously irresponsible conduct' can be attributed to 'a persistent disorder or disability of mind', and the latter is therefore the presumed target of intervention. However, this putative mental disorder lacks any criteria other than its persistence and its power to cause seriously antisocial conduct. In the absence of independent criteria, the disorder must be inferred in circular fashion from the behaviour it supposedly causes, and in this respect, it is a legal fiction. It is therefore misleading to describe people who 'suffer from' this disorder as 'psychopaths'. Not only is the label pejorative, it spuriously implies a homogeneous group who have something in common beyond their antisocial behaviour. In fact, as the Butler Committee observed: 'The class of persons to whom the term "psychopathic disorder" relates is not a single category identifiable by any medical, biological, or psychological criteria' (Home Office/ Department of Health and Social Security, 1975). Heterogeneity has been amply confirmed in psychological research with special hospital patients (Blackburn, 1975, 1986, 1992).

In practice, psychiatrists attempt to translate the legal concept into clinical concepts of psychopathic personality, but the diverse meanings attached to this term undermine its potential scientific and clinical utility. Blackburn (1988) distinguishes three different uses of the term. First, as developed in late nineteenth century German psychiatry, 'psychopathic' had the etymologically correct meaning of *psychologically damaged* or abnormal, and psychopathic personalities were a miscellaneous group whose personality deviations caused suffering to themselves or others (Schneider, 1923/1950). The legacy of this concept is the broad class of personality disorders in the International Classification of Diseases (ICD-9, 1978) and DSM-III-R (American Psychiatric Association, 1987). ICD-9 in fact retains the concept of *psychopathy* as a generic description of disorders of personality, whether or not these are expressed in antisocial behaviour.

In Anglo-American psychiatry, however, 'psychopathic' has been narrowed to mean antisocial or *socially damaging*. This second use emphasises socially deviant behaviour rather than personality disorder, and is exemplified in the English legal category of psychopathic disorder. In the United States, psychopath became synonymous with sociopath, fostering a stereotype of the sadistic killer or the vicious rapist which continues to be profitably exploited by the media. The DSM-III-R category of *antisocial personal disorder* (APD), which is one of the eleven categories of personality disorder, is primarily a catalogue of socially offensive behaviour rather than a description of personality, and reference to personality traits is limited to irritability and aggressiveness, impulsivity, recklessness, and lack of remorse. Wulach (1983) suggests that this concept was influenced by the growing climate of negative attitudes towards rehabilitation of offenders, and notes that the stereotypic criminal it portrays discourages opportunities for treatment.

A third use is a hybrid which identifies a specific and narrow category of antisocial person by reference to personality traits (Cleckley, 1941/1976; Gough, 1948; McCord and McCord, 1964). Cleckley, for example, rejected detailed classifications of personality disorders, seeing most categories as neurotic or psychotic disorders, but he proposed a 'distinct clinical entity' of psychopathic personality defined by 16 criteria, such as superficial charm, unreliability, lack of remorse, egocentricity, and interpersonal unresponsiveness. McCord and McCord (1964) also identify a specific category, describing the psychopath as 'an asocial, aggressive, highly impulsive person, who feels little or no guilt, and is unable to form lasting bonds of affection with other human beings'. This specific conception owes more than a little to the psychoanalytic notion of an individual who lacks conscience or superego, and is sometimes referred to as the primary or 'classical' concept of psychopathy. This concept has been favoured in psychological research (Hare, 1986), although some writers distinguish between primary and secondary psychopaths on the basis of the presence of anxiety (Blackburn, 1975; Lykken, 1957).

However, from a clinical standpoint, focus on this more specific concept of psychopathic personality has two disadvantages. First its relation to the classification of personality disorders more generally remains unclear. While it correlates quite highly with the category of APD in DSM-III, some of the criteria emphasised by Cleckley appear in other categories, such as histrionic, narcissistic, and borderline disorders. Blackburn (1988) suggests that this problem can be resolved if personality disorders are classified in dimensional terms, rather than as discrete categories. Psychopathy would thus be more appropriately conceptualised as one superordinate dimension representing attributes of several personality disorders, which are distinguished from each other by an orthogonal personality dimension.

A second disadvantage is that given the heterogeneity of antisocial populations identified legally as psychopathic, only a minority meets these criteria for psychopathic personality. For example, Blackburn (1975) found that only a quarter of legal psychopaths admitted to a special hospital showed characteristics approximating to the more specific category of primary psychopath, and similar findings are reported for 'psychopaths' admitted to the Henderson unit, a therapeutic community in England (Copas, O'Brien, Roberts, and Whiteley, 1984). Harris, Rice, and Cormier (1989) also note that although two-thirds of patients admitted to a Canadian maximum security hospital were diagnosed as 'antisocial personality', less than a quarter met DSM-III criteria for APD. It can, of course, be argued that this heterogeneity of 'psychopathic' populations reflects the unreliability of psychiatric diagnosis and a failure to agree strict criteria. On the other hand, it highlights the association of persistent antisocial behaviour with other forms of personality disorder. To restrict clinical attention to a more narrowly defined category of primary psychopath or APD would deny many offenders access to clinical services from which they might benefit.

This is not to deny the relevance of the 'classical' concept of psychopathy to research and clinical work with offenders, and traits held to define it, such as egocentricity, impulsivity, or lack of empathy continue to be regarded as significant factors in criminal behaviour more generally (Gottfredson and Hirschi, 1990). However, clinical attention would seem to be more appropriately focused on those offenders who exhibit some form of personality disorder, and not simply those who are psychopathic or antisocial personalities in the narrower sense (Blackburn, 1988, 1992). It needs to be recognised, nevertheless, that personality disorder and mental illness are not mutually exclusive, and that the two frequently co-exist. Studies of Special Hospital samples in England, for example, indicate that although the majority of patients are identified as mentally ill, more than two-thirds meet criteria for one or more personality disorders (Blackburn, Crellin, Morgan, and Tulloch, 1990; Tyrer, 1988). In this respect, the legal category of psychopathic disorder is not synonymous with personality disorder.

This argument has implications for the goals of clinical intervention. If socially deviant behaviour is a function of personality disorder, the concern of clinicians is to reduce the likelihood of further deviant acts by modifying the offender's inflexible and maladaptive traits. How these are conceptualised will vary with the orientation of the therapist. Cognitive-behavioural therapists, for example, increasingly relate them to cognitive-affective processes and interpersonal skills.

There are, however, disagreements about what should be targeted and how successful outcome should be evaluated. Some behaviourists propose that criminal behaviour is the appropriate target of intervention. Crawford (1984), for example, argues that concepts of 'mental abnormality' have no utility for a deterministic behavioural science, and that a behavioural analysis calls for examination of the development of the offending behaviour. However, as

Andrews, Bonta, and Hoge (1990) note, antisocial attitudes and psychopathic personality traits have been shown to be significant mediators of criminal behaviour, and many therapists would now see attention to cognition as necessary in all interventions with offenders. Crawford's view also raises ethical problems, since it allows for no criteria for judging which offenders should be subject to psychological intervention. Crime is defined by the state, not by behavioural or medical science, and the implication that all offenders are potential subjects for psychological intervention reduces the role of the psychologist to that of agent of social control.

Robertson (1989), in contrast, argues against recidivism as an outcome criterion, suggesting that treatment in the form of hospitalisation contributes only a small part of the variance in reoffending. However, this prejudges the empirical question of what influences outcome, and seems to rest on a medical conception of treatment as symptom removal, rather than a psychological conception of intervention as the provision of skills for avoiding offending.

Since it is mental disorder rather than offending which justifies the diversion of mentally disordered offenders to the mental health system, alleviation of the disorder is a necessary outcome criterion, but reduced recidivism will be one indication of successful outcome in the case of personality disorder. Reduced recidivism is therefore a necessary but not sufficient outcome criterion. The primary need is to identify and target the *mediators* of antisocial behaviour, and to establish which treatments influence these mediators.

ASSESSMENT ISSUES

Clinical evaluations of offenders considered psychopathic or personality disordered may be undertaken for forensic purposes, such as to advise on treatability or dangerousness, or for the more central clinical purposes of treatment planning and monitoring. These circumstances entail different kinds of obligation to the client, but in general will draw on similar assessment procedures.

Such offenders will usually have committed a serious violent or sexual offence, and a primary consideration is therefore their propensity to commit further similar offences. A wide range of procedures has been developed to assess proneness to aggression (Blackburn, 1989) and deviant sexual behaviour (Maletzky, 1991), and clinicians working with offenders need to be familiar with these. Since these methods raise issues beyond the assessment of psychopathy, they are not considered here.

Assessment of Psychopathy and Personality Disorders

Many violent and sexual offenders either deny their offence or minimise its effects, and do not readily become engaged in assessment and treatment. Traditional characteristics of classical psychopaths are that they lie easily and are manipulative, and some workers advocate that their accounts are not to be trusted. It is, however, important to avoid moralistic stereotypes, which can become self-fulfilling prophecies, and to recognise that without an element of trust between clinician and client, neither effective assessment nor treatment is possible. Clinicians therefore need to avoid the extremes of gullible acceptance and hostile suspiciousness.

Violent offenders frequently have wide-ranging problems, and a comprehensive assessment needs to cover early development and relationships, and to examine social, cognitive, and affective levels of functioning as well as criminal behaviour. Assessment of these relies on a combination of interviews, psychometric measures, and file information recording social, psychiatric, and criminal history and the observations of significant others.

Behaviour therapists usually approach assessment through a *functional analysis*, which seeks to determine the personal and environmental factors of which the antisocial behaviour is a function. Initial interviews thus entail analysis of events preceding, during, and following the offence, including the roles of mood, alcohol, the nature of the assault, and the offender's feelings about the victim and their behaviour. Functional analysis is often contrasted with traditional psychodiagnosis, and dispositional concepts of personality do not marry readily with such an approach, which focuses on the immediate antecedents and consequences of deviant acts. However, to the extent that the analysis is concerned with the tendency to *repeat* deviant acts, it cannot avoid reference to the more general dispositions a person brings to a situation. These represent the products of prior learning which mediate new experiences, including socially deviant acts. Assessment should therefore also investigate lifestyle factors conducive to deviant behaviour, such as attitudes to self and others, interpersonal style, recreations, and substance use. Information from independent sources, such as family members, court records, and victims should also be sought.

The classification and assessment of disorders of personality has been facilitated by the development of operational criteria in DSM-III-R. Although this classification of dysfunctional traits is not sacrosanct, and falls short of an optimal scientific system, it provides a useful first step in identifying dispositions which might mediate socially deviant behaviour. Some measures are now available for assessing these, probably the best known being the *Millon Clinical Multiaxial Inventory* (MCMI: Millon, 1983), which aims to assess the DSM-III personality disorders as well as clinical syndromes. Personality disorder scales have also been developed for the original MMPI (Morey, Waugh, and Blashfield, 1985), and structured interviews are discussed by Widiger and Frances (1987) and Tyrer (1988).

Several more specific measures of psychopathy are available, although these reflect differing assumptions about psychopathy and the preferences of different investigators for particular forms of measurement. These methods are discussed by Brantley and Sutker (1984), who emphasise the need for multimethod, multimeasure strategies. Most research during the past three decades has relied on one or more of the following measures.

(1) *Cleckley's criteria.* Lykken (1957), and subsequently Hare (1986) popularised Cleckley's concept as a basis for identifying psychopaths in

deviant populations. Assessment usually entails a global rating of the extent to which an individual meets Cleckley's 16 criteria, rather than detailed ratings of the specific criteria. Satisfactory interrater reliabilities have been achieved, but use of this measure has rested on the untested assumption that Cleckley's concept is valid, and his criteria internally consistent.

(2) *Psychopathy Checklist (PCL)*. In an attempt to produce a more objective scale, Hare (1980; Hare, Harpur, Hakstian, Forth, Hart, and Newman, 1990) developed a checklist from factor analyses of ratings of Cleckley's criteria and other attributes of psychopaths suggested by the literature. Items reflect both a history of social deviance and deficiencies in interpersonal sensitivity emphasised by Cleckley, and are rated from case history data and a structured interview. The scale has satisfactory reliabilities, and correlates highly with global Cleckley ratings. Offenders scoring high and low on the scale have been shown to differ on a variety of behavioural and laboratory measures, supporting its construct and predictive validity. Recent analyses indicate that two oblique factors are distinguishable (Hare *et al.*, 1990). One is an interpersonal dimension of selfish, callous and remorseless use of others, the other a dimension of socially deviant lifestyle.

(3) *MMPI scales*. Scale 4 of the MMPI (*Pd*: Psychopathic deviate) was developed empirically against a criterion group of psychologically disturbed delinquents, and is usually the scale on which offender samples score highest. While it has been used in some studies as a measure of psychopathic personality, its content is primarily concerned with nonconformity and conflict with family and authority, and seems more appropriately construed as social rule-breaking. A more specific criterion is the combined elevation of scales 4 and 9 (*Ma*: Hypomania), the latter relating to impulsivity or 'acting out'. This pattern conforms to the notion of primary psychopath, since it reflects relatively low scores on scales measuring emotionality. When combined with elevations on scales assessing anxiety (7: Psychasthenia; 0: Social Introversion), moodiness (2: Depression) or deviant perceptual and interpersonal experiences (6: Paranoia; 8: Schizophrenia), it suggests traits of the secondary psychopath.

Cluster analyses of MMPI profiles of offenders in the Mental Health Act category of psychopathic disorder (Blackburn, 1975) identified the 4–9 profile as one of four main patterns, and Blackburn (1982) developed the SHAPS (Special Hospitals Assessment of Personality and Socialisation) to measure the main variables contributing to differentiation between these patterns. This 10-scale questionnaire is based mainly on MMPI items, but most of the variance is summarised by two factors, for which scales have been developed (Blackburn, 1987). The first (Belligerence) measures impulsivity and hostility versus conformity, the second (Withdrawal) measuring shyness and poor self-esteem versus sociability and confidence. Primary and secondary psychopaths are identified in the empirical classification by high scores on the first factor, but opposite extremes on the second.

(4) *Socialisation scale*. The 54-item *So* scale from Gough's California Psychological Inventory (Gough, 1969) measures the extent to which a person has internalised social values and considers them personally binding. Gough (1948) proposed that the central feature of psychopathy is an inability to take the role of 'the generalised other', and there is evidence that *So* indexes role-taking ability (Rosen and Schalling, 1974). Low scores have therefore been used by several investigators as a criterion of psychopathy, while Heilbrun (Heilbrun and Heilbrun, 1985) has employed the sum of *Pd* minus *So* for this purpose.

(5) *Quay's behaviour classification dimensions*. Quay (1977, 1987) has identified dimensions of deviant behaviour through factor analyses of self-report, case history, and behaviour rating data in delinquent populations. The four main dimensions are currently described as unsocialised aggression or psychopathy (UA), anxiety-withdrawal-dysphoria (AW), attention deficit (AD), and socialised aggression (SA). The first two factors appear consistently in all measurement media, and have been used in a number of studies to distinguish psychopathic and neurotic delinquents. Factors can be measured by composite scores derived from different assessment media, but more commonly by rating scales of the Behaviour Problem Checklist (Quay, 1977). Evidence on validity has accumulated in several studies which demonstrate differential performance of groups in response to laboratory experiments and criminal justice interventions (Quay, 1987). The UA and AW factors also have counterparts in adult populations (Quay, 1984). The Adult Internal Management System (AIMS) identifies five factors, labelled aggressive-psychopathic, manipulative, situational, inadequate-dependent, and neurotic-anxious, which are measured by a rating scale and case history checklist. This classification is currently used by several American prisons to facilitate 'internal management', which divides prisoners into more homogeneous and manageable subgroups (Levinson, 1988). It has successfully identified groups differing in response to institutional regimes, and reduced the level of serious institutional incidents.

These various measures have been found to correlate with each other, but correlations are not sufficiently high for them to be regarded as interchangeable. The 'psychopaths' of one investigator do not, then, necessarily correspond to those of another. For example, Kuriychuk (1990) found a correlation of 0.48 between Hare's PCL and Blackburn's Belligerence scale in a sample of 60 Canadian prisoners and staff. Hare (1985) compared scores on several of the above measures in 274 prison inmates. Intercorrelations between Cleckley ratings, PCL score, and DSM-III diagnosis of APD ranged from 0.57 to 0.80, while correlations of these three with *Pd*, *So*, and *Pd* minus *So* ranged from 0.21 to 0.44. Factor analysis clearly separated the observer measures from self-report scales, and Hare suggests that the latter are not useful in assessing psychopathy among inmates. This conclusion, however, is unwarranted, since observer ratings and self-reports tap different personal attributes and any assessment of personality which ignores the person's self-image and self-presentation is inevitably one-sided. Since psychopathy is a theoretical construct rather than a palpable entity, there can be no 'true' measure, and adequate assessment ideally requires multiple measures (Brantley and Sutker, 1984; Widiger and Frances, 1987).

Several of these scales were developed primarily for research use, and they may therefore be used to identify subject groups in treatment research. They may also be used in predicting treatment outcome, for example in assessing responsivity to different treatment methods. However, not all of them permit the monitoring of treatment effects or the evaluation of change. Many items of Hare's PCL, for example, relate to past history. Similarly the criteria for APD are predominantly historical items, and this category is therefore of limited use to therapists.

There are also limits to the utility of global measures which yield only a diagnostic categorisation, since clinical programmes are likely to target specific attributes such as impulsivity or proneness to anger. It is therefore desirable to employ more specific measures of deviant attributes which are sensitive to change. Cognitive-behavioural programmes with offenders have increasingly focused on targets which enter into descriptions of psychopathic personality, such as egocentricity, lack of empathy, or level of moral development. Available measures of these and related variables are described by Ross and Fabiano (1985).

Assessing Treatability

The prediction of dangerousness remains a central consideration in the discharge of psychopathic offenders, but as was noted earlier, treatability has become a more important criterion for their admission to psychiatric facilities (Heilbrun, Bennett, Evans, Offutt, Reiff, and White, 1988; Quinsey, 1988). The available evidence, however, suggests that clinical judgements about treatability are even less reliable than those of dangerousness (Quinsey, 1988). Dell and Robertson (1988), for example, found that psychiatrists admitting legal psychopaths to Broadmoor Special Hospital had specified a purpose or form of treatment for less than a quarter, and were generally at a loss as to what treatment to provide. A study at another Special Hospital similarly found that a purpose of admission had been stated for only 43% of patients in the category of psychopathic disorder who were deemed treatable, and a comparison of demographic, psychiatric, and criminological variables revealed virtually no differences between those admitted as treatable and those rejected as untreatable (Collins, 1991).

Two problems in particular limit the accuracy of treatability decisions. First is uncertainty about treatment goals and outcome criteria. Clearly, to assess treatability, we need to be able to specify the nature of the disorder to be treated, the targets of therapeutic change, and the nature of the interventions which will achieve those changes. Dell and Robertson (1988) argue that these requirements are not met, since forensic psychiatry lacks a relevant *medical* formulation of psychopathy. However, if medical in this context means organically based, this represents a narrow reductionist view of the scope of forensic psychiatry, which has always embraced psychological as well as biological models of disorder.

Although there is a lack of an agreed theory of psychopathic personality or of personality disorders more generally, current psychological therapies usually identify specific goals and anticipated outcomes.

A second problem is that treatability decisions parallel dangerousness evaluations in blurring the distinction between assessment and prediction (Heilbrun *et al.*, 1988). The evaluation of treatability requires a distinction between the prediction of a treatment outcome and the assessment of *amenability to treatment* as a constellation of personal and situational characteristics. The former demands empirical evidence on treatment efficacy, which is examined below. The latter requires a reliable measure which takes account of (i) the appropriate fit between treatment goals and patient deficits; (ii) history of the patient's response to treatment; (iii) motivation; (iv) contra-indications. It must also consider the availability of treatment and environmental resources. Heilbrun *et al.* (1988) describe preliminary attempts to construct such a measure, which, however, foundered on the quality of file information available.

TREATMENT OF PSYCHOPATHY AND PERSONALITY DISORDER

The commonly expressed view that psychopaths are untreatable rests more on anecdote than firm evidence, and the treatment literature is plagued by the inconsistent use of the term 'psychopath'. A further problem in most reports is that the theoretical link between treatment technique and outcome is usually obscure. Demonstration of treatment efficacy requires not only that treatment be shown to reduce recidivism, but also that this is a consequence of changes in psychological mediators. Few programmes reported, however, clearly specify targets other than antisocial behaviour, and as was noted above, failure to identify treatment goals continues to be widespread in clinical practice. Psychodynamic programmes, for example, tend to identify global goals, such as improved social responsibility or self-control, but provide no reliable means of determining their attainment. At the other extreme, behavioural programmes have often been concerned with concrete targets such as institutional compliance, grooming habits, or skills whose relevance to either antisocial behaviour or personality disorder is unclear (Emery and Marholin, 1977; Hollin, 1990).

It was suggested earlier that the appropriate clinical focus is on personality disorders, and differentiation of these disorders is therefore necessary not only as a first step in identifying individual treatment targets, but also to identify amenability to different treatment methods. Personality disorders represent learned dysfunctional behaviour patterns rather than discrete disease categories. Personal change rather than 'cure' is therefore the appropriate goal, although the provision of specific coping skills may often be the most attainable target. However, systematic outcome research on the treatment of different forms of personality disorder remains rare, reflecting the lack of clinical interest in personality disorders other than psychopathic personality prior to the advent of DSM-III (Beck and Freeman, 1990; Widiger and Frances, 1985). This discussion will of necessity focus on the clinical literature dealing with 'psychopaths' or 'antisocial personalities', but it must be emphasised that conclusions about the treatability of the classical psychopath rest mainly on studies of poor methodology conducted with vaguely defined samples.

There have been several follow-up studies of discharged mentally disordered offenders, which typically find that legal psychopaths are at greater risk of reoffending than those deemed mentally ill (Bailey and MacCulloch, 1992; Murray, 1989). However, these studies primarily address the question of predicting dangerousness, and evidence of the impact of particular treatment interventions is meagre. From a search of 295 reports on the treatment of antisocial personality, Levine and Bornstein (1972) identified only ten studies which approached methodological requirements (homogeneous samples, untreated controls, follow-up, and specific outcome criteria), most of which concerned juvenile offenders in penal settings. Eight described significant effects on antisocial behaviour, and the authors note that this limited evidence does not support the view that antisocial personalities are unamenable to change. However, none of these studies employed a reproducible criterion of antisocial personality, and it is doubtful whether any dealt with homogeneous samples. For example, almost 60% of the 'character and behaviour disorders' of one of these studies (Colman and Baker, 1969) had primary diagnoses of schizophrenia or neurosis.

The problem of diagnosis is emphasised by Suedfeld and Landon (1978), who reviewed the literature on individual and group therapy, milieu therapy, somatic treatment, and behaviour modification with 'psychopaths' reported up to 1975. Most reports concerned the treatment of delinquents and adult criminals, and consistently inadequate criteria of psychopathy precluded anything more than the following tentative conclusions: therapy should be conducted with firm rules and non-gullible supportiveness; drugs may enable the psychopath to achieve rapport with therapists; a therapeutic community may be helpful; and psychopaths may 'burn out' with age. Only a handful of relevant studies has appeared since these reviews. These are examined in the following discussion, although some of the earlier reports are included for illustrative purposes.

Psychopharmacological Treatment

Major and minor tranquillisers are often administered in psychiatric hospitals to manage violent incidents. The rationale is the non-specific one of calming or sedating the patient, which can be justified when the safety of others is threatened. There is, however, currently little rationale for drug treatment of personality disorders, and drugs are not used widely in clinical practice. Dell and Robertson (1988), for example, found that only 14% of legal psychopaths at Broadmoor had been prescribed medication. Nevertheless, conditions requiring pharmacological treatment, such as epilepsy or mood disorders, sometimes co-occur with personality disorders, and Widiger and Frances (1985) suggest that there may be some potential for the use of drugs as an adjunct to psychological treatment in view of the evidence for biological influences on personality.

Biological models of psychopathic personality also continue to receive some attention, and would imply a possible role for pharmacological agents.

Findings from the scattered clinical literature on pharmacological attempts to improve compliance in personality disorders are generally inconclusive (Kellner, 1978; Suedfeld and Landon, 1978). Keller found little evidence for the effectiveness of neuroleptics or minor tranquillisers, but suggests that some drugs might benefit sociopaths showing uncontrollable aggression, impulsiveness, or mood lability. Lithium, for example, originally used to treat mania, has been found to reduce serious institutional rule infractions among aggressive prisoners (Sheard, Marini, Bridges, and Wagner, 1976). O'Callaghan (1988), however, notes that the quality of evidence supporting the pharmacological control of violence is poor, and suggests that while controlled studies with psychiatric patients support the use of major tranquillisers, the effects of stimulants, anticonvulsants, beta blockers, and lithium are merely suggestive.

There is, however, a longstanding interest in the possible use of stimulants to facilitate compliance and new learning in view of relatively consistent evidence that agents such as methylphenidate and dextramphetamine reduce impulsive antisocial behaviour in hyperactive children. Satterfield (1978) suggests that this effect is achieved via an increase in cortical arousal, which reduces motor restlessness and improves concentration. He proposes that adult psychopaths are also underaroused, and that pharmacologically increased arousal may be a necessary adjunct to educational and other therapeutic efforts.

However, the hypothesis that psychopaths are underaroused has not fared well from research (Blackburn, 1993), and evidence for positive effects of stimulants on antisocial adults is limited to uncontrolled case studies. In an early study, Hill (1947) followed up eight patients who had briefly received amphetamine, and concluded that it was of little value for inadequate, passive, hysterical, or neurasthenic personalities, but that there were beneficial effects for aggressive characters capable of warm interpersonal relationships. This does not, however, describe the classical psychopath. Stringer and Josef (1983) also reported the use of methylphenidate with two patients diagnosed APD who had a childhood history of attention deficit disorder. Both were more co-operative and less aggressive while receiving the drug, but this did not outlast treatment.

Given the lack of evidence that drug administration facilitates the learning of adaptive coping skills, pharmacological treatment seems unlikely to have a role in clinical programmes for psychopaths beyond that of ameliorating other psychiatric symptoms or temporarily controlling violence. In the latter context, the use of a 'chemical straitjacket' raises ethical issues because of the potential for punitive use and the neglect of environmental causes of violence. The voluntary acceptability of drugs such as lithium is also limited by unpleasant side-effects (Sheard *et al.*, 1976).

Individual and Group Psychodynamic Psychotherapy

Psychodynamic therapies are frequently employed in secure psychiatric settings. Dell and Robertson (1988) found that 71% of psychopathic disorder patients at Broadmoor had received group psychotherapy and 43% individual psycho-therapy, compared with 41% who had been involved in social skills training or other behavioural therapies, although this pattern is not necessarily typical of all such institutions. Psychodynamic therapists explicitly emphasise personality structure, and see problems of violence, sex offending, and psychopathy in similar terms. Chronic antisocial behaviour is held to reflect distortions in development and primitive defences against trusting relationships resulting from early rejection and abuse. Therapy aims to promote self awareness, empathy, self-control, and social responsibility by means of the therapeutic relationship.

The traditional psychoanalytic view is that the psychopath is untreatable because of the absence of neurotic conflicts, and there seems general agreement that the psychopath's resistance to treatment, manipulativeness and use of primi-tive defences, difficulties in forming a therapeutic alliance, and strong counter-transference reactions pose significant obstacles to the attainment of insight or self-awareness through the transference relationship. However, some psycho-therapists do not draw a firm line between psychopaths and acting-out neurotics, believing that psychopaths have some trace of anxiety or depression (e.g. Schmideberg, 1961; Vaillant, 1975). Psychopaths may therefore be treatable under certain conditions.

Although there is no uniform approach, psychotherapists working with violent offenders identify similar goals, strategies, and problems (Carney, 1977, 1978; Madden, 1986; Vaillant, 1975). Getting the patient to accept responsibility for his situation and for change is a particular focus, but a core issue is to establish trust. This is both a prerequisite for therapy and a target of change for individuals who are likely to view relationships as dangerous. It requires the therapist to show acceptance of the patient, though not his deeds, while at the same time setting limits and external controls, and therapists are more directive than is traditional in psychotherapy. Therapy entails establishing awareness of feelings by over-coming defences against fears of intimacy and low self-esteem, and this is achieved by encouraging verbalisations of destructive fantasies, tolerating expressions of uncomfortable feelings, and reflecting these. Disclosure of anxieties arising from early traumatic relationships may be particularly facilitated by the dynamics of a small group. A primary goal is to provide insight to help the patient tolerate 'the unfinished business' of early trauma (Cox, 1980). However, Cox acknowledges that this itself is unlikely to stop the patient offending.

Two issues recur in discussions of therapy with this group, which have some relevance for other approaches. First is the problem of patient motivation and capacity for change. Antisocial patients usually enter therapy only under pressure from families or the courts, and even among involuntarily detained patients, attendance may be erratic and dropout rates high. Group therapy is considered less threatening, and the most appropriate medium. However, patients may passively resist therapeutic involvement, or 'con' the therapist with superficial gestures of self-awareness. Failure of the patient to express strong emotion is prognostically unfavourable, and Lion (1978) believes that change is unlikely without the development of a depressive reaction, signifying emerging guilt.

Nevertheless, change is limited by the patient's ego strength, and a 'symptom oriented solution' may be the most realistic goal (Carney, 1977).

A second issue is the demands made on the therapist. Treatment requires regular sessions extending over a year or more, and continued therapist support may be necessary for much longer. While the development of a trusting relationship requires honest acceptance from the therapist, the focus on the patient's destructiveness may generate an intense countertransference, often taking the form of fear of the patient. Therapists therefore need to explore and verbalise their own feelings, preferably with other therapists.

There are few evaluations of the effectiveness of psychotherapy with personality disordered offenders, but several therapists describe partial evaluations. In a forerunner to cognitive therapy, Thorne (1959) saw 'sociopathic reactions' in Adlerian terms as an offensive-defensive lifestyle protected by egocentric attitudes and blame-avoidance. Individual outpatient therapy emphasised limit setting, acceptance of responsibility for negative consequences, insight into self-defeating behaviour, reality testing, and the discovery that 'honesty is the best policy'. Thorne claimed that this approach was successful in all of seven patients treated, although this was a selected group in private practice for whom treatment lasted up to 10 years in some cases.

A more typical group of institutionalised young adult offenders diagnosed as sociopaths was examined by Persons (1965), who conducted a controlled study of 20 sessions of individual 'eclectic' psychotherapy. Subjects were randomly assigned to therapy or no therapy controls, and administration of self-report tests of psychopathy and anxiety before and after treatment demonstrated significant effects of therapy on adjustment. Those in therapy also had significantly fewer disciplinary reports, but evaluation of behavioural effects was limited to the duration of therapy. Vaillant (1975) is also relatively optimistic about treatment prospects. He questions Cleckley's claim that psychopaths lack anxiety and motivation for change, seeing this as a stereotype of 'a patient fleeing therapy'. He suggests that the behaviour of antisocial personalities represents immature defences against fears of dependency and intimacy, and reports four case studies in which inpatient containment, firm behavioural control, confrontation rather than interpretation, and peer group support were apparently successful in achieving personality change.

Carney (1977) describes an uncontrolled follow-up of group therapy in an outpatient clinic. Personality disordered offenders attended as a condition of probation, and after an average of 13 months treatment, were followed up for some 9 months. Significant improvements were found in ratings of community adjustment, and recidivism rate was a relatively low 28%. However, no changes were found on psychological tests. Carney suggests that while therapy did not change personality, it achieved control over violent behaviour. Woody, McClellan, Luborsky, and O'Brien (1985), however, are more pessimistic. Among outpatient drug abusers undergoing cognitive or supportive-expressive psychotherapy, APD patients showed little change on a variety of psychiatric and psychological measures in comparison with APD patients who were also depressed. The authors suggest that difficulties in forming a relationship with the therapist militate against successful treatment of APD. Nevertheless, moderate improvements in the areas of employment and illegal behaviour were found for this group.

Most psychotherapists consider individual and outpatient treatment to be inappropriate for antisocial personalities, and regard structured group therapy in a residential setting as the treatment of choice (Carney, 1978; Cox, 1980; Frosch, 1983). Jew, Clanon, and Mattocks (1972) found that imprisoned personality disordered offenders in group therapy for at least a year had a significantly better success on parole than untreated offenders during the first year following release (74% vs 67%), but this modest difference subsequently disappeared. The authors suggest that lack of parole support facilities may have been critical. Apparently supporting this, Carney (1978) reports low recidivism rates for 'defective delinquents' treated at Patuxent by a combination of individual and group therapy followed by three years of supervised parole. Of those completing treatment, only 7% reoffended, in comparison with 37% for the institution as a whole. However, the outcome data from Patuxent have been challenged (Holden, 1978).

Therapeutic Communities

The therapeutic community (TC) is a generic term for several kinds of therapeutic organisation in which group processes are the primary treatment medium (Kennard, 1983). Although secure hospitals often claim to offer 'milieu therapy', this is usually a euphemism for an orderly regime, and more pertinent to the present discussion are the democratic-analytic and the concept-based TCs. The former, which is more common in Britain, is usually a small community of adolescents or young adults with neurotic problems or personality disorders, which aims to resolve inner conflicts and promote responsible social behaviour through exposure to a combination of democratic power sharing, permissiveness, communalism, and reality confrontation. The best known example is the Henderson Hospital, associated with the work of Maxwell Jones (1963), but these principles are also utilised by Grendon Underwood Prison (Gunn, Robertson, Dell, and Way, 1978) and the Barlinnie unit in a Scottish prison (Cooke, 1989).

Concept-based TCs are more common in America, and are hierarchically organised communities originating in self-help philosophies. They are mainly concerned with rehabilitating alcohol or drug abusers, staff members usually being ex-addicts. This kind of TC has been established in several American prisons (Wexler, Falkin, and Lipton, 1990). Kennard (1983) suggests that despite the differing models, TCs share the following basic features: (i) an informal atmosphere; (ii) regular community meetings; (iii) sharing the work of running the community; (iv) recognition of residents as auxiliary therapists. The general assumption is that the delegation of responsibility to residents in a 'living and learning' environment which encourages open expression of feelings and exploration of relationships will facilitate self-control.

There are several descriptive accounts of TCs for personality disordered offenders (e.g. Roosenburg, 1966) but fewer reports of outcome. TCs have been found to benefit psychological adjustment in the short term by reducing anxiety and depression (Fink, Derby,and Martin, 1969; Gunn *et al.*, 1978) and increasing self-esteem and self-perceived conformity and independence (Norris, 1983). Their impact in resocialising offenders is more equivocal. Craft, Stephenson, and Granger (1964) randomly allocated young legal psychopaths to a TC or a traditional authoritarian ward. After one year, there were few differences on a range of psychological tests, but those in the authoritarian unit showed a greater increase in IQ. They had also reoffended less at 14-month follow-up, and only a quarter were in need of continued care, compared with half of those from the TC. Craft (1984) describes subsequent work with similar results at Garth, an open hospital for offenders suffering from psychopathic disorder or subnormality under the Mental Health Act. Again, a patriarchal, disciplined regime produced more favourable results than a similar institution focusing on education and counselling. Craft notes good results for a substantial minority, and records that 58% did not reoffend. However, he considers treatment 'success' to be debatable, since few patients were subsequently married, employed or fully self-supporting. Nevertheless, institutional care provided a necessary asylum.

While the low intelligence of Craft's patients may partly account for their favourable response to a disciplined regime, a controlled evaluation at an English approved school by Cornish and Clarke (1975) also failed to demonstrate any benefits of a TC. 'Suitable' boys were randomly assigned to either a TC or a traditional unit, while 'unsuitable' boys also went to a traditional unit. At a 2-year follow-up, reconviction rates for the three units were indistinguishable, ranging from 68% to 70%. A 10-year follow-up of prisoners discharged from Grendon Underwood similarly found no reduction in recidivism, 92% of the TC prisoners having a further conviction compared with 85% of a comparison group (Robertson and Gunn, 1987).

Follow-up of 'psychopaths' admitted to the Henderson Hospital further suggests a high failure rate. Using a criterion of no further hospitalisations or criminal offences within 3 to 5 years as indicating success, Copas *et al.* (1984) found that 36% of those admitted were successful compared with 19% of a group not admitted for various reasons, although success rates increased with length of stay. They also found that secondary psychopaths derived the least benefit, and that the more successful patients already possessed an adequate repertoire of interpersonal skills and were the least unsocialised to begin with. Similar findings are reported from Canada. Harris, Rice, and Cormier (1989) carried out a 10-year follow-up of violent recidivism among offenders who had been patients for at least 2 years in a TC in a maximum security hospital. They found that 77% of those scoring highly on Hare's PCL were violent recidivists compared with 24% of those scoring low. Ogloff, Wong, and Greenwood, (1990) also found that offender patients in a TC who had high scores on the PCL stayed in treatment for a shorter time than those with medium or low scores, and were rated as lower in motivation and improvement.

These latter findings, however, imply that some personality disordered offenders respond favourably, and a few studies suggest more positive benefits of the TC on offenders. Peer modelling was emphasised in a unit for habitually violent prisoners in an Indian prison, where the majority of inmates were conforming and 'provided a good example' (Sandhu, 1970). Of 18 psychopaths who stayed for an average of 9 months, 13 were said to be successful on staff judgements of attitude to work and general conduct. A preliminary evaluation of the Barlinnie unit also provides evidence of reduced violence following admission and a lower than expected recidivism rate at follow-up (Cooke, 1989), although numbers are small and a comparison group lacking.

McCord (1983) reports significantly reduced recidivism among pre-adolescent 'psychopaths' exposed to milieu therapy which emphasised 'disciplined love'. However, continued support seems to have been available after institutional release for treated delinquents, but not for the comparison group. More definitive is a large-scale study of a concept-based prison TC for drug abusers in New York State (Wexler, Falkin, and Lipton, 1990). Over a follow-up period of some three years, rearrest rates for males were 27% for those completing the programme, 35% for those in a less structured milieu programme, and 41% of prisoners volunteering for the TC but not participating. Wexler, Falkin, and Lipton believe that their hierarchical TC contains the ingredients now considered necessary for successful rehabilitation (e.g. Andrews, Bonta, and Hoge, 1990), such as a social learning model, a high degree of structure, and prosocial modelling. Whether these ingredients were lacking in the less successful TCs merits attention, but these findings can only be tentatively generalised to personality disordered offenders.

Despite the limited evidence for its success, the TC continues to have vocal supporters. The humane, democratic, treatment-oriented approach contrasts with the punitive and degrading features of many custodial institutions, and in this respect the TC commends itself as 'a paradigm of prison management' (Robertson and Gunn, 1987). Nevertheless, its ideological and aesthetic appeal may overshadow issues of rehabilitative efficacy. There is no evidence that the TC is superior to other therapeutic modalities in promoting psychological adjustment, and the evidence suggests that most TCs do not affect criminality. Robertson and Gunn (1987) argue that reoffending has more to do with problems of marital adjustment, accommodation, or employment faced by the offender after release than with what happens in treatment. However, such problems may reflect skill deficits as much as opportunities, and Harris, Rice, and Cormier (1989) note that the TC they investigated gave no emphasis to skills training or to the learning of anticriminal attitudes. One problem shared with other psychodynamic methods is the lack of specificity inherent in the goals of 'insight' or 'responsibility', and Kennard (1983) suggests that TCs might benefit from addressing the more specific deficits dealt with by behavioural methods.

Cognitive-behavioural Approaches

The development of behavioural interventions with mentally disordered offenders and penal populations has paralleled that in mental health services generally. Early applications focused on the use of operant methods for managing behavioural deficits or disruptive institutional behaviour and the combination of contingency management with modelling and role play to enhance social skills. In the Special Hospitals early examples of skills training programmes were described for aggressive offenders by Howells (1976) and for sex offenders by Crawford and Allen (1979). More recent training methods emphasise linguistic procedures which target cognitive mediators of deviant behaviour, such as distortions in thinking and cognitive-affective linkages, or deficits in problem-solving processes. The repertoire of psychologists working with psychopathic offenders is therefore now likely to include techniques such as self-control training, anger management, cognitive restructuring, and inter-personal problem-solving training, as well as a range of specific techniques for dealing with deviant sexual and aggressive behaviour. Grounds, Quayle, France, Brett, Cox, and Hamilton (1987), for example, describe an eclectic programme for psychopathic disorder patients at Broadmoor in which individual and group therapy is integrated with cognitive-behavioural methods. The latter include social skills training, anger management, sex education, and cognitive therapy for depression and sexual problems. As yet, there is little evidence for the long-term maintenance of changes achieved by these approaches, and virtually none on their impact on recidivism, although Crawford demonstrated that social skills developed by sex offenders were maintained at 2-year follow-up within the institution.

Behavioural methods have been applied to deviant behaviour in psychiatric populations likely to contain many with personality disorders, but few of these programmes identify their clients in terms of psychopathic personality or person-ality disorder. Behaviour therapists may therefore frequently deal with person-ality disorders, but choose to call them something else. What are commonly identified as social skill deficits, for example, include social avoidance and anxiety, lack of assertiveness, and inappropriate anger expression, which appear among the criteria for personality disorders. However, despite the aversion of behaviour therapists to dispositional concepts, some have attempted to incor-porate clinical concepts of personality disorder into a behavioural framework, usually by translating them into terms of skill deficits. Marshall and Barbaree (1984), for example, conceptualise personality disorders as unskilful social behavioural repertoires which fail to engender rewarding or non-aversive outcomes from others.

A few behavioural programmes applied with undifferentiated personality disorders have been reported successfully to reduce social dysfunction. Jones, Stayer, Wichlacz, Thomes, and Livingstone (1977), for example, describe a short-term token economy ward for military personnel diagnosed as personality disorders. A combination of individualised contingency contracting and the reinforcement with points for appearance, work, and educational achievement led to significantly more of those treated remaining on active duty than untreated controls. Moyes, Tennent, and Bedford (1985) also found that a programme combining a token economy, individualised contingency management, and social skills training reduced aggressive and disruptive behaviour and self-mutilation in youths described as behaviour and character disordered. It also delayed sub-sequent involvement with the police. However, an ambitious token economy programme described by Cavior and Schmidt (1978), in which offenders were also assigned to differential treatment on the basis of Quay's behaviour classification system, failed to produce any significant reduction in recidivism, or any differential effects for psychopaths.

Applications of more cognitively oriented methods to personality disorders have received some attention, but outcome data are currently few. Templeman and Wollersheim (1979) described a programme for psychopaths which employed fixed role therapy and problem-solving training through self-instruction to teach clients to obtain their goals of obtaining sensation and self-gratification in socially acceptable ways, but reported no outcome data. In another approach, Frederiksen and Rainwater (1981) conceptualised explosive personality disorder in terms of negative interpersonal expectations and deficient assertion. They treated voluntary patients with a short but intensive programme of social skills training, cognitive restructuring, and self-control of problem drinking, and found reductions in explosive outbursts for those followed up. However, drop-out rate was high, and some of those completing treatment continued to have social difficulties.

Anger problems are among the criteria defining passive-aggressive, borderline, and antisocial personality disorders, and anger is now commonly regarded as a significant mediator of antisocial aggression, and a target for cognitive-behavioural intervention (Levey and Howells, 1990). The most widely used approach is Novaco's anger management programme, which involves cognitive restructuring and coping skills training, the package being used on an individual or group basis. It has been shown to be effective as a stress management procedure which reduces interpersonal conflict in a variety of populations, such as married couples, child-abusing parents, and criminal justice personnel. However, while its popularity in penal settings appears to be growing, reports of its utility with offenders are confined to a few studies of delinquents, and only one controlled study with personality disordered offenders has been described. This involved a brief, six-session programme for patients in a forensic psychiatric unit, most of them diagnosed as APD (Stermac, 1986). Training produced effects on self-reported anger and coping strategies, but longer term behavioural effects were not examined. While the utility of anger management for dealing with disruptive behaviour in institutions now seems established (Levey and Howells, 1990), its longer term impact on violent offenders who are disordered remains to be investigated.

Cognitive-behavioural approaches which view personality disorders in terms of skill deficits follow the molecular emphasis of traditional learning theory based therapies, and eschew any broader conceptualisation of personality. However, Beck and Freeman (1990) note findings in the treatment literature suggesting that the presence of personality disorder reduces the effectiveness of programmes which focus on skills training alone. They argue for a more molar approach, proposing that personality traits are overt expressions of tacit or deep cognitive schemata which dictate a generalised behavioural strategy. Each personality disorder is held to be characterised by a distinct cognitive profile reflecting a composite of beliefs, attitudes, affects, and strategies organised around a general theme of the nature of the self and others. For example, passive-aggressive personalities are held to be dominated by beliefs that others interfere with their freedom of action, and that they must do things their own way. In the case of antisocial personalities, core beliefs relate to looking out for oneself and an entitlement to break rules, resulting in a strategy of attacking or exploiting others.

This conceptualisation of antisocial personality disorder gives less weight to an absence of 'superego' than to an egocentric level of moral development in which self-serving beliefs minimise future consequences. Therapy aims to enhance cognitive functioning by utilising self-serving motivation. The clinician attempts to guide the client from a strategy of unqualified self-interest to one of qualified self-interest which takes account of the needs of others, by means of guided discussions, structured cognitive exercises, and behavioural experiments. Beck and Freeman (1990) report experience of the success of cognitive therapy with antisocial outpatients. However, available empirical data are limited to those of Woody *et al.* (1985) described earlier, whose findings offer only qualified support.

The preceding approach introduces systematic theory into an area of practice which has largely relied on technique-driven strategies. However, it rests on a direct translation of DSM-III descriptions of personality disorder categories into belief systems which would appear to underlie them, and is not derived from any established theory of personality or empirical research. A related theory, which does have empirical support, conceptualises personality disorders as dysfunctional *interpersonal styles* supported by biased expectations, which function as self-fulfilling prophecies through their effects on others (Blackburn, 1992; Carson, 1979). From this perspective, therapy needs to focus on disconfirming interpersonal expectations, and some cognitive therapists propose that this can be achieved by using the therapist–client relationship as a mechanism for change (Safran, 1990). This approach offers a rapprochement with psychodynamic therapies. However, it also implies that therapy cannot be wholly person-centred, and must take account of the social environment. In the case of institutionalised offenders, it would suggest programming the environment to provide not only disconfirming experiences, but also opportunities for developing new interpersonal skills.

It will be apparent that the application of cognitive-behavioural methods to personality disordered offenders is at an early stage of development. This partly reflects the relatively recent introduction of many of these procedures, but it also reflects the traditional antipathy of behaviour therapists to personality constructs. However, recent social cognitive approaches emphasise dispositions traditionally associated with psychopathy as mediators of antisocial behaviour, and a number of interventions which target these characteristics have successfully reduced recidivism in young delinquents. Particularly prominent have been skills training and educational programmes which focus on impulsivity and self-control, egocentricity and social role-taking and the development of moral reasoning (for reviews, see Blackburn, 1993; Hollin, 1990; Ross and Fabiano, 1985). Since these attributes are central to the classical concept of psychopathy, the extension of these methods to personality disordered offenders would appear to hold some promise.

A CASE HISTORY

The following case history illustrates the cognitive-behavioural treatment of a patient in a Special Hospital, who was categorised as suffering from psychopathic disorder. Psychologically, he is describable as a secondary psychopath.

Martin was a young man with several convictions since age 13 for minor thefts, obscene telephone calls, and indecent exposure, and had previously served two short prison sentences. His most recent incidents of indecent exposure were accompanied by physical assaults on his female victims and threats with a knife, and the offence prior to his arrest also involved a threat to rape. Psychiatrists who examined him in prison found him to be depressed, to have longstanding social and sexual difficulties, and to suffer from a personality disorder. He also described violent fantasies of raping and killing females, and in view of the apparent escalation of violence in his offences, he was considered to be dangerous and in need of treatment.

He was an anxious man, who readily described his social and sexual difficulties and acknowledged a need for psychological help. Assessment following his admission extended over several interviews, and included the administration of psychological tests (MCMI, SHAPS, Beck Depression Inventory, nurse rating scales). His mood, urges to expose himself, violent fantasies, and self-esteem, were also regularly monitored by idiographic scales (PQRST). Results confirmed frequent depressed mood and continuing violent fantasies, and indicated that his social dysfunctions centred on passive-aggressive, avoidant, schizoid, and antisocial traits. His extensive sexual problems included anxieties about social and sexual interaction with females, erectile failure when attempting intercourse, excessive masturbation, and urges to expose himself which he continued to experience in hospital. He was also frequently tense, and felt a failure in most areas of his life. He had an unstable employment history, partly due to his lack of skills, but also to his impulsively leaving his jobs, and had been inclined to get into financial difficulties due to heavy gambling and drinking.

His mother had died when he was a child, and he saw his father as a remote figure, his elder sister having been the dominant figure in his formative years. These family relationships appeared to be significant in his psychosexual development, which was characterised by a low level of masculine identity and an overidealisation of females. This was reflected in nursing observations that he tended to be timid and avoidant with both his peers and male staff, but very dependent on female staff. He was also noted to be stubborn, and sometimes unco-operative, though not particularly aggressive. These interpersonal characteristics were consistent with personality test data, and it was clear that any potential for violence centred on females and his exhibitionism. However, while the two were associated, frequent episodes of indecent exposure had preceded aggression to females by several years, and analysis of these suggested a chain of events usually triggered by depressed mood. More recently, this mood was related to the termination of a brief affair with a younger girl, Linda, which he attributed to her becoming a 'prostitute', an interpretation resulting from her interest in wearing heavy make-up and provocative clothes. He felt intense hatred to all women he perceived as prostitutes, and this occasioned his recent assaults.

Martin's problems were interpreted as a failure of social development consequent on uncertainties relating to attachment to females following the death of his mother, the absence of masculine role modelling, and the development of a self-defeating life-style in which he was unable to generate positive reinforcement in his relationships. In this context, his indecent exposure, gambling, drinking, and also his violent sexual fantasies can be construed as negatively reinforced ways of coping with failure experiences and resulting low self-esteem. In addition, however, his hostile preoccupation with 'prostitutes' represented distorted attributions following the breakup of the only heterosexual relationship he had found rewarding. The treatment plan therefore targeted his beliefs about prostitutes, depressed mood, social and sexual skill deficits, his urges to expose himself, and his passive-aggressive coping style.

Initial treatment employed cognitive therapy procedures, in which the sources of his beliefs about prostitutes were examined. Although Martin made no connection between these and his feelings about Linda, it was apparent that they represented distorted overgeneralisations, and therapy sessions focused on his relationship with Linda and his explanation for its termination. Alternatives to his belief that she had left him because she became 'corrupted' were debated, and the cues on which he based his perception of prostitutes challenged. The aim was to help him discover that his beliefs about prostitutes derived from an inappropriate interpretation of Linda's behaviour. While progress seemed slow, and he frequently reported feeling angry about prostitutes, a change occurred after some four months of therapy, when he produced old letters from Linda which he asked the therapist to destroy. His reasons indicated a more realistic reappraisal of her behaviour, and he was encouraged to destroy the letters himself. He also reported reduced hostility towards prostitutes and a feeling that he had been 'stupid'.

His sexual fantasies also ceased to contain violence, but episodes of depressed mood and urges to exhibit himself continued. Cognitive procedures were extended to his depression, which tended to be elicited by social failures and self-denigration. Attempts were made to identify small success experiences, and these were facilitated by having him join a social skills training group, in which he not only performed well, but also formed friendships with other group members. It was, in fact, observed that he possessed a number of positive skills which were masked by social anxiety. As he began to make less negative appraisals of his own behaviour, this decreased in intensity, and his depressive moods became less frequent. After nine months of treatment, further psychological testing revealed significant reductions in depression and anxiety, and improved self-esteem, although some dysfunctional traits were still evident. Therapy sessions were reduced in frequency, subsequently focusing on problems in his past relationships with females, and since his knowledge of sexuality proved to be deficient, he joined a sex education class. Some of his heterosexual interaction problems were dealt with in the social skills training group which contained female therapists, but the learning of new skills in this area was limited by the absence of opportunities for meeting females informally, since the hospital housed only male patients.

The problem of his continuing exposure urges remained to be dealt with, and he reported that these formed much of his masturbatory fantasy. They increased when he became infatuated with a female nurse, and there was a crisis when he actually exposed himself to her. An attempt was therefore made to deal with his exhibitionism by means of covert sensitisation. Tape recordings were made describing the sequence of antecedent events and thoughts leading to exposure in incidents reported by Martin. Consequences he identified as aversive (shame, physical pain, fear of arrest) were described at critical points in the behaviour sequence. A final scenario described him exercising control over his urges early in the sequence, and the rewarding consequences of this. Tapes were played for an hour in 12 weekly sessions, and Martin also listened to them on his own between sessions. His self-monitoring of urges to expose himself revealed a decline from an average of two to three daily prior to treatment to less than one a month six months after treatment, and no further incidents occurred. While his urges were not completely eliminated, he described them as controllable and less powerful.

Individual sessions throughout treatment also focused on his stubborn passive resistance when frustrated, and his loss of a favoured job as a result of this behaviour provided an opportunity to examine the contribution of rigid beliefs to previous social and employment failures. Problem-solving techniques, in which he generated and rehearsed alternative solutions to frustration, were used to develop more adaptive coping strategies, with beneficial effects. Further testing confirmed not only the maintenance of earlier therapeutic gains, but also less pronounced schizoid, passive-aggressive, and antisocial traits. His visible progress therefore led to agreement for outings to shops, restaurants, and pubs to observe his coping with everyday situations and to prepare him for discharge. It was agreed that little further progress could be expected in hospital, and that he no longer presented a danger to women, and he was subsequently transferred to a regional secure unit. Two years later, he wrote to report that he had held a responsible job for a year, and had formed a satisfying relationship with a woman he was about to marry. He again described his previous deviant behaviour as 'stupid', and felt that his treatment in hospital had enabled him to 'grow up'.

In some respects, this case is typical of psychopathic offenders admitted to Special Hospitals. Martin's deviant behaviour was not an isolated problem, but rather has to be seen in the context of multiple and longstanding cognitive, affective, and social dysfunctions. Therapy therefore had multiple targets, and called for intensive therapeutic involvement over an extended period. It is not, of course, possible to attribute his improvement specifically to the techniques employed, although they provided a necessary structure to therapy. Nevertheless, it is unlikely that the significant changes demonstrated and maintained would have occurred without psychological intervention.

There are, however, two critical factors which contributed to successful outcome. First, Martin was not a 'classical' psychopath, having some capacity for warmth and concern for others, and also being well motivated to change. Second, his offences had not resulted in serious injury to anyone, making it easier to progress his rehabilitation to a more open environment after the relatively short period of detention (for a Special Hospital) of three years.

CONCLUSIONS

Quinsey (1988) observed that systematic treatment programmes for mentally disordered offenders are not only rare, but that evaluations of their effects are typically conspicuous by their absence. This remains the case for offenders described as 'psychopathic'. Few new findings have emerged from the recent treatment literature to add to the tentative observations of Suedfeld and Landon (1978), and the number of methodologically adequate reports remains so small that only two conclusions can be drawn. First, while classical psychopaths have been shown to respond poorly to some traditional therapeutic interventions, it has yet to be established that 'nothing works' with this group. Second, some offenders with personality disorders do appear to change with psychological treatment. No particular approach has consistently been found to be beneficial, but procedures which structure the therapeutic environment, such as the token economy and the therapeutic community, and eclectic psychotherapy, group therapy, social skills training, and cognitive restructuring can all claim examples of positive effects. Social cognitive interventions being developed with offenders generally seem particularly relevant to personality disorders.

Given the range of programmes which have achieved effects, it may be that specific techniques are less important than certain conditions of service delivery which promote change. Common ingredients of more successful programmes appear to be inpatient containment, treatment staff who are warm but directive and set limits, procedures which challenge egocentric and antisocial beliefs, the programming of new cognitive and interpersonal skills through prosocial modelling and skills training, intensive treatment, and structured support beyond programme termination. While evidence that these conditions are critical to the treatment of psychopathic offenders is piecemeal, recent evaluations indicate that many of them are basic to successful offender rehabilitation generally (Andrews, Bonta, and Hoge 1990; Gendreau and Ross, 1987).

However, offenders do not respond in a uniform fashion to all treatment approaches. We do not as yet know which disorders within the heterogeneous category of psychopathic disorder or 'antisocial personalities' respond to which interventions, and until clinically relevant discriminations are made within this group, practice in this area will remain in a theoretical vacuum.

REFERENCES

American Psychiatric Association (1987). *Diagnostic and Statistical Manual of Mental Disorders* (third edn, revised). Washington, DC: American Psychiatric Association.

Andrews, D. A., Bonta, J., and Hoge, R. D. (1990). Classification for effective rehabilitation: Rediscovering psychology. *Criminal Justice and Behavior*, **17**, 19–52.

Bailey, J., and MacCulloch, M. (1992). Characteristics of 112 cases discharged directly to the community from a new Special Hospital and some comparisons of performance. *Journal of Forensic Psychiatry*, **3**, 91–112.

Beck, A. T., and Freeman, A. (1990). *Cognitive Therapy of Personality Disorders*. New York: Guilford.

Blackburn, R. (1975). An empirical classification of psychopathic personality. *British Journal of Psychiatry*, **127**, 456–60.

Blackburn, R. (1982). The Special Hospitals assessment of personality and socialisation (SHAPS). Unpublished manuscript, Park Lane Hospital, Liverpool.

Blackburn, R. (1986). Patterns of personality deviation among violent offenders: Replication and extension of an empirical taxonomy. *British Journal of Criminology*, **26**, 254–69.

Blackburn, R. (1987). Two scales for the assessment of personality disorder in antisocial populations. *Personality and Individual Differences*, **8**, 81–93.

Blackburn, R. (1988). On moral judgements and personality disorders: The myth of the psychopathic personality revisited. *British Journal of Psychiatry*, **153**, 505–12.

Blackburn, R. (1989). Psychopathy and personality disorder in relation to violence. In K. Howells and C. R. Hollin (eds), *Clinical Approaches to Violence*. Chichester: Wiley.

Blackburn, R. (1992). Criminal behaviour, personality disorder, and mental illness: The origins of confusion. *Criminal Behaviour and Mental Health*, **2**, 66–77.

Blackburn, R. (1993). *The Psychology of Criminal Conduct: Theory, Research and Practice*. Chichester: Wiley.

Blackburn, R., Crellin, M. C., Morgan, E. M., and Tulloch, R. M. B. (1990). Prevalence of personality disorders in a Special Hospital population. *Journal of Forensic Psychiatry*, **1**, 43–52.

Bowden, P. (1992). Pioneers in forensic psychiatry. James Cowles Prichard: moral insanity and the myth of psychopathic personality. *Journal of Forensic Psychiatry*, **3**, 113–36.

Brantley, P. J., and Sutker, P. B. (1984). Antisocial behaviour disorders. In H. E. Adams and P. B. Sutker (eds), *Comprehensive Handbook of Psychopathology*. New York: Plenum.

Carney, F. L. (1977). Outpatient treatment of the aggressive offender. *American Journal of Psychotherapy*, **31**, 265–74.

Carney, F. L. (1978). Inpatient treatment programs. In W. H. Reid (ed.), *The Psychopath: A Comprehensive Study of Antisocial Disorders and Behaviors*. New York: Brunner/ Mazel.

Carson, R. C. (1979). Personality and exchange in developing relationships. In R. L. Burgess and T. L. Huston (eds), *Social Exchange in Developing Relationships*. New York: Academic Press.

Cavior, H. E. and Schmidt, A. A. (1978). Test of the effectiveness of a differential treatment strategy at the Robert F. Kennedy Centre. *Criminal Justice and Behavior*, **5**, 131–9.

Chiswick, D. (1987). Managing psychopathic offenders: A problem that will not go away. *British Medical Journal*, **295**, 159–60.

Cleckley, H. (1941). *The Mask of Sanity* (sixth edn 1976). St Louis: Mosby.

Colman, A. D., and Baker, S. L. (1969). Utilisation of an operant conditioning model for the treatment of character and behavior disorders in a military setting. *American Journal of Psychiatry*, **125**, 101–9.

Collins, P. (1991). The treatability of psychopaths. *Journal of Forensic Psychiatry*, **2**, 103–10.

Cooke, D. (1989). Containing violent prisoners: An analysis of the Barlinnie Special Unit. *British Journal of Criminology*, **29**, 129–43.

Copas, J. B., O'Brien, M., Roberts, J., and Whiteley, S. (1984). Treatment outcome in personality disorder: The effects of social, psychological, and behavioural measures. *Personality and Individual Differences*, **5**, 565–73.

Cornish, D. B., and Clarke, R. V. G. (1975). *Residential Treatment and its Effects on Delinquency*. London: HMSO.

Cox, M. (1980). Personal reflections upon 3000 hours in therapeutic groups with sex offenders. In D. J. West (ed.), *Sex Offenders in the Criminal Justice System*. Cropwood Conferences Series No. 12. Cambridge: Institute of Criminology.

Craft, M. (1984). The results of treatment. In M. Craft and A. Craft (eds), *Mentally Abnormal Offenders*. London: Bailliere Tindall.

Craft, M., Stephenson, G., and Granger, C. (1964). A controlled trial of authoritarian and self-governing regimes with adolescent psychopaths. *American Journal of Ortho-psychiatry*, **64**, 543–54.

Crawford, D. A. (1984). Behaviour therapy. In M. Craft and A. Craft (eds), *Mentally Abnormal Offenders*. London: Bailliere Tindall.

Crawford, D. A., and Allen, J. V. (1979). A social skills training program with sex offenders. In M. Cook and G. Wilson (eds), *Love and Attraction*. Oxford: Pergamon.

Dell, S., and Robertson, G. (1988). *Sentenced to Hospital: Offenders in Broadmoor*. Maudsley Monographs No. 32. Oxford: Oxford University Press.

Emery, R. E., and Marholin, D. (1977). An applied behavior analysis of delinquency: The irrelevancy of relevant behavior. *American Psychologist*, **32**, 860–73.

Fink, L. F., Derby, W. N., and Martin, J. P. (1969). Psychiatry's new role in corrections. *American Journal of Psychiatry*, **126**, 542–6.

Frederiksen, L. W. and Rainwater, N. (1981). Explosive behavior: A skill development approach to treatment. In R. B. Stuart (ed.), *Violent Behavior: Social Learning Approaches to Prediction, Management and Treatment*. New York: Brunner/ Mazel.

Frosch, J. P. (1983). The treatment of antisocial and borderline personality disorders. *Hospital and Community Psychiatry*, **34**, 243–8.

Gendreau, P., and Ross, R. R. (1987). Revivification of rehabilitation: Evidence from the 1980s. *Justice Quarterly*, **4**, 349–407.

Gottfredson, M. R., and Hirschi, T. (1990). *A General Theory of Crime*. Stanford: Stanford University Press.

Gough, H. G. (1948). A sociological theory of psychopathy. *American Journal of Sociology*, **53**, 359–66.

Gough, H. G. (1969). *Manual for the California Psychological Inventory*. Palo Alto, Ca.: Consulting Psychologists Press.

Grounds, A. T. (1987). Detention of 'psychopathic disorder' patients in Special Hospitals: Critical issues. *British Journal of Psychiatry*, **151**, 474–8.

Grounds, A. T., Quayle, M. T., France, J., Brett, T., Cox, M., and Hamilton, J. R. (1987). A unit for 'psychopathic disorder' patients in Broadmoor hospital. *Medicine, Science and The Law*, **27**, 21–31.

Gunn, J., Robertson, G., Dell, S., and Way, C. (1978). *Psychiatric Aspects of Imprisonnent*. London: Academic Press.

Hare, R. D. (1980). A research scale for the assessment of psychopathy in criminal populations. *Personality and Individual Differences*, **1**, 111–19.

Hare, R. D. (1985). A comparison of procedures for the assessment of psychopathy. *Journal of Consulting and Clinical Psychology*, **53**, 7–16.

Hare, R. D. (1986). Twenty years of experience with the Cleckley psychopath. In W. H. Reid, D. Dorr, J. Walker and J. W. Bonner (eds), *Unmasking the Psychopath: Antisocial Personality and Related Syndromes*. New York: Norton.

Hare, R. D., Harpur, T. J., Hakstian, A. R., Forth, A. E., Hart, S. D., and Newman, J. P. (1990). The revised Psychopathy Checklist: Reliability and factor structure. *Psychological Assessment: A Journal of Consulting and Clinical Psychology*, **2**, 338–41.

Harris, G. T., Rice, M. E., and Cormier, C. A. (1989). Violent recidivism among psychopaths and nonpsychopaths treated in a therapeutic community. *Research Reports*, vol. 6, No. 1. Mental Health Centre, Penetanguishene, Ontario.

Heilbrun, A. B., and Heilbrun, M. R. (1985). Psychopathy and dangerousness: Comparison, integration, and extension of two psychopathic topologies. *British Journal of Clinical Psychology*, **24**, 181–95.

Heilbrun, K., Bennett, W. S., Evans, J. H., Offutt, R. A., Reiff, H. J., and White A. J. (1988). Assessing treatability in mentally disordered offenders: A conceptual and methodological note. *Behavioral Sciences and the Law*, **6**, 479–86.

Higgins, J. (1984). The mentally abnormal offender and his society. In M. Craft and A. Craft (eds), *Mentally Abnormal Offenders*. London: Bailliere Tindall.

Hill, D. (1947). Amphetamine in psychopathic states. *British Journal of Addiction*, **44**, 50–4.

Holden, C. (1978). Patuxent: Controversial prison clings to belief in rehabilitation. *Science*, **199**, 665–8.

Hollin, C. R. (1990). *Cognitive-Behavioral Interventions with Young Offenders*. New York: Pergamon.

Home Office/Department of Health and Social Security (1975). *Report of the Committee on Abnormal Offenders*. London: HMSO.

Howells, K. (1976). Interpersonal aggression. *International Journal of Criminology and Penology*, **4**, 319–30.

Jew, C. C., Clanon, T. L., and Mattocks, A. L. (1972). The effectiveness of group psychotherapy in a correctional institution. *American Journal of Psychiatry*, **129**, 602–5.

Jones, F. D., Stayer, S. J., Wichlacz, C. R., Thomes, L., and Livingstone, B. L. (1977). Contingency management of hospital diagnosed character and behavior disorder soldiers. *Journal of Behavior Therapy and Experimental Psychiatry*, **8**, 333.

Jones, M. (1963). The treatment of character disorders. *British Journal of Criminology*, **3**, 276–82.

Kellner, R. (1978). Drug treatment of personality disorders and delinquents. In W. H. Reid (ed.), *The Psychopath: A Comprehensive Study of Antisocial Disorders and Behaviors*. New York: Brunner/Mazel.

Kennard, D. (1983). *An Introduction to Therapeutic Communities*. London: Routledge & Kegan Paul.

Kuriychuk, M. (1990). The assessment of psychopathy and risk-taking behavior. Unpublished PhD dissertation, Queen's University, Kingston, Ontario.

Levey, S., and Howells, K. (1990). Anger and its management. *Journal of Forensic Psychiatry*, **1**, 305–27.

Levine, W. R., and Bornstein, P. E. (1972). Is the sociopath treatable? The contribution of psychiatry to a legal dilemma. *Washington University Law Quarterly*, 693–717.

Levinson, R. B. (1988). Developments in the classification process: Quay's AIMS approach. *Criminal Justice and Behavior*, **15**, 24–38.

Lion, J. R. (1978). Outpatient treatment of psychopaths. In W. H. Reid (ed.), *The Psychopath: A Comprehensive Study of Antisocial Disorders and Behaviors*. New York: Brunner/Mazel.

Lykken, D. T. (1957). A study of anxiety in the sociopathic personality. *Journal of Abnormal and Social Psychology*, **55**, 6–10.

Madden, D. J. (1986). Psychotherapeutic approaches in the treatment of violent persons. In L. H. Roth (ed.), *Clinical Treatment of the Violent Person*. New York: Guilford.

Maletzky, B. M. (1991). *Treating the Sex Offender*. Newbury Park, Ca.: Sage.

Marshall, W. L., and Barbaree, H. E. (1984). Disorders of personality, impulse, and adjustment. In S. M. Turner and M. Hersen (eds), *Adult Psychopathology and Diagnosis*. New York: Wiley.

McCord, W. M. (1983). *The Psychopath and Milieu Therapy*. New York: Academic Press.

McCord, W. M., and McCord, J. (1964). *The Psychopath: An Essay on The Criminal Mind*. New York: Van Nostrand.

Millon, T. (1981). *Disorders of Personality: DSM-III, Axis II*. New York: Wiley.

Millon, T. (1983). *Millon Clinical Multiaxial Inventory* (third edn). Minneapolis: Interpretive Scoring Systems.

Morey, L. C., Waugh, M. H., and Blashfield, R. K. (1985). MMPI scales for DSM-III personality disorders: Their derivation and correlates. *Journal of Personality Assessment*, **49**, 245–51.

Moyes, T., Tennent, T. G., and Bedford, A. P. (1985). Long-term follow-up study of a ward-based behaviour modification programme for adolescents with acting-out and conduct problems. *British Journal of Psychiatry*, **147**, 300–5.

Murray, D. J. (1989). *Review of Research on Re-offending of Mentally Disordered Offenders*. Research and Planning Unit Paper 55. London: Home Office.

Norris, M. (1983). Changes in patients during treatment at the Henderson Hospital therapeutic community during 1971–1981. *British Journal of Medical Psychology*, **56**, 135–43.

O'Callaghan, M. A. J. (1988). Bio-social influences on the control of aggression/ aggressive behaviour in mental health settings. In T. E. Moffitt and S. A. Mednick (eds), *Biological Contributions to Crime Causation*. Dordrecht: Martinus Nijhoff.

Ogloff, J. R., Wong, S., and Greenwood, A. (1990). Treating criminal psycopaths in a therapeutic community program. *Behavioral Sciences and the Law*, **8**, 181–90.

Peay, J. (1988). Offenders suffering from psychopathic disorder: The rise and demise of a consultation document. *British Journal of Criminology*, **28**, 67–81.

Persons, R. W. (1965). Psychotherapy with sociopathic offenders: An empirical evaluation. *Journal of Clinical Psychology*, **21**, 205–7.

Pichot, P. (1978). Psychopathic behaviour: A historical overview. In R. D. Hare and D. Schalling (eds), *Psychopathic Behaviour: Approaches to Research*. Chichester: Wiley.

Quay, H. C. (1977). Measuring dimensions of deviant behavior: The Behavior Problem Checklist. *Journal of Abnormal Child Psychology*, **5**, 277–87.

Quay, H. C. (1984). *Managing Adult Inmates*. American Correctional Association.

Quay, H. C. (1987). Patterns of delinquent behavior. In H. C. Quay (ed.), *Handbook of Juvenile Delinquency*. New York: Wiley.

Quinsey, V. L. (1988). Assessment of the treatability of forensic patients. *Behavioral Sciences and the Law*, **6**, 443–52.

Robertson, G. (1989). Treatment for offender patients: How should success be measured? *Medicine, Science, and the Law*, **29**, 303–7.

Robertson, G., and Gunn, J. (1987). A ten year follow-up of men discharged from Grendon prison. *British Journal of Psychiatry*, **151**, 674–8.

Roosenburg, A. M. (1966). *The Unwilling Patient*. London: Institute for the Scientific Treatment of Delinquency.

Rosen, A., and Schalling, D. (1974). On the validity of the California Psychological Inventory Socialisation scale: A multivariate approach. *Journal of Consulting and Clinical Psychology*, **42**, 757–65.

Ross, R. R., and Fabiano, E. A. (1985). *Time to Think: A Cognitive Model of Delinquency Prevention and Offender Rehabilitation*. Johnson City, Ten.: Institute of Social Sciences and Arts.

Safran, J. D. (1990). Toward a refinement of cognitive therapy in light of interpersonal theory: 1. Theory. *Clinical Psychology Review*, **10**, 87–105.

Sandhu, H. J. (1970). Therapy with violent psychopaths in an Indian prison community. *International Journal of Offender Therapy*, **14**, 138–44.

Satterfield, J. H. (1978). The hyperactive child syndrome: A precursor of adult psychopathy? In R. D. Hare and D. Schalling (eds), *Psychopathic Behaviour: Approaches to Research*. Chichester: Wiley.

Schmideberg, M. (1961). Psychotherapy of the criminal psychopath. *Archives of Criminal Dynamics*, **4**, 724–35.

Schneider, K. (1923). *Psychopathic Personalities* (ninth edn 1950). London: Cassell.

Sheard, M. H., Marini, J. L., Bridges, C. I., and Wagner, E. (1976). The effect of lithium on impulsive aggressive behaviour in man. *American Journal of Psychiatry*, **133**, 1409–13.

Stermac, L. E. (1986). Anger control treatment for forensic patients. *Journal of Interpersonal Violence*, **1**, 446–57.

Stringer, A. Y., and Josef, N. C. (1983). Methylphenidate in the treatment of aggression in two patients with antisocial personality disorder. *American Journal of Psychiatry*, **140**, 1365–6.

Suedfeld, P., and Landon, P. B. (1978). Approaches to treatment. In R. D. Hare and D. Schalling (eds), *Psychopathic Behaviour: Approaches to Research*. New York: Wiley.

Sutherland, E. H. (1950). The diffusion of sexual psychopath laws. *American Journal of Sociology*, **56**, 142–8.

Templeman, T. L., and Wollersheim, J. P. (1979). A cognitive-behavioral approach to the treatment of psychopathy. *Psychotherapy: Theory, Research and Practice*, **16**, 132–9.

Thorne, F. C. (1959). The etiology of sociopathic reactions. *American Journal of Psychotherapy*, **13**, 319–30.

Tyrer, P. (1988). *Personality Disorders: Diagnosis, Management and Course*. London: Wright.

Vaillant, G. E. (1975). Sociopathy as a human process: A viewpoint. *Archives of General Psychiatry*, **32**, 178–83.

Walmsley, R. (1991). *Managing Difficult Prisoners: The Parkhurst Special Unit*. Home Office Research Study 122. London: HMSO.

Wexler, H. K., Falkin, G. P., and Lipton, D. S. (1990). Outcome evaluation of a prison therapeutic community for substance abuse treatment. *Criminal Justice and Behavior*, **17**, 71–92.

Widiger, T. A., and Frances, A. (1985). Axis II personality disorders: Diagnostic and treatment Issues. *Hospital and Community Psychiatry*, **36**, 619–27.

Widiger, T. A., and Frances, A. (1987). Interviews and inventories for the measurement of personality disorders. *Clinical Psychology Review*, **7**, 47–75.

Woody, G. E., McClellan, A. T., Luborsky, L., and O'Brien, C. P. (1985). Sociopathy and psychotherapy outcome. *Archives of General Psychiatry*, **42**, 1081–6.
Wulach, J. (1983). Diagnosing the DSM-III antisocial personality disorder. *Professional Psychology: Research and Practice*, **14**, 330–40.

Part 3
Overview and Prognosis

9

A Clinical Approach to the Mentally Disordered Offender: An Overview and some Major Issues

THE LATE SALEEM A. SHAH
National Institute of Mental Health, Rockville, USA

INTRODUCTION

Concerns about protection of the community from harm are shared in all societies and constitute a plenary responsibility of the State. Such public safety or *police power* functions provide one major rationale for coercive interventions and are handled primarily, but not exclusively, through the criminal justice system. Another basis for the State's use of coercive powers resides in its traditional authority to care for those who are unable to care for themselves, the benevolent *parens patriae* function. To varying degrees several other societal systems—such as health, mental health, education, and social welfare—also assist in the regulation of behavior and related social control functions (see, e.g. Cummings, 1968). While the rationales for the State's police power and *parens patriae* interventions seem clear in theory, in many public policies and in actual practice the bases and objectives are blurred, overlap, or may be combined.

It has also been noted that while the criminal justice and mental health systems separately can exert powerful social control over individuals, when they are combined to deal with certain socially-deviant persons (prototypically mentally disordered offenders) the nature and extent of the coercive control can very markedly be enhanced (e.g. Allen, 1964; Morris, 1968; Shah, 1970). Understandably, therefore, issues pertaining to the involuntary confinement, handling and treatment of mentally disordered offenders raise a number of longstanding and vexing philosophical, public policy, ethical, and practical dilemmas.

Clinical Approaches to the Mentally Disordered Offender
Edited by K. Howells and C. R. Hollin published 1993 John Wiley & Sons Ltd

Maintaining order and public safety is not, however, the only societal goal to be considered. It must be balanced against other important societal values and goals—for example, respecting the autonomy and rights of individuals. The balancing of these competing, often conflicting, goals not only varies across national contexts and different types of political arrangements, but also within societies as a reflection of changing sociopolitical climates. This balance should be consonant with the major values and ideals professed by the society (e.g. fundamental fairness and justice); it should also comply with international and regional human rights principles, covenants, and related instruments (e.g. Center for Human Rights, 1988; Council of Europe, 1965; United Nations, 1991).

This chapter provides an overview of several issues involving the use of clinical approaches with mentally disordered offenders (MDOs) and addresses some definitional issues; the major categories of MDOs; the conceptualization of behaviour and implications for assessment, treatment, and handling; programmatic and service delivery issues; implications of the outcome evidence regarding services to MDOs; and same ethnical and policy dilemmas. Some recommendations for programs and policies are noted.

A key point emphasized in this chapter is that assertions of benevolence and therapeutic intent should not be allowed to obscure careful attention to some fundamental policy issues concerning political authority—viz. the circumstances under which the State is justified in using its coercive powers, the nature and extent of such intrusions, and the manner in which such exercises of power should be constrained and regulated. An important consideration is that broadly-shared principles of 'fundamental fairness' (more commonly referred to as 'due process' in the US context), 'fundamental justice' (in the Canadian context), and 'natural justice' (in the UK context) should be applied—*regardless* of whether the coercive interventions are based on punitive, public safety, or therapeutic purposes.

DEFINITION ISSUES AND RELATED MATTERS

Clarification of Key Terms and Phrases

The phrase 'clinical approach' is used here in its relevant dictionary meaning—namely, approaches relating to or conducted as if in a clinic. Since the original Greek word from which 'clinic' is derived pertains to medical practice at the bedside of sick persons, the clear connotation is that recipients of *clinical* services are persons who, in this context, suffer from some mental illness or disorder. In the broader mental health context, however, clinical services are directed at a much wider range of maladaptive or problem behaviors and for the alleviation of psychological distress. These problems may not be of a nature or severity to warrant a diagnosis of *mental disorder*. Clinical services are also provided to address a variety of problems involving intrafamily and interpersonal conflicts, stress management, anger control, and deficits in social and vocational skills.

Clinical approaches, concerned with individuals who manifest various illnesses, symptoms and problems, need to be distinguished from *public health* approaches. The latter focus on larger population groups with respect to such things as the assessment of health and mental health needs, identification of environmental factors that contribute to or otherwise influence various conditions and disorders (viz. risk factors), the conceptualization and application of several levels of prevention (primary, secondary, and tertiary), and the systematic assessment of treatment interventions. There is a considerable body of literature on community and public health approaches in the mental health field (e.g. Caplan, 1964; Lamb, 1988; Moos, 1976). These approaches have considerable relevance for the roles and functions of mental health professionals, especially in institutional settings such as correctional facilities and security or special mental hospitals.

It should be emphasized that clinical and community mental health approaches should not be tied exclusively to a particular model (e.g. 'medical', 'psychological', or 'social'), or to a singular focus on the treatment of 'mental disorders'. These models are generally linked to particular disciplinary, theoretical, or ideological perspectives, associated key concepts, as well as various guild interests— which considerations can obstruct the cost-effective utilization of a wide range of useful treatment, habilitative, and rehabilitative services.

In the discussion that follows, *criminal commitment* will refer to the involuntary psychiatric hospitalization of persons who were charged with violating criminal statutes, *civil commitment* will refer to the involuntary hospitalization of persons who have not been charged with criminal conduct.

Major Categories of Mentally Disordered Offenders

The law's concern with mental disorder is not with simply *any* discernible departure from notions of 'normality', regardless of how one may wish to define it. Rather, the concern typically focuses on the *nature and severity of the resulting dysfunctions* in specific reference to a variety of legal issues, questions, role expectations and functioning (Morse, 1978; Shah, 1986). In the context of the criminal process, several important considerations underlie this concern. For example: (i) proceeding against mentally impaired and 'unfit' defendants offends the moral dignity and fairness of the legal process; (ii) the defendant's mental dysfunctioning could seriously weaken the reliability and accuracy of legal fact-finding; (iii) mentally impaired defendants may not be able to make key decisions regarding their legal defense or treatment—that is, the ability to exercise autonomy and decisional competence; and (iv) the imposition of criminal sanctions would not be fair or just when criminal culpability is lacking due to severe mental impairment (Bonnie, 1990).

By way of a quick overview, the 31 773 mentally disordered offenders who were admitted to public and private inpatient psychiatric facilities (including psychiatric units of general hospitals) in the US in 1980, were distributed across various categories: almost 58% were evaluated and/or adjudicated for incompetency to stand trial (category 1 below), 8% were evaluated and/or adjudicated for a defense of insanity (category 2), 32% were mentally disordered prisoners (category 4), and only 3% were in category 5, namely, persons evaluated and/or adjudicated as mentally disordered sex offenders (Steadman, Rosenstein, MacAskill, and Manderscheid 1988). Not included in these figures for psychiatric facilities were mentally disordered persons in jails and prisons (category 3)—the largest group of MDOs.

The following categories include persons who had been charged with crimes and were involuntarily hospitalized (i.e. criminally committed) for evaluation, confinement and treatment, also those incarcerated in correctional institutions (see Kerr and Roth, 1986; Monahan and Steadman, 1983). (The term 'offender' is being used loosely since some of the categories involve persons who have been charged with but *not* convicted of criminal acts, hence they are not 'offenders' in the strict sense of that term.)

1. *Persons who have been adjudicated as mentally incompetent or unfit to proceed in the criminal process.* In Common Law countries the general, albeit short-hand, reference often is to the issue of competency to stand trial or fitness to plead. However, since questions about a defendant's mental competence can arise at several points in the criminal process—such as, competence to be arraigned, to enter a plea, to waive various legal rights (e.g. the right to legal counsel, the privilege against self-incrimination, etc.)—the appropriate encompassing phrase would be mental competency or fitness to proceed in the criminal process.

2. *Persons who have been adjudicated as not criminally responsible or as having diminished responsibility because of serious mental disorder at the time of the offense.* In legal systems that do not have a special defense of non-responsibility because of severe mental disability at the time of the offense (viz. the insanity defense), functionally equivalent dispositions are typically made to divert seriously mentally disabled persons from the imposition of criminal sanctions—e.g. prosecution may be waived and the persons transferred to the mental health system for confinement and treatment. In some US jurisdictions the legal concept of Diminished Capacity serves to reduce the severity of the crime that can be charged (e.g. from murder to manslaughter), and in others Diminished Responsibility and related doctrines can mitigate severity of punishment. These *convicted* persons typically go to penal facilities (Brakel, Parry, and Weiner, 1985; Shah, 1986).

3. *Offenders confined in correctional institutions.* By the close of 1990 the institutional correctional population in the US had rather handily surpassed the one million figure: at year-end, State and Federal prisons had 771 243 inmates (Bureau of Justice Statistics Bulletin, 1991a), and at midyear 1990 (29 June 1990) the estimated number of persons held in local jails (those convicted as well as those awaiting trial) was 405 320 (Bureau of Justice Statistics Bulletin, 1991b). (The prevalence of mental disorders among jail and prison inmates is discussed later.)

US courts have held that provision of adequate health care in correctional facilities is constitutionally required (e.g. *Estelle* v. *Gamble*, 1976; *Bowring* v. *Godwin*, 1977). (See Cohen, 1988, for a detailed discussion of relevant legal issues pertaining to mentally disordered prisoners.)

4. *Psychotic and other seriously disordered prisoners who are transferred to security mental hospitals or units.* As noted above, 32% of the 31 773 mentally

disordered persons admitted to inpatient psychiatric facilities in 1980 were in this category. Mentally disordered prisoners who object cannot be transferred (typically to security hospitals or units) without being afforded several minimal due process safeguards that the US Supreme Court held in *Vitek* v. *Jones* (1980) to be constitutionally required (e.g. written notice, hearing, opportunity to present evidence and to cross-examine witnesses, an independent decision maker, etc.).

5. *Special categories of offenders who are considered to be mentally ill, dangerous and in need of mental health treatment in secure settings.* In several US jurisdictions there are special statutes directed at persons designated as 'mentally disordered sex offenders', 'sexually dangerous persons', 'sexual psychopaths', etc. Similar provisions for the confinement and treatment of offenders believed to be mentally ill and dangerous and/or to pose serious recidivism risks are to be found in several other countries (e.g. Ashworth and Gostin, 1984; Krul-Steketee, 1987).

During the past three decades such laws have received much criticism in the US and several national commissions and professional groups have recommended their repeal—most recently the American Bar Association Criminal Justice Mental Health Standards (1989). Some of these laws were found to be unconstitutional, a few were repealed, and the remaining have undergone considerable revisions. At present statutes in only six US jurisdictions permit indeterminate periods of confinement (see, generally, Brakel, Parry and Weiner, 1985).

A couple of points merit emphasis. First, although persons in the foregoing categories can be lumped together as 'mentally disordered offenders', the reasons and purposes for their criminal commitments relate to particular legal and policy issues, have varying implications for psycholegal assessments and treatment interventions, and hence differ in legally-relevant outcome criteria. Second, in most instances the *legal* determinations are neither equivalent to nor do they necessarily have direct implications for specific *clinical* dispositions. For example, the mental disorder and associated disabilities that are adjudged to make a defendant 'unfit' to proceed in the criminal process, are *not* equivalent to the requisite criteria for involuntary hospitalization and neither are the treatment outcome criteria similar.

CONCEPTUAL ISSUES AND PROBLEMS

The discussion now moves to the manner in which behavior and associated assessment and treatment tasks are conceptualized and operationalized, and some important implications of an interactional perspective.

The Conceptualization of Behavior

A key consideration in the assessment, prediction, treatment and management of mentally disordered offenders concerns the manner in which behavior is conceptualized. Behavior, whether evaluated and labelled as 'normal,' 'deviant,' or as 'disordered', is often viewed (explicitly or implicitly) as a function largely of the individual; that is, of his or her personality, psychodynamics, or other trait-oriented notions. Hence, patterns of behavior may be seen as fairly stable and consistent characteristics of the individual's personality. Assumptions may also be made that particular samples of the individual's behavior (e.g. assaults and violence) are characteristic of the person and thus likely to be displayed across settings. Moreover, labels that are applied to aspects of the individual's behavior may, through a conceptual short-cut, come to be applied to the person. Thus, not only are certain acts of the individual 'dangerous,' but the person himself comes to be viewed, labelled, and handled as 'dangerous.'

Considerable theoretical work and empirical research over the past several decades have brought into question certain basic assumptions about the global dispositional approaches inherent in trait-oriented notions of behavior. These studies show rather modest levels of cross-setting consistencies in behavior. Hence, while recognizing the reality and stability of individual differences, greater attention has been focused on the influence of the specific context, setting and situation in which the behaviors occur; more particularly, to the complex and reciprocal interactions between persons and the environmental contexts in which they function. The reference here is not just to the objective and physical aspects of the environments and situations, but also to the ways in which these are perceived, constructed, and interpreted by individuals (i.e. their 'psychological environments') (see e.g. Bandura and Walters, 1968; Bowers, 1973; Ekehammar, 1974; Endler and Magnusson, 1976; Lewin, 1935; Mischel, 1968, 1973).

Much research has also addressed the characteristics of environments and their effects on behavior (e.g. Barker, 1968; Moos, 1973, 1976). These efforts have included assessments of therapeutic and correctional environments (Moos, 1974, 1975) and some studies have shown relationships between characteristics of treatment environments and outcomes (e.g. Collins, Ellsworth, Casey, Hyer *et al.*, 1985; Ellsworth, Collins, Casey, Schoonover *et al.*, 1979; Moos and Schwartz, 1972).

The interactional conceptualization of behavior has important implications for various clinical assessment, prediction, treatment and management tasks. For example, assessments of a person's 'dangerousness' (i.e. the likelihood of engaging in dangerous acts) and 'readiness for release' cannot adequately be undertaken without *also* taking into account and evaluating the particular environmental context in which the person will be functioning (e.g. the problem-aggravating as well as the positive and supportive features likely to be present). It follows, therefore, that the likelihood of future dangerous behavior and other problems will seldom be a function *solely* of patients' characteristics (e.g. their psychopathologies and dysfunctions). The likelihood will also reflect on the availability and adequacy of graduated release planning, after care programs, and social supports in the community; hence, on policy decisions regarding allocation of resources for such programs.

How is Treatment to be Conceptualized, Defined and Implemented?

The manner in which 'treatment' is conceptualized will be influenced in large measure by such things as how the target conditions and problems are viewed (e.g. as 'crime,' 'mental disorder,' or 'handicap') and the particular social systems that are involved—e.g. criminal justice, corrections, mental health, and social welfare. When the key defining label involves the concepts of 'disease' or 'disorder', the health and mental health systems play a dominant role and the conceptualization of problems and treatments will largely be in reference to the above and related medical and psychiatric concepts.

Some complications arise, however, when the concepts of 'disease' and 'disorder' and some of their connotations in the field of medicine are applied to the mental health area (e.g. King, 1954). The concept of disease can be related to several alternative paradigms and involves issues that are in part scientific, in part sociological, and in part political—that is, mental health interventions in the service of social control (Klerman, 1977). It has also been emphasized that, notwithstanding frequent references to treatment needs and patient welfare, public safety and social control remain dominant concerns in the handling of MDOs. Indeed, it is with MDOs—generally perceived by lay, professional, and policy-making groups as especially dangerous—that the confounding of 'therapeutic' and 'incapacitative' functions permits more powerful social control than would generally have been possible through penal sanctions (Shah, 1989, 1990).

Considering the marked variations in the nature, range, and severity of symptoms among persons with the same mental disorder, the diagnosis alone rarely provides sufficient information about the seriousness of specific deficits and dysfunctions, or about interventions that are relevant to particular legal questions. Treatment of MDOs typically involves a range of mental health and related interventions to address, for example, not only the positive and negative psychotic symptoms and related rehabilitative needs, but also various informational, cognitive, affective, and life skill competencies relevant to specific *legal* questions—for example, fitness to proceed in the criminal process (e.g. Poythress and Miller, 1991; Quinsey, 1988; Rice, Harris, Quinsey, and Cyr, 1990). Thus, as will be discussed later, we need to think more specifically in terms of *psycholegal* assessments and treatments.

The various services noted above have developed within different traditions, involve a number of disciplines, conceptual models, interventions, and service providers, and encompass several systems. These services cannot, therefore, be squeezed within any single model—'medical', 'psychological' or 'social'.

PROGRAMMATIC AND SERVICE-DELIVERY ISSUES

This section will provide an overview of some recent prevalence studies of mental disorders among correctional inmates, and then discuss some implications for the roles and functions of mental health professionals in correctional institutions and security or special hospitals.

The Prevalence of Mental Disorders in Prisons and Jails

Various studies have suggested that about 8% of prisoners in state facilities in the US suffer from serious psychiatric disorders, while 15–20% are in need of mental health care and treatment at some point during their incarceration (Roth, 1986). In the UK, Gunn, Robertson, Dell, and Way (1978) found that 31% of sentenced prisoners could be regarded as psychiatric cases. It is difficult, however, to make meaningful comparisons of various results or generalizations because of variations in study samples, clinical assessment procedures, the particular prevalence rates used, and other methodological constraints.

During the 1980s the five-site Epidemiologic Catchment Area (ECA) program of the National Institute of Mental Health (NIMH), involving more than 20 000 subjects (see e.g. Regier, Myers, Kramer, Robins et al., 1984), stimulated the development of a standardized assessment instrument, the Diagnostic Interview Schedule (DIS) based on DSM-III (Robins, Helzer, Croughan, and Ratcliff, 1981), to facilitate large-scale prevalence studies. Several recent investigations have utilized the DIS with large and representative samples of correctional inmates (e.g. Neighbors, 1987; Regier, Boyd, Burke, Rae et al., 1988; Regier, Farmer, Rae, Locke et al., 1990; Teplin, 1990a, b). These studies provide clear evidence of high rates of mental disorder among correctional inmates.

Some initial reports from the ECA program indicate that the *lifetime* prevalence rate for any alcohol, drugs, and mental disorder among penal institutional populations (82%) was more than double that (32.2%) found in community samples (Regier et al., 1988, 1990). Even though the high rates among prisoners were primarily attributable to antisocial personality disorders (about ten times higher than community samples) and substance abuse and dependence (at least three times higher), rates were also higher for many of the major mental disorders. Using the DIS, fairly similar results have been reported in Michigan (Neighbors, 1987) and North Carolina (Collins and Schlenger, 1983), and by Canadian investigators (Hodgins and Côté, 1990).

Gunn, Maden, and Swinton, (1991) surveyed a representative sample of sentenced male prisoners in England and Wales (N = 1769) to ascertain current prevalence of mental disorder, using the International Classification of Diseases, ICD-9 (World Health Organization, 1978), and found 37% to have a diagnosable psychiatric disorder. Of these, 2% were suffering from psychoses, 6% from neuroses, 10% from personality disorders, and 23% from substance dependence and/or abuse.

The *lifetime* prevalence rates for mental disorders do not, of course, address the question of *current* functioning and treatment needs. The Michigan study (involving a probability sample of 1240 prisoners) also assessed *current* disorder and found that 10.4% of the inmates had psychotic disorders and 29% had current mood disorders. With regard to functioning during the past month, almost 20% were judged to be severely impaired and 47% as moderately impaired (Neighbors, 1987).

Steadman, Fabisiak, Dvoskin, and Holohean (1987) surveyed a sample of 3684 New York State prison inmates to assess current levels of *mental and functional disability* (not diagnosed mental disorders) to determine need for services. They estimated 8% of the prison population to have 'very substantial' psychiatric and functional disabilities that would clearly warrant some type of mental health services; an additional 16% had 'significant' psychiatric and functional disabilities requiring at least periodic mental health services.

Rates for most mental disorders are also very high in US jails (city and county correctional facilities that house criminal defendants awaiting trial as well as convicted offenders sentenced to terms of less than a year). Since many pretrial detainees with serious mental disorders may not yet have been screened out, the prevalence rates in jails will generally be higher as compared to prisons (e.g. Jemelka, Trupin, and Chiles, 1989). Systematic screening of a random sample of 728 male detainees in a large urban jail revealed that the observed rates of schizophrenia, major depression, and mania were two to three times higher than in the general population—using both *current* (within two weeks of interview) and *lifetime* prevalence rates (Teplin, 1990b). Moreover, in view of the fast turnover of detainees, problems of overcrowding, and limited mental health resources, it is here that even major mental disorders are more likely to go undetected and untreated (Teplin, 1990a).

Co-morbidity has been another noteworthy finding. Some form of substance abuse or dependence was identified in about 84% of individuals with antisocial personality (Regier *et al.*, 1990) and among 72% of the currently severely ill in an urban jail (Abram and Teplin, 1991). Such co-morbidity further complicates treatment and management (e.g. Abram, 1989; Helzer and Pryzbeck, 1988).

In sum, although there are many differences among jails and prisons both within and across jurisdictions, significant levels of psychiatric morbidity are likely to be found among inmates of correctional institutions. Still, this does not provide a complete picture of the extent of psychiatric morbidity and psychological breakdown and distress, or about the disturbed, disruptive, chronically maladaptive, suicidal and self-destructive behaviors that create problems for inmates, for staff, as well as for the penal institutions (Toch and Adams, 1989; Toch, Adams, and Grant, 1989).

Roles and functions of mental health professionals

Considering the very significant amounts of psychiatric morbidity among inmates of correctional institutions, the stresses and strains associated with penal incarceration, and the limited mental health resources available, some critically important policy and practical questions need to be addressed regarding the most appropriate and effective roles for mental health professionals in these facilities.

Five major roles and functions can be identified: (i) Assessment and evaluation for a variety of administrative decisions and determinations of clients' needs; (ii) crisis interventions for acute morbidity and stress, self-injurious behaviors, violence victimization, etc.; (iii) treatment interventions for serious mental disorders as well as a broad array of psychological, social, and rehabilitative programs; (iv) consultation and training for facility line staff to enhance skills in the early recognition of major mental disorders, the management of mentally disturbed and/or disruptive inmates, etc.; and (v) program planning, development, and evaluation for such things as needs assessment, projection of trends, program planning and evaluation, and research (Clements, 1987).

A number of problems have been identified regarding the optimal utilization of mental health resources in correctional facilities. For example, in many instances available resources are disproportionately consumed by various and sundry—even repetitious—evaluations, the actual need for and utility of which may well be questioned. While diagnostic labels can readily be applied and treatment recommended, resources are often lacking to implement such recommendations (Clingempeel, Mulvey, and Reppucci, 1980). Obviously, clients cannot benefit from treatment that was not provided; nor do benefits necessarily follow when interventions believed to have value remain untested.

Questions also arise about the primary roles of mental health staff in penal institutions and how the scarce available resources might most cost-effectively be allocated across the various functions. To what extent, for example, should mental health staff concentrate their treatment services on the major and treatable mental disorders? And, should not greater attention be given to the use of community mental health approaches to identify and ameliorate some of the unnecessarily repressive and iatrogenic features of institutional milieus in penal and security hospital settings?

IMPLICATIONS OF THE OUTCOME EVIDENCE

Outcomes must be evaluated in reference to clearly articulated objectives and associated criteria. There also needs to be clear conceptualization and description of what constitutes the 'treatment' that is to be evaluated. Simply calling something 'treatment' does not make it therapeutic. Most treatment programs for MDOs may well have difficulty providing a clear conceptualization and description of what precisely constitutes the 'treatment,' especially in reference to specific legal questions and concerns such as competency or fitness to stand trial.

Two general observations might initially be made. First, systematic evaluations of various mental health and related services functions and programs are rare, and second, clinical practices are typically not well informed by relevant research. Considering the range and diversity of programs for mentally disordered offenders and the relative paucity of rigorous outcome research, one is reminded of Raimy's characterization of the state of psychotherapy research four decades ago as—'undefined techniques applied to unspecified problems, with unpredictable outcome' (Raimy, 1950, p. 93).

Outcome Domains

Outcome is a multidimensional concept that must be assessed in reference to several criteria and associated measures. Hargreaves and Shumway (1989) have provided a framework that includes four domains: (i) clinical—the reduction, elimination or alleviation of symptoms of psychopathology or the cure of specific mental disorders; (ii) rehabilitative—the restoration and/or improvement of self-care, as well as social, vocational, and occupational functioning; (iii) humanitarian—an increase in the sense of well-being and personal fulfillment of both patient and family members; and (iv) public safety—the prevention of harm to the patient, family, and/or the community.[1]

With regard to mentally disordered offenders, the outcome framework needs to be broadened to ensure that these domains take *legal* problems into account. Since important legal and human rights considerations must be addressed when involuntary interventions are involved, a fifth domain, legal and human rights, needs to be added to assess adherence to relevant provisions under national, regional, and international laws and covenants. For example, in addition to protections afforded under mental health laws, such provisions would include relevant fundamental laws (e.g. the Canadian Charter of Rights and Freedoms (1983), Federal and various State constitutions in the US),[2] the European Convention on Human Rights (Council of Europe, 1965),[3] and several international instruments such as the Universal Declaration of Human Rights, the International Covenant of Civil and Political Rights, the International Declaration of the Rights of Disabled Persons (Center for Human Rights, 1988), and the recently adopted Principles for the Protection of Persons with Mental Illness and for the Improvement of Mental Health Care (United Nations, 1991—hereinafter referred to as the UN Principles).

The following section will briefly highlight some implications of extant outcome evidence concerning assessment and treatment services for MDOs.

Psycholegal Assessments

This term refers to various mental health evaluations undertaken in connection with specific legal determinations affecting MDOs. An important question concerns the extent to which the usual assessment instruments (e.g. clinical interviews, mental status evaluations, psychological tests, etc.) are conceptually relevant to particular functional capacities, and whether the clinical data, inferences and conclusions sufficiently address the legal questions involved.

---

[1] The 'public safety' domain combines coercive interventions based on police power (protection of the community) and those based on *parens patriae* objectives (caring for those unable to care for themselves). This is clearly problematic for assessing outcomes. To ensure conceptual and doctrinal clarity, precision in the identification of treatment objectives, and use of appropriate outcome measures, it is essential to distinguish the *parens patriae* and police power objectives. Measures of treatment effectiveness with regard to the care, treatment, and welfare of the patient are quite different from those pertaining to protection of the community from serious criminal and violent acts. Failure to make such distinctions perpetuates the confounding of social control and therapeutic objectives.
[2] Some of the major reforms of mental health laws in the US over the past 25 years have resulted from efforts to seek judicial redress for violations of constitutionally-protected rights; various legislative revisions typically followed (Shah, 1981). Similar developments have been taking place in Canada (Verdun-Jones, 1991).
[3] There is a growing body of relevant case law emanating from the European Court of Human Rights (Harding, 1989); several of the decisions have been followed by legislative revisions in the countries involved.

Clinical diagnoses and assessments do *not* translate directly or readily into specific capacities and functional abilities related to particular legal questions. For example, a diagnosis of schizophrenia does not necessarily indicate a lack of fitness to proceed or non-responsibility for crime. The focus of psycholegal assessments must remain the nature and severity of functional disabilities in reference to particular legal issues and associated standards and criteria.

Grisso (1986a) has pointed out that psycholegal assessments need to take into account and reflect proper understanding of such things as: (i) specific legal constructs, questions, and related capacities and functional abilities; (ii) relevant legal standards and criteria for making such determinations; (ii) translation of legal concepts and questions into related psychological capacities and functional abilities; (iv) selection of appropriate instruments to assess these capacities and functional abilities; (v) relating results of the assessments to specific legal questions and associated standards; and (vi) reporting findings in clear language and in sufficient detail for decisionmakers to apply them to ultimate legal and policy judgements.

Such assessments need, therefore, to be improved with respect of their relevance (e.g. reflecting clear understanding of and conceptual relevance to particular legal questions); scientific integrity (e.g. using standardized assessment with reliability and validity information available); and clarity of role within the legal process (e.g. providing understandable description and explanation of psychopathology and indicating specific areas of impaired functioning and their relevance to legal questions, but leaving 'ultimate legal and/or normative judgements' to the appropriate legal decisionmakers) (Grisso, 1986b, 1987).

An important implication of the outcome evidence regarding psycholegal assessments is that much greater effort needs to focus on the development and construction of instruments (e.g. standardized and structured psychiatric interviews, rating scales, and psychological tests) that are conceptually related to the legal constructs, capacities, and functional abilities to be measured. Several psycholegal instruments have been developed during the past two decades—e.g. the Competency to Stand Trial Assessment Instrument and Competency Screening Test (Lipsitt, Lelos, and McGarry, 1971; Laboratory of Community Psychiatry, 1973), the Interdisciplinary Fitness Interview (Golding, Roesch, and Schreiber, 1984), and Rogers Criminal Responsibility Assessment Scales (Rogers, 1984). (For further information see also: Grisso and Siegel, 1986; Melton, Petrila, Poythress, and Slobogin, 1987.)

Treatment Interventions

The term 'treatment' requires clarification when used in reference to mentally disordered offenders. As Poythress and Miller (1991) have noted, from a *traditional perspective* one could focus on most of the persons in the major categories listed earlier (cf. pp. 213–215) as mental patients who happened to have become involved with the legal system. Hence, they would receive the customary treatments for those disorders, with outcome being assessed primarily in terms of the usual clinical criteria such as symptom reduction and improved role functioning.

An alternative and *narrower perspective* of treatment would focus on interventions and outcomes that pertain specifically to the legal questions involved—e.g. incompetency to stand trial, non-responsibility for crime, or sexual psychopathy. In contrast to the 'traditional perspective', the focus of treatment interventions in this approach would be the deficits and dysfunctions related to the particular legal questions, and outcome criteria would focus heavily, albeit not solely, on the legally-relevant functioning. Considering the vast range of problems and legal concerns encompassed by the various categories of MDOs, it is safe to say that no single or uniform set of treatment interventions will apply.

In recent years increasing attention has focused on the important construct of 'treatability', especially with regard to mentally disordered offenders (MDOs). For example, with the exception of the need for and effectiveness of the phenothiazines for treating psychotic disorders, consensus is lacking among clinicians—even *after* a case has been discussed—about the applicability or efficacy of specific treatments (e.g. Quinsey and Maguire, 1983; Quinsey, 1988). Referring to various programs for MDOs, Quinsey (1988) concluded that:

> Today, treatment programs in secure psychiatric institutions are noteworthy primarily by their absence, poor implementation, unevaluated status, lack of conceptual sophistication, and incomplete description and documentation. (p. 444)

This assessment is as accurate as it is succinct.

More conceptually-relevant and cost-effective treatment approaches have been developed and should receive greater attention (e.g. Pendleton, 1980; Siegel and Elwork, 1990).

ETHICAL AND POLICY DILEMMAS

The many ethical dilemmas involved in the delivery of services to mentally disordered offenders are compounded when the services are provided in coercive contexts and the resultant complexities are further exacerbated when social control concerns are combined and conflated with treatment objectives.

Some Ethical Dilemmas

A number of sources are available in the US to inform and sensitize mental health professionals and to provide guidance regarding ethical issues and standards of practice. There are, for example, the ethical principles of the major professional organizations (e.g. American Psychiatric Association, 1989; American Psychological Association, 1990) which are periodically revised and updated (Pope and Vetter, 1992). Mechanisms are also available for handling complaints, adjudication, and imposing various sanctions (e.g. American Psychological Association, 1991). Several issues and problems pertaining to MDOs were also cogently addressed by an American Psychological Association Task Force on the Role of Psychology in the Criminal Justice System (American Psychological Association,

1978—hereinafter referred to as the Task Force Report; see also Monahan, 1980a).

More specialized guidelines have been developed by the American Academy of Psychiatry and the Law (1991). Other fairly comprehensive Specialty Guidelines for Forensic Psychologists have been developed by the American Psychology–Law Society and the Division of Psychology and Law of the American Psychological Association (Committee on Ethical Guidelines for Forensic Psychologists, 1991—hereinafter referred to as the Specialty Guidelines). Also informative and useful for legal and mental health professionals are the ABA Criminal Justice Mental Health Standards (American Bar Association, 1986), which resulted from a major undertaking involving many national experts from the legal and mental health fields.

These ethical principles and standards provide both general and fairly specific guidelines for the delivery of mental health services to MDOs. Although the number and complexity of ethical dilemmas associated with the handling of MDOs could easily take up an entire chapter, three of the more salient ones will briefly be discussed: (i) Problems of dual or multiple relationships and role conflicts; (ii) confidentiality; and (iii) professional competence and relevant expertise.

Problems of dual or multiple relationships

The traditional 'doctor–patient' relationship, involving a primary concern with the interests and welfare of patients, typifies services that are provided essentially on a voluntary basis and in which mental health professionals function as agents of the patients. Such a relationship clearly does *not* exist when the services (evaluation, consultation, treatment, and rehabilitation) are provided on an involuntary basis, in coercive contexts (e.g. when the person is involved with the criminal justice system or faces involuntary hospitalization), at the request of various third parties, and for purposes other than the care and treatment of the patient. In these situations several other parties and interests are also involved— the society, the criminal justice or health/mental health systems, and the particular institution or facility, as well as the convenience and preferences of staff.

It is seldom clear in cases of dual or multiple relationships where precisely, in theory or in practice, mental health professionals' allegiances and obligations lie, how the conflicting role demands are handled and resolved, and more importantly to what extent patients have been informed about these matters. Various ethical principles, as well as notions of fundamental fairness, require that mental health professionals provide such information to patients *before* initiating evaluative or therapeutic services. For example, Principle 5 (Welfare of the Consumer) of the Ethical Principles of Psychologists (American Psychological Association, 1990) states:

> Psychologists respect the integrity and protect the welfare of the people and groups with whom they work. When conflicts of interest arise between clients and

psychologists' employing institutions, psychologists clarify the nature and direction of their loyalties and responsibilities and keep all parties informed of their commitments. (p. 393)

Section (b) of this Principle points out that:

When a psychologist agrees to provide services to a client at the request of a third party, the psychologist assumes the responsibility of clarifying the nature of the relationships to all parties concerned. (p. 393)

Similarly, the Specialty Guidelines (1991) emphasize that:

Forensic psychologists have an obligation to ensure that prospective clients are informed of their legal rights with respect to the anticipated forensic service, of the purposes of any evaluation, of the nature of procedures to be employed, of the intended uses of any product of their services, and of the party who has employed the forensic psychologist. (Sub-section E, p. 659)

Other types of conflicts also need to be identified and resolved, for example, combining the roles of therapist and evaluator. Although therapists typically have much relevant information about the patient, problems of conflicting loyalties and interests are raised if they also try to serve as independent evaluators for assessments of 'dangerousness' and/or readiness for release. Several questions arise, such as: Might the dual roles necessitate violations of confidentiality and/or complicate the nature of subsequent therapeutic relations with the patient? Can mental health professionals be sufficiently objective in trying to balance the interests of the patient as well as those of the institution or society?

Confidentiality

It must be remembered that confidentiality is a right of clients who disclose personal information. Thus, when mental health professionals are not functioning primarily as agents of patients, the usual assumptions and understandings about confidentiality do not apply—but patients may be unaware of this and its implications. General notions of fair-play, relevant ethical guidelines, and considerations of 'fundamental fairness' require that patients be informed about the nature and limits of, as well as any exceptions to, confidentiality in a particular context. Even after initial disclosure about the lack of confidentiality in court-ordered and other evaluations, patients may slip into assumptions or expectations of confidential communications with their 'doctor' (mental health professional). Thus, it may be necessary to remind them about the lack of confidentiality during the course of the evaluation and/or other services.

The relevant guidelines are instructive. For example, Section 4-6 of the annotations for psychiatrists (American Psychiatric Association, 1989) states:

Psychiatrists are often asked to examine individuals for security purposes, to determine suitability for various jobs, and to determine legal competence. The psychiatrist must fully describe the nature and purpose and lack of confidentiality of the examination to the examinee at the beginning of the examination. (p. 6)

Similarly, Section V (Confidentiality and Privilege) of the Specialty Guidelines (1991) advises that:

> Forensic psychologists have an obligation to be aware of the legal standards that may affect or limit the confidentiality or privilege that may attach to their services or their products, and they conduct their professional activities in a manner that respects those known rights and privileges. (Sub-section A, p. 660)

Principle 6 (Confidentiality) of the recently adopted UN Principles (1991) also recommends that the 'right of confidentiality of information' be respected (p. 325).

In view of the involvement of MDOs in the criminal process and the coercive context in which services are generally delivered, mental health professionals need to be especially sensitive to issues of confidentiality and diligent about explaining its absence or limitations to clients.

Professional competence

Two concerns will be noted. First, when mental health professionals interact with the legal system they have a professional and ethical obligation to educate themselves about relevant legal issues and their implications for various service functions (e.g. psycholegal evaluation, treatment, and consultation). Such knowledge is especially important in view of the potential impact of the services on the lives and liberties of MDOs.

A related concern that has been the subject of much commentary (Chiswick, 1985; Grounds, 1987; Halleck, 1984; Morse, 1978; Shah, 1969, 1974) is when mental health professionals go beyond providing information about the mental functioning of patients and proceed to render conclusory opinions on ultimate legal issues (e.g. fitness to proceed or criminal responsibility) or normative and public policy determinations (e.g. 'dangerousness' and readiness for release). In these instances, they not only exceed the bounds of their expertise but arrogate roles and responsibilities that properly belong to triers of fact (judges and juries) and/or other designated decisionmakers.

Relevant guidance is provided however. For example, Principle 2 (Competence) of the Ethical Principles of Psychologists (American Psychological Association, 1990) points out that:

> The maintenance of high standards of competence is a responsibility shared by all psychologists in the interest of the public and the profession as a whole. *Psychologists recognize the boundaries of their competence and the limitations of their techniques.* ... They maintain knowledge of current-scientific and professional information related to the services they render. (pp. 390–1, emphasis added)

The ABA Criminal Justice Mental Health Standards (1986), the Task Force

Report (1978), and the Specialty Guidelines (1991) have also addressed this issue. Although, as citizens, mental health professionals hold certain views on various normative and policy questions, they do not have any special expertise in these matters and hence should eschew providing conclusory opinions in their role as 'expert' consultants or witnesses.

One might wonder why mental health professionals are so willing to assume these dubious roles on moral and political questions. It would appear that the demand characteristics of the situations, ready and uncritical acceptance of inaccurate (but flattering) attributions of 'expertise,' and elements of personal and professional narcissism, combine to make it difficult for many persons to resist such temptations. Almost 40 years ago in reference to the practice of psychotherapy, Judd Marmor (1953) observed that the constant exercise of authority carried with it 'the occupational hazard of tending to create unrealistic feelings of superiority in the authority figure' (p. 270). This hazard may well be greater for mental health professionals working in the forensic area.

Some Policy Dilemmas

Space limitations permit brief discussion of just three policy dilemmas and problems that involve the mental health system and mental health professionals: (i) normative and policy issues addressed as scientific or technical questions; (ii) assessments of 'dangerousness' and readiness for release; and (iii) the confounding of incapacitation and treatment. While mental health professionals and their organizations cannot shoulder responsibility for the establishment of these policies (although their views and preferences may well be quite influential), as key functionaries involved in their implementation they need to be sensitive to and concerned about some problematic implications for their roles and functions.

Normative and policy issues addressed as scientific or technical questions

As noted above, a major ethical and policy dilemma pertains to the confounding of technical expertise with normative judgments. The problem is not just the limited and uncertain nature of relevant scientific knowledge—which limitations should, of course, explicitly be indicated. The fundamental problem is that mental health professionals are permitted, even solicited, to offer conclusory opinions on matters that require legal, moral, and policy judgments. This point was explicated several years ago by Judge Bazelon in *Washington* v. *United States* (1967) in reference to judgments of criminal responsibility:

> With the relevant information about the defendant, and guided by the legal principles enunciated by the courts, the jury must decide, in effect, whether or not the defendant is blameworthy. Undoubtedly, the decision is often painfully difficult, and perhaps its very difficulty accounts for the readiness with which we have encouraged the expert to decide the question. But our society has chosen not to give this decision to psychiatrists or to any other professional elite but rather to twelve lay representatives of the community. (pp. 453–4)

The issue of dangerousness was discussed in very similar fashion by the New Jersey Supreme Court (*Krol* v. *State*, 1975):

> The determination of dangerousness involves a delicate balancing of Society's interest in protection from harmful conduct against the individual's interest in personal liberty and autonomy. This decision, while requiring the court to make use of the assistance which medical testimony may provide, is ultimately a legal one, not a medical one. (p. 302)

Such guidance notwithstanding, Monahan (1980b) has observed that to avoid dealing with various complex and difficult questions of law, judges frequently solicit conclusory opinions, and, 'oblivious to the limits of their expertise, mental health professionals sink to the occasion' (p. v).

One can only speculate about why policies permit, or even invite, such practices. It may well be that the conclusory opinions by mental health professionals serve to sanitize and euphemize public safety concerns with a 'clinical' and 'scientific' gloss, and thereby help to mask and avoid addressing the vexing legal and moral conflicts in more forthright fashion.

Halleck (1984) has wondered about the willingness of psychiatrists to become involved in certain 'double-agent' and social control roles, and points out that such roles 'can provide psychiatrists with power, a certain amount of prestige, and, at times, considerable financial remuneration' (p. 281). Moreover, such roles can be harmful to patients as well as to the profession. These observations and cautions also apply to other mental health professionals.

Assessments of 'dangerousness' and readiness for release

Earlier in this chapter it was pointed out that these assessments cannot be based simply on characteristics of individuals. They must also take into account the environmental and situational contexts in which persons will be functioning, including the availability of a graduated range of less restrictive alternatives, aftercare, followup, supervision and treatment in community settings, and other social support programs. Moreover, while public safety is a dominant concern, the rights of patients must also be recognized. For example, Principle 9 of the UN Principles (1991) states that 'Every patient shall have the right to be treated in the least restrictive environment ...' (p. 326).

These assessments place undue reliance on longer-term predictions of dangerousness and tend to focus almost exclusively on patient characteristics. To address the primary goal of community protection, however, one should not rely solely or too heavily on a particular means (long-term predictions of dangerousness) toward that end.

As compared with the long and indeterminate confinement of MDOs in security hospitals, public safety objectives can also be addressed through a variety of less drastic, less restrictive, and less costly means, such as: graduated release programs making greater use of civil, general, and local hospitals; community-based residential treatment and supportive living facilities; and carefully designed programs of monitored conditional release and intensive case management in the community. (There is much discussion in the clinical literature about the poor motivation of many MDOs to become involved in treatment and related programs. It must be pointed out, however, that very similar problems of poor motivation are often presented by mental health facilities and professionals in their reluctance to accept and work with MDOs.)

In contrast to the difficulties and systematic errors inherent in longer term predictions, close monitoring and intensive case management under conditional release programs provide opportunities for *ongoing* and frequent assessments (e.g. weekly or as often as indicated) of patients' functioning, compliance with treatment and related conditions, and potential problems. Such conditional release programs for criminally committed MDOs must also have provisions that permit prompt revocation (during the period of jurisdiction) when key conditions are violated and the likelihood of serious risks to the community or the patient becomes evident.

For example, Oregon's Psychiatric Security Review Board legislation for the management of insanity acquittees explicitly states that its primary purpose is protection of the community. However, this is nicely balanced with attention to the rights of patients—for example, provision of various due process safeguards, durational limits on the length of confinement and/or community supervision (linked to the maximum penal sentence that could have been imposed had the person not been acquitted), and allocation of resources for conditional release supervision and treatment in the community (e.g. Bloom, Williams, Rogers, and Barbur, 1986; Bloom, Williams, and Bigelow, 1991). The cost of managing patients on conditional release in this program has been estimated to be about 14% of the cost of secure hospitalization (Bigelow, Bloom, and Williams, 1990).

Several conditional release programs for criminally committed patients (most notably insanity acquittees) have been in use in various US jurisdictions (e.g. Lamb, Weinberger, and Gross, 1988; Silver, Cohen, and Spodak, 1989), and key features in the design and implementation of such programs have been described (Griffin, Steadman, and Griffin, 1991). In sum, while the knowledge and means for more cost-effective and 'less restrictive' alternatives certainly exist, the requisite political will is often lacking.

The confounding of 'incapacitation' and 'treatment'

A longstanding and pervasive problem involves policies whereby MDOs (e.g. those found unfit to proceed and insanity acquittees) who are diverted to the mental health system for treatment may face longer periods of confinement in security hospitals than if they had been convicted and sentenced to prison. Extended and indeterminate periods of psychiatric incapacitation can be achieved when labels of 'mental disorder' and 'dangerous' are attached and treatment purposes are invoked.

The moral and policy dilemmas are further compounded when adequate treatment resources are not available, issues of 'treatability' are skirted, and the *effectiveness* of treatment for certain types of MDOs (e.g. 'psychopaths', 'sexual psychopaths', and those with severe personality disorders) remains to be demonstrated. The provision of adequate, or even abundant, amounts of ineffective treatment, together with use of prolonged and indeterminate periods of confinement, point to incapacitative rather than therapeutic purposes.

Public safety concerns can and should more forthrightly be addressed. The clearest and strongest rationale for extended periods of confinement for persons who have repeatedly endangered the community (e.g. by serious and violent criminal conduct) is provided by their pattern of behaviour—not by diagnostic labels, clinical judgments, or the expedient of invoking treatment objectives. To guard against uses and misuses of the mental health system for extended confinement of MDOs in security hospitals, the principle of Proportionality (viz. the requirement that punishments be proportional to the seriousness of the offense) should also be applied to criminal defendants who are diverted to the mental health system.

The provision of durational limits for *criminally* committed patients would be more consistent with principles of fundamental fairness and justice. Such policies would also afford 'equal protection' of the laws to these MDOs, as compared with offenders who are sentenced to penal confinement. The establishment of durational limits would also encourage governments to allocate needed resources for the development and enhancement of community-based programs for the aftercare, supervision, and treatment of MDOs.

There will undoubtedly be MDOs (e.g. persons found unfit to proceed and insanity acquittees) who may require continued hospitalization after the period of their criminal commitment has expired. As in the case of prisoners, the durational limit pertains to the *criminal* commitment. Further outpatient or inpatient treatment can certainly be provided to those who need it either on a voluntary basis or, when so indicated, through the use of the usual *civil* commitment (involuntary hospitalization) provisions. Indeterminate incapacitation that cannot be applied to convicted offenders in the name of punishment should not be inflicted on criminally committed MDOs in the name of treatment. Such policies bring disrepute to the primarily benevolent, care-giving, and therapeutic purposes and functions of the mental health system.

A recent decision by the Supreme Court of Canada (*Regina* v. *Swain*, 1991) addresses the issues of proportionality and durational limits *vis-à-vis* insanity acquittees and affords greater protection of their rights. This decision also provides an interesting contrast to the narrowly split (5 : 4) decision of the US Supreme Court in *Jones* v. *United States* (1983), where the majority upheld the constitutionality of the indeterminate hospitalization of an insanity acquittee who had been charged with attempted petit larceny, a misdemeanour punishable by a maximum prison sentence of one year.

In *Swain* (1991), the Supreme Court of Canada held that a provision of the Canadian criminal code, providing for the automatic and indefinite detention of defendants acquitted by reason of insanity of an indictable offence, infringed the accused's rights to fundamental justice enshrined in Section 7 of the Canadian

Charter of Rights and Freedom (1983). This section pertains to 'Life, liberty, and security of persons' and proclaims that:

> Everyone has the right to life, liberty and security of the person and the right not to be deprived thereof except in accordance with the principles of fundamental justice. (p. 5)

This landmark decision nicely underscores the point that it is not just the assertion of lofty moral and legal principles and rules that is important, but their effective implementation and enforcement.

CONCLUSION

As this overview of the field has indicated, there have been many major developments with regard to improvements in our knowledge and understanding of the tasks and functions of mental health professionals in working with mentally disordered offenders (e.g. better conceptualization of psycholegal assessments and treatments, and improved knowledge about the prevalence of mental disorders among inmates of correctional institutions). Other impressive developments have focused on reforms of mental health laws and brought greater attention to human rights issues. In this context, I have emphasized here that, in using various clinical approaches with MDOs, mental health professionals need to be alert to various ethical and policy dilemmas as well as sensitive to their roles and functions when social control and treatment goals are combined and/or conflated.   .

With regard to vexing policy questions involving moral disputes, Nettler (1984) has rightly observed that the usual calls for 'more research' and studies reflect a trite mode of pacification and resolve nothing. Instead, he urges:

> Honest confrontation of moral differences can be recommended for its own sake or as a means of clarifying what we are doing, but it does not dissolve the conflict. The constant emollient of moral quarrels is hypocrisy, sometimes abetted by apathy and compromise. (p. 391)

Thus, while more research is certainly needed on a number of conceptual, empirical, and technical questions associated with the handling and treatment of mentally disordered offenders, the noted ethical, moral, and policy dilemmas involving various functions of the mental health system and the roles of mental health professionals require more forthright attention—*not* therapeutic 'emollients'.

AUTHOR'S NOTE

The views expressed here are mine and not necessarily those of the National Institute of Mental Health.

I should like to acknowledge with thanks the helpful comments of my colleagues Alyson Muff and Ecford Voit to an earlier draft.

REFERENCES

Abram, K. M. (1989). The effect of co-occurring disorders on criminal careers: Interaction of antisocial personality, alcoholism, and drug disorders. *International Journal of Law and Psychiatry*, **12**, 133–48.

Abram, K. M., and Teplin, L. A. (1991). Co-occurring disorders among mentally ill jail detainees: Implications for public policy. *American Psychologist*, **46**, 1036–45.

Allen, F. (1964). *The Borderland of Criminal Justice*. Chicago: University of Chicago Press.

American Academy of Psychiatry and the Law (1991). Ethical Guidelines for the Practice of Forensic Psychiatry. (Adopted, May 1987, revised October 1989 and October 1991.) Baltimore, MD: Author.

American Bar Association (1986). *ABA Criminal Justice Mental Health Standards*. Washington, DC: Association.

American Psychiatric Association (1989). The Principles of Medical Ethics: With Annotations Especially Applicable to Psychiatry. Washington, DC: Author.

American Psychological Association (1978). Report of the Task Force on the Role of Psychology in the Criminal Justice System. *American Psychologist*, **33**, 1099–113.

American Psychological Association (1990). Ethical principles of psychologists. *American Psychologist*, **45**, 390–5.

American Psychological Association (1991). Report of the ethics committee, 1989 and 1990. *American Psychologist*, **46**, 750–7.

Ashworth, A., and Gostin, L. (1984). Mentally disordered offenders and the sentencing process. *Criminal Law Review*, April, 195–212.

Bandura, A., and Walters, R. H. (1968). *Social Learning and Personality Development*. New York: Holt, Rinehart & Winston.

Barker, R. (1968). *Ecological Psychology: Concepts and Methods for Studying the Environment of Human Behavior*. Palo Alto, CA: Stanford University Press.

Bigelow, D. A., Bloom, J. D., and Williams, M. H. (1990). Costs of managing insanity acquittees under a Psychiatric Security Review Board system. *Hospital and Community Psychiatry*, **41**, 613–14.

Bloom, J. D., Williams, M. H., and Bigelow, D. A. (1991). Monitored conditional release of persons found not guilty by reason of insanity. *American Journal of Psychiatry*, **148**, 444–8.

Bloom, J. D., Williams, M. H., Rogers, J. L., and Barbur, P. (1986). Evaluation and treatment of insanity acquittes in the community. *Bulletin of the American Academy of Psychiatry and the Law*, **14**, 231–44.

Bonnie, R. J. (1990). The competence of criminal defendants with mental retardation to participate in their own defense. *The Journal of Criminal Law and Criminology*, **81**, 419–46.

Bowers, K.S. (1973). Situationism in psychology: An analysis and a critique. *Psychological Review*, **80**, 307–36.

Bowring v. *Godwin*, 551 F. 2d 44 (4th Cir. 1977).

Brakel, S. J., Parry, J., and Weiner, B. A. (1985). *The Mentally Disabled and the Law* (revised edn). Chicago: University of Chicago Press.

Bureau of Justice Statistics Bulletin (1991a). Prisoners in 1990. Washington, DC: US Department of Justice.

Bureau of Justice Statistics Bulletin (1991b). Jail Inmates, 1990. Washington, DC; US Department of Justice.

Canadian Charter of Rights and Freedoms (1983). *The Canadian Bar Review*, **61**, 4–11.

Caplan, G. (1964). *Principle of Preventive Psychiatry*. New York: Basic Books.

Center for Human Rights (1988). *Human Rights: A Compilation of International Instruments*. New York: United Nations.

Chiswick, D. (1985). Use and abuse of psychiatric testimony. *British Medical Journal*, **290**, 975–7.

Clements, C. B. (1987). Psychologists in adult correctional institutions. In E. K. Morris, and C. J. Braukmann (eds), *Behavioral Approaches to Crime and Delinquency*. New York: Plenum, pp. 521–41.

Clingempeel, W. G., Mulvey, E., and Reppucci, N. D. (1980). A national study of ethical dilemmas of psychologists in the criminal justice system. In J. Monahan (ed.), *Who is the Client?* Washington, DC: American Psychological Association, pp. 126–53.

Cohen, F. (1988). *Legal Issues and the Mentally Disordered Prisoner*. National Institute of Corrections. Washington, DC: US Department of Justice.

Collins, J. F., Ellsworth, R. B., Casey, N. A., Hyer, L., Hickey, R. H., Schoonover, R. A., Twemlow, S. W., and Nesselroade, J. R. (1985). Treatment characteristics of psychiatric programs that correlate with patient community adjustment. *Journal of Clinical Psychology*, **41**, 299–308.

Collins, J. J., and Schlenger, W. E. (1983). The prevalence of psychiatric disorder among admissions to prison. Paper presented at the 35th annual meeting of the American Society of Criminology, Denver, CO.

Committee on Ethical Guidelines for Forensic Psychologists (1991). Specialty Guidelines for Forensic Psychologists. *Law and Human Behavior*, **15**, 655–65.

Council of Europe, (1965). *European Convention of Human Rights: Collected Texts*. Strasbourg: Council of Europe.

Cummings, E. (1968). *Systems of Social Regulation*. New York: Atherton Press.

Ekehammar, B. (1974). Interactionism in personality from a historical perspective. *Psychological Bulletin*, **81**, 1026–48.

Ellsworth, R.B., Collins, J. F., Casey, N. A., Schoonover, R. A., Hickey, R. H., Hyer, L., Twemlow, S. W., and Nesselroade, J. R. (1979). Some characteristics of effective psychiatric treatment programs. *Journal of Consulting and Clinical Psychology*, **47**, 799–817.

Endler, N. S., and Magnusson, D. (1976). Toward an interactional psychology of personality. *Psychological Bulletin*, **83**, 956–74.

Estelle v. *Gamble*, 429 US 97 (1976).

Golding, S., Roesch, R., and Schreiber, J. (1984). Assessment and conceptualization of competency to stand trial: Preliminary data on the Interdisciplinary Fitness Interview. *Law and Human Behavior*, **8**, 321–34.

Griffin, P. A., Steadman, H. J., and Griffin, K. (1991). Designing conditional release systems for insanity acquittees. *Journal of Mental Health Administration*, **18**, 231–41.

Grisso, T. (1986a). *Evaluating Competencies: Forensic Assessments and Instruments*. New York: Plenum.

Grisso, T. (1986b). Psychological assessment in legal contexts. In W. J. Curran, A. L. McGarry, and S. A. Shah (eds), *Forensic Psychiatry and Psychology*. Philadelphia, PA: F. A. Davis, pp. 103–28.

Grisso, T. (1987). Psychological assessments for legal decisions. In D. W. Weisstub (ed.), *Law and Mental Health: International Perspectives*, vol. 3, New York: Pergamon, pp. 125–57.

Grisso, T., and Siegel, S. K. (1986). Assessment of competency to stand trial. In W. J. Curran, A. L. McGarry, and S. A. Shah (eds), *Forensic Psychiatry and Psychology*. Philadelphia, PA: F. A. Davis, pp. 145–65.

Grounds, A. T. (1987). Detention of 'psychopathic disorder' patients in special hospitals: Critical issues. *British Journal of Psychiatry*, **151**, 474–8.

Gunn, J., Maden, T., and Swinton, M. (1991). How many prisoners should be in hospital? *Research Bulletin* (Home Office Research & Statistics Department), No. 31, 9–15.

Gunn, J., Robertson, G., Dell, S., and Way, C. (1978). *Psychiatric Aspects of Imprisonment*. London: Academic Press.

Halleck, S. L. (1984). The ethical dilemmas of forensic psychiatry: A utilitarian approach. *Bulletin of the American Academy of Psychiatry and the Law*, **12**, 279–88.

Harding, T. W. (1989). The application of the European Convention of Human Rights to the field of psychiatry. *International Journal of Law and Psychiatry*, **12**, 245–62.

Hargreaves, W. A., and Shumway, M. (1989). Effectiveness of mental health services for the severely mentally ill. In C. A. Taube, D. Mechanic, and A. A. Hohmann, (eds), *The Future of Mental Health Services Research*. National Institute of Mental Health. DHHS Public. No. (ADM)89-1600. Washington, DC: US Govt. Printing Office, pp. 253–83.

Helzer, J. E., and Pryzbeck, T. R. (1988). The co-occurrence of alcoholism with other psychiatric disorders in the general population and its impact on treatment. *Journal of Studies on Alcohol*, **49**, 219–24.

Hodgins, S., and Côté, G. (1990). Prevalence of mental disorders among penitentiary inmates in Quebec. *Canada's Mental Health*, March 1990, 1–4.

Jemelka, R., Trupin, E., and Chiles, J.A. (1989). The mentally ill in prisons: A review. *Hospital and Community Psychiatry*, **40**, 481–91.

Jones v. *United States*, 103 S.Ct. 3043 (1983).

Kerr, C. A., and Roth, J. A. (1986). Populations, practices, and problems in forensic psychiatric facilities. *Annals of the American Academy of Political & Social Sciences*, **484**, 127–43.

Klerman, G. L. (1977). Mental illness, the medical model, and psychiatry. *Journal of Medicine and Philosophy*, **2**, 220–43.

King, L. S. (1954). What is disease? *Philosophy of Science*, **21**, 193–203.

Krul-Steketee, J. (1987). The psychiatric patient in legislation on mental health: principal legal regulations. In D. N. Weisstub (ed.), *Law and Mental Health: International Perspectives*, vol. 3. New York: Pergamon Press, pp. 33–7.

Laboratory of Community Psychiatry, Harvard Medical School (1973). *Competency to Stand Trial and Mental Illness*. DHEW Public. No. (ADM) 77-103. Rockville, MD: National Institute of Mental Health.

Lamb, H.R. (1988). Community psychiatry and prevention. In J. A. Talbott, R. E. Hales, and S. C. Yudofsky (eds), *Textbook of Psychiatry*. Washington, DC: American Psychiatric Press, pp. 1141–60.

Lamb, H. R., Weinberger, L., and Gross, B. (1988). Court-mandated out-patient treatment for persons found not guilty by reason of insanity: A five-year follow-up. *American Journal of Psychiatry*, **139**, 892–7.

Lewin, K. (1935). *A Dynamic Theory of Personality*. New York: McGraw-Hill.

Lipsitt, P. D., Lelos, D., and McGarry, A. L. (1971). Competency for trial: A screening instrument. *American Journal of Psychiatry*, **128**, 105–9.

Marmor, J. (1953). The feeling of superiority: An occupational hazard in the practice of psychotherapy. *American Journal of Psychiatry*, **110**, 370–6.

Melton, G. B., Petrila, J., Poythress, N.G., and Slobogin, C. (1987). *Psychological Evaluations for the Courts: A Handbook for Mental Health Professionals and Lawyers*. New York: Guilford Press.

Mischel, W. (1968). *Personality and Assessment*. New York: Wiley.

Mischel, W. (1973). Toward a cognitive social learning reconceptualization of personality. *Psychological Review*, **80**, 252–83.

Monahan, J. (ed.) (1980a). *Who is the Client? The Ethics of Psychological Intervention in the Criminal Justice System*. Washington, DC: American Psychological Association.

Monahan, J. (1980b). Foreword. In R. Roesch, and S. L. Golding, *Competency to Stand Trial*. Urbana, IL: University of Illinois Press.

Monahan, J., and Steadman, H. J. (eds) (1983). *Mentally Disordered Offenders: Perspectives from Law and Social Science*. New York: Plenum.

Moos, R. H. (1973). Conceptualization of human environments. *American Psychologist*, **28**, 652–65.

Moos, R. H. (1974). *Evaluating Treatment Environments: A Social Ecological Approach*. New York: Wiley.

Moos, R. H. (1975). *Evaluating Correctional and Community Settings*. New York: Wiley.

Moos, R. H. (1976). *The Human Context: Environmental Determinants of Behavior*. New York: Wiley.

Moos, R. H., and Schwartz, J. (1972). Treatment environment and treatment outcome. *Journal of Nervous and Mental Disease*, **154**, 264–75.

Morris, N. (1968). Psychiatry and the dangerous criminal. *Southern California Law Review*, **41**(3), 514–47.

Morse, S. J. (1978). Law and mental health professionals: The limits of expertise. *Professional Psychology*, **9**, 389–99.

Neighbors, H. W. (1987). The prevalence of mental disorder in Michigan prisons. *DIS Newsletter*, IV, 2, 8–11. (Department of Psychiatry, Washington University School of Medicine, St Louis, MO.)

Nettler, G. (1984). On 'rehabilitation.' *Law and Human Behavior*, **8**, 383–93.

Pendleton, L. (1980). Treatment of persons found incompetent to stand trial. *American Journal of Psychiatry*, **137**, 1098–100.

Pope, K. S., and Vetter, V. A. (1992). Ethical dilemmas encountered by members of the American Psychological Association: A national survey. *American Psychologist*, **47**, 397–411.

Poythress, N. G., and Miller, R. D. (1991). The treatment of forensic patients: Major issues. In S. A. Shah, and B. D. Sales (eds) *Law and Mental Health: Major Developments and Research Needs*. National Institute of Mental Health. DHHS Public. No. (ADM)91-1875. Washington, DC: US Govt. Printing Office, pp. 81–114.

Quinsey, V. L. (1988). Assessment of the treatability of forensic patients. *Behavioral Sciences and the Law*, **6** (4), 443–52.

Quinsey, V. L., and Maguire, A. (1983). Offenders remanded for a psychiatric examination: Perceived treatability and disposition. *International Journal of Law and Psychiatry*, **6**, 193–205.

Raimy, V. C. (ed.) (1950). *Training in Clinical Psychology*. Englewood Cliffs, NJ: Prentice-Hall.

Regier, D. A., Myers, J. K., Kramer, M., Robins, L. N., Blazer, D. G., Hough, R. L., Eaton, W. W., and Locke, B. Z. (1984). The NIMH Epidemiologic Catchment Area (ECA) Program: Historical context, major objectives, and study population characteristics. *Archives of General Psychiatry*, **41**, 934–41.

Regier, D. A., Boyd, J. H., Burke, J. D., Rae, D. S., Myers, J. K., Kramer, M., Robins, L. N., George, L. K., Karno, M., and Locke, B. Z. (1988). One-month prevalence of mental disorders in the United States. *Archives of General Psychiatry*, **45**, 977–86.

Regier, D. A., Farmer, M. E., Rae, D. S., Locke, B. Z., Keith, S. J., Judd, L. L., and Goodwin, F. K. (1990). Comorbidity of mental disorders with alcohol and other drug abuse. *Journal of the American Medical Association*, **264**, 2511–18.

Regina v. *Swain*, 63 C.C.C. (3d) 481 (1991).

Rice, M. E., Harris, G. T., Quinsey, V. L., and Cyr, M. (1990). Planning treatment programs in secure psychiatric facilities. In D. N. Weisstub, (ed.), *Mental Health and Law: International Perspectives*, vol. 5, New York: Pergamon, pp. 162–230.

Robins, L. N., Helzer, J. E., Croughan, J., and Ratcliff, K. S. (1981). National Institute of Mental Health Diagnostic Interview Schedule: Its history, characteristics, and validity. *Archives of General Psychiatry*, **38**, 381–9.

Rogers, R. (1984). *Rogers Criminal Responsibility Assessment Scales*. Odessa, FL: Psychological Assessment Resources.

Roth, L. H. (1986). Correctional psychiatry. In W. J. Curran, A. L. McGarry, and S. A. Shah (eds), *Forensic Psychiatry and Psychology*. Philadelphia, PA: F. A. Davis, 1986, pp. 429–68.

Shah, S. A. (1969). Crime and mental illness: Some problems in defining and labelling deviant behavior. *Mental Hygiene*, **53**, 21–33.

Shah, S. A. (1970). Community mental health and the criminal justice system: Some issues and problems. *Mental Hygiene*, **54**(1), 1–12.

Shah, S. A. (1974). Some interactions of law and mental health in the handling of social deviance. *Catholic University Law Review*, **23**, 674–719.

Shah, S. A. (1981). Legal and mental health system interactions: Major developments and research needs. *International Journal of Law and Psychiatry*, **4**, 219–270.

Shah, S. A. (1986). Criminal responsibility. In W. J. Curran, A. L. McGarry, and S. A. Shah (eds), *Forensic Psychiatry and Psychology*. Philadelphia, PA: F.A. Davis Company, pp. 167–208.

Shah, S. A. (1989). Mental disorder and the criminal justice system: Some overarching issues. *International Journal of Law and Psychiatry*, **12**, 231–44.

Shah, S. A. (1990). Therapeutic sanctions and fundamental notions of justice. In C. Kelk, F. Koenraadt, and A. W. M. Mooij, (eds), *Harmonie en Tegenspraak* (Harmony and Contradiction). Arnhem, Netherlands: Gouda Quint BV, pp. 317–29.

Siegel, A. M., and Elwork, A. (1990). Treating incompetence to stand trial. *Law and Human Behavior*, **14**, 57–65.

Silver, S. B., Cohen, M. I., and Spodak, M. K. (1989). Follow-up after release of insanity acquittees, mentally disordered offenders, and convicted felons. *Bulletin of the American Academy of Psychiatry and the Law*, **17**, 387–400.

Steadman, H. J., Fabisiak, S., Dvoskin, J., and Holohean, E. J. (1987). A survey of mental disability among state prison inmates. *Hospital and Community Psychiatry*, **38** (10), 1086–90.

Steadman, H. J., Rosenstein, H. J., MacAskill, R. L., and Manderscheid, R. W. (1988). A profile of mentally disordered offenders admitted to inpatient psychiatric services in the United States. *Law and Human Behavior*, **12**, 91–9.

Teplin, L. A. (1990a). Detecting disorder: The treatment of mental illness among jail detainees. *Journal of Consulting and Clinical Psychology*, **58**(2), 233–6.

Teplin, L. A. (1990b). The prevalence of severe mental disorder among male urban jail detainees: Comparison with the Epidemiologic Catchment Area program. *American Journal of Public Health*, **80**(6), 663–9.

Toch, H., and Adams, K. (1989). *The Disturbed Violent Offender*. New Haven: Yale University Press.

Toch, H., Adams, K., with Grant, J. D. (1989). *Coping: Maladaptation in Prisons*. New Brunswick, New Jersey: Transation Publishers.

United Nations (1991). The protection of persons with mental illness and the improvement of mental health care. Resolution No. 46/119, adopted on 17 December 1991.

Verdun-Jones, S. N. (1991). From the Courts—Canada: *Regina v. Swain* (1991). *International Bulletin of Law and Mental Health*, **3**, 19–21.

Vitek v. *Jones*, 445 US 480 (1980).

World Health Organization (1978). *Mental Disorders: Glossary and guide to their classification in accordance with the Ninth Revision of the International Classification of Diseases*. Geneva: WHO.

10

A Clinical Approach to the Mentally Disordered Offender: Prognosis

CLIVE R. HOLLIN and KEVIN HOWELLS

As is abundantly clear to anyone who has seriously worked in the field, the study of crime and criminal behaviour is a far from simple affair. An appealing, if taxing, aspect of criminology is the need to read across disciplines: thus, as a psychologist, not only is it necessary to be conversant with psychological research and theory as applied to criminal behaviour, but one also needs to be aware of developments in several disciplines, including sociology, law, economics, philosophy, and biology. Without claiming specialist knowledge in these disciplines, it is, by and large, a manageable if demanding task to keep abreast of the field. However, when it comes to the specific instance of the mentally disordered offender the complexity of the issues involved is multiplied yet further. In no particular order we have picked out from what has gone before some of the points that seem crucial to the future development of an understanding of the mentally disordered offender.

The immediate issue is how to disentangle the role that mental disorder plays in the commission of any particular crime. This point is important at several levels. From a legal point of view it asks questions about responsibility: can the mentally disordered offender be held accountable for his or her actions? If the foundation of the legal system is that individuals must be shown to have acted with criminal intent, then can a mentally disordered person be said to have knowingly committed a crime? This issue was graphically illustrated in the trial of Peter Sutcliffe, the 'Yorkshire Ripper'. During Sutcliffe's trial the jury was directed to decide on the accuracy of the diagnosis of the psychiatrists who had proclaimed that Sutcliffe was mentally ill. Further, they were asked to consider whether, even if the psychiatric diagnosis was accurate, Sutcliffe's state of mind

Clinical Approaches to the Mentally Disordered Offender
Edited by K. Howells and C. R. Hollin © 1993 John Wiley & Sons Ltd

at the time of committing the offences was such that he did not know what he was doing was wrong. It is now a matter of history that the jury decided that Sutcliffe was fit to stand trial, and that he was found guilty and sentenced to life imprisonment. Three years later he was transferred to a Special Hospital because he was mentally ill (see Prins, 1986).

An understanding of mental disorder and criminal behaviour will only come about through well-designed and controlled empirical studies. For example, recent Canadian research has not only given strong estimates of the rate of mental disorder among some offender groups, but also begins to offer an insight into the relationship between mental disorder and the type and nature of the offence (Hodgins, 1992; Hodgins and Côté, in press a, b). The complexity of the issues involved is shown by findings that reveal that many offenders actually show a multiplicity of disorders (Abram and Teplin, 1991; Hodgins and Côté, in press a). Thus, in the Canadian study, of the offenders diagnosed as schizophrenic almost 65% were also diagnosed as showing antisocial personality disorder; almost 76% were alcohol abusers or alcohol-dependent; and over 70% were drug abusers or drug-dependent. A similar pattern emerged for offenders diagnosed as clinically depressed. Thus attempts at causal explanations must deal with the links between mental disorder, personality disorder, and alcohol and drug abuse.

The need to disentangle the role of mental disorder in criminal behaviour is of crucial importance with respect to the management of the individual concerned. Those individuals sentenced under criminal law will experience a different outcome to those individuals who are judged to be in need of treatment.

From a treatment perspective, it is likely that clinicians will need to develop sophisticated programmes to remediate not only, say, mental disorder (which will probably involve pharmacological as well as psychological components), but also to change enduring personality dispositions and patterns of drug and alcohol abuse. Of course, as highlighted repeatedly in this book, the question of the effectiveness of intervention programmes remains open. It is doubtless true that successful treatment initiatives have been designed and carried out with mentally disordered offenders. The burning question is which interventions, delivered under what conditions, work best for which particular mentally disordered offenders? While reviewers can offer narrative reviews leading to helpful guidelines for practitioners, the time is surely drawing near when a meta-analysis of the field needs to be conducted. In this sense the position is analogous to that in the field of working with young offenders. While there has traditionally been a strong lobby for the effectiveness of clinically orientated intervention (e.g. Gendreau and Ross, 1987), the publication of several meta-analyses (e.g. Andrews, Zinger, Hoge, Bonta, Gendreau, and Cullen, 1990; Lipsey, 1992) settled the argument (in as much as arguments can ever be settled in the human sciences) by showing that given certain conditions intervention could be effective. A similar analysis in the field of clinical interventions with mentally disordered offenders would doubtless prove of similar benefit, both theoretically and practically, in informing clinical approaches to the mentally disordered offender.

REFERENCES

Abram, K. M., and Teplin, L. A. (1991). Co-occurring disorders among mentally ill jail detainees. *American Psychologist*, **46**, 1036–45.

Andrews, D. A., Zinger, I., Hoge, R. D., Bonta, J., Gendreau, P., and Cullen, F. T. (1990). Does correctional treatment work? A clinically relevant and psychologically informed meta-analysis. *Criminology*, **28**, 369–404.

Gendreau, P., and Ross, R. R. (1987). Revivification of rehabilitation: Evidence from the 1980s. *Justice Quarterly*, **4**, 349–407.

Hodgins, S. (1992). Mental disorder, intellectual deficiency and crime: Evidence from a birth cohort. *Archives of General Psychiatry*, **49**, 476–483.

Hodgins, S., and Côté, G. (in press, a). Major mental disorder among Canadian penitentiary inmates. In C. D. Webster, L. Stermac, and L. Stewart (eds), *Clinical Criminology*.

Hodgins, S., and Côté, G. (in press, b). The criminality of mentally disordered offenders. *Criminal Justice and Behavior*.

Lipsey, M. W. (1992). Juvenile delinquency treatment: A meta-analytic inquiry into the variability of effects. In T. D. Cook, H. Cooper, D. S. Cordray, H. Hartmann, L. V. Hedges, R. J. Light, T. A. Louis, and F. Mosteller (eds), *Meta-analysis for Explanation: A Casebook*. New York: Russell Sage Foundation.

Print, H. (1986). *Dangerous Behaviour, the Law, and Mental Disorder*. London: Tavistock.

Author index

Subject index

Indexes compiled by Liz Granger